In South Africa, this is not simply a brick.

Expand your business horizons by seeing the true potential in things. Combine our **sound macro-economic fundamentals** and **improved international credit ratings**[*] with a regulatory framework that guarantees **protection of property** and **intellectual rights**, and the groundwork for success is laid. With links to **all major shipping routes** and **free trade agreements** to ensure cost-efficiency, South Africa is ready to help you grow your business beyond your wildest expectations. Set your business on a solid foundation. Put it on South African soil.

www.southafrica.info

For more information visit www.southafrica.info. This advertisement was developed by the International Marketing Council of South Africa.

[*]Moody's Credit Ratings

THINK OF IT AS THE LONG HAUL TO FREEDOM.

A visit to Joburg is not only an escape from all that is familiar, it is an escape from all your previous expectations of an African city. Only in Joburg will you find the perfect marriage of Western, Eastern, and African cultures and influences, resulting in a unique fusion that is reflected in the cuisine, architecture, fashion, the arts and music. So whatever it may be, chances are your choice of daytime or night time activities will be nothing like you've ever experienced before. Take a long good look at Joburg, because you'd have to go a long way to find this much freedom of choice anywhere else.

JOBURG! AFRICA AT ITS BEST

www.joburgtourism.com
www.joburg.org.za

Pocket Guide to SOUTH AFRICA

Pocket Guide to South Africa 2005/06
Third edition

Published by STE Publishers
on behalf of Government Communications (GCIS)
Private Bag X745, Pretoria 0001, South Africa
Tel: +27 12 314 2911
Fax: +27 12 323 0557
Website: www.gcis.gov.za

ISBN: 1-919855-71-8

Editor: Delien Burger

Assistant editors: Elias Tibane and Louise van Niekerk

Proofreader: Kathleen Bartels for Wordsmiths

Design and layout: Adam Rumball

Cover photographs: Satour

Publishing consultant: Zann Hoad – Sharp Sharp Media

Printed and bound in South Africa by Formeset Printers

STE Publishers Tel: +27 11 484 7824
PO Box 93446, Yeoville 2143, South Africa

Sharp Sharp Media Tel: +27 11 442 8707
49 Rothsay Ave, Craighall Park 2096, South Africa

The editorial staff has taken all reasonable care to ensure correctness of facts and statistics. However, any person requiring confirmation of any data in the *Pocket Guide to South Africa*, or more detailed and specific information, should consult the relevant department/institution. This information is also available at Government Online [www.gov.za].

Unless otherwise specified, information contained in this book was the latest available as at October 2005.

Contents

Foreword by President Thabo Mbeki	6
South Africa at a glance	8
South Africa today	9
History	15
South Africa's people	23
Government	31
Provinces	45
Economy	57
National finances	73
Doing business in South Africa	85
Foreign affairs	99
Communications	111
Transport	123
Agriculture, forestry and land	133
Minerals and mining	145
Energy and water	155
Education	165
Science and technology	173
Housing	183
Safety, security and defence	189
Justice and correctional services	197
Social development	209
Environment	213
Arts and culture	225
Tourism	233
Health	247
Sport and recreation	257

Pocket Guide to South Africa 2005/06

South Africa has entered the second year of the Second Decade of Freedom, fully geared to meet the popular mandate to halve unemployment and poverty by 2014.

Government has adopted a detailed programme of action encompassing attention to improving the capacity of the State; building a growing economy which benefits all; expanding social services; and entrenching peace, security and democratic governance in our region and continent.

This programme outlines detailed steps that need to be taken in each area of social endeavour and, where appropriate, with timelines for each project.

It is in part a measure of the encouraging possibilities that our country faces that what is now the longest recorded

Foreword

upward economic trend in our history, gathered further momentum during the past year.

However, rather than merely celebrate this positive environment, government has joined hands with social partners to develop a comprehensive initiative that will raise the range of growth to higher levels, and do so in a manner that benefits all South Africans. The Accelerated and Shared Growth Initiative for South Africa is centred on higher rates of public and private investment as well as expanding work opportunities.

As the *Pocket Guide to South Africa* goes to print, the initiative is being developed in further detail and government is consulting with social partners to ensure that the final product unites all of us in pursuit of common development and growth objectives.

The *Pocket Guide* highlights the policies and programmes that have brought our country to the point at which we can proclaim with confidence that tomorrow looks much brighter than yesterday.

Together we can and shall indeed do the many more things that need to be done to build a South Africa that truly belongs to all.

President Thabo Mbeki
November 2005

Pocket Guide to South Africa 2005/06

Size	1 219 090 km²
Key economic sectors	Mining services and transport, energy, manufacturing, tourism, agriculture
Population	46,9 million (mid-2005)
Official languages	English, isiZulu, isiXhosa, isiNdebele, Afrikaans, siSwati, Sesotho sa Leboa, Sesotho, Setswana, Tshivenda and Xitsonga
Government	Constitutional multiparty, three-tier (local, provincial, national) democracy.
Major cities	Johannesburg, Cape Town, Durban, Pretoria, Port Elizabeth, Bloemfontein, East London, Kimberley. There are nine provinces
Currency	100 cents equals one rand
Time	GMT +2 hours
Distances	Cape Town to Johannesburg 1 400 km (880 miles) Johannesburg to Durban 600 km (380 miles) Port Elizabeth to Bloemfontein 700 km (440 miles)
Transportation	Excellent roads, rail and air facilities (both domestic and international)
Telecommunications	World-class infrastructure. Internet access is widely available. There are three mobile (cellular) networks
Value-added tax	Levied at 14%. Tourists may apply for tax refunds on purchases over R250 on departure
Health	Top quality care is available throughout the country, although basic in rural areas. Inoculations are only required for those travelling from yellow-fever areas. Malaria precautions are necessary in some areas
Total GDP (2004)	US$213,1 billion*
GDP per capita (2004)	US$4 500*
Real GDP growth (2004)	3,7%
Inflation (CPIX)	4,3%

* Based on a mid-2005 exchange rate of R6,45 to the US$

For further information on South Africa, visit
www.southafrica.info and www.gov.za

South Africa today

In 1994, a new democratic South African state was born with an inheritance which was anything but auspicious. The first years of democracy saw the introduction of a new constitutional and legislative framework. The Constitution was adopted in 1996 and an average of 90 Acts of new legislation were introduced per year in the first 10 years.

Within that framework, the South African polity has seen progress in:
- voice and accountability
- political stability
- government effectiveness
- regulatory quality
- integrity and legitimacy of the State and the rule of law
- efforts to expose and deal with corruption.

Black people had previously been denied the vote and meaningful access to the economy. From the sports fields to the factory floors, schoolrooms to neighbourhoods, South Africans were divided along racial lines, a divide enforced by repression and the denial of human rights.

The economy, isolated for years by the international community, was stagnating while debt was ballooning.

The economic recovery that began in late 1999 – already the longest business cycle upswing on record – gathered further momentum in 2004 and the first half of 2005. The pace of economic growth was expected to be just above 4% during 2006 and to reach between 4,5% and 5% a year in 2007 and 2008.

Since 1994, in line with the Reconstruction and Development Programme (RDP), government has set out to dismantle apartheid social relations and to create a democratic society based on equity, non-racialism and non-sexism.

Governance and administration

Since 1994, the Public Service has been transformed. On 31 March 2005, 73,9% of the Public Service was African, 3,7% Asian, 8,9% coloured and 13,5% white. With regard to gender, 53,3% was female and 46,7% male. However, at senior management level, 54% were African, 7,5% Asian, 7,7% coloured and 30% white. The gender breakdown for senior management was 28,5% female and 71,5% male.

Government's imbizo outreach programme, including meetings with provincial and local government executives, enables communities to interact directly with government to help speed up the implementation of programmes to improve their lives.

Better service delivery

Policy and implementation are more integrated thanks to the Government's cluster approach, improved provincial and local government co-ordination and a national development framework. The fight against corruption has been given muscle with legislation, national campaigns, whistle-blowing mechanisms and special courts.

Important initiatives include community development workers and the Batho Pele Gateway Portal.

Social cluster

Social grants have been equalised between the races and the number of those benefiting has risen. Beneficiaries of social grants increased from 3,8 million in April 2001 to more than 10 million in September 2005.

South Africa today

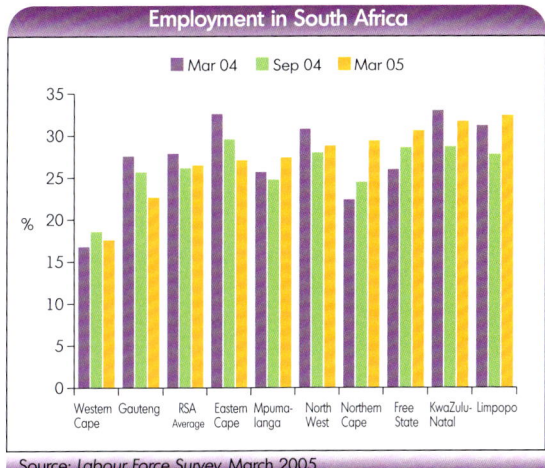

Source: *Labour Force Survey, March 2005*

By September 2005, about 6,3 million children were receiving the Child Support Grant (CSG), 286 131 the Foster Care Grant, and 87 093 the Care Dependency Grant.

Millions who previously had no access to electricity, water or sanitation now enjoy these services.

Other achievements:
- Women and children under six enjoy free healthcare.
- Between April 1994 and June 2005, a total of 2,4 million housing subsidies were approved. During this period, 1,7 million housing units were provided to more than seven million people.
- By 28 February 2005, 57 908 land claims had been settled, benefiting 863 138 beneficiaries who had obtained 854 444 hectares of land.

Since 1994, government has made steady progress in raising the proportion of spending on social services that goes to the poorest 40% of the people.

Welfare and social assistance, education, land restitution and housing have evolved into strongly redistributive expenditure programmes, bringing the average value of services, of the social wage, that goes to the poorest 40% of households to an estimated R956 a month.

Economy cluster

Performance of the economy

- Stability

  Resources have been freed up for social expenditure by reducing interest repayments thanks to lesser debt. Growth of the South African economy has averaged 3,2% a year over the past four years. A continued expansion of between 4% and 4,5% is expected over the next three years, signalling a significant step-change in the pace of economic growth. At the same time, consumer price inflation decreased to 4,3% for the year to December 2004, and is expected to remain comfortably within the 3% to 6% target range over the period ahead.

- Economic reform

  Trade and industry have been restructured to make the country more competitive, while labour reform has created an environment in which both employers and workers have greater certainty and security.

- Employment

  The March 2005 *Labour Force Survey* conducted by Statistics South Africa indicated that over half-a-million (500 000) additional jobs were created between March 2004 and March 2005 – surpassing the number of new entrants (400 000) into the labour market.

South Africa is playing an energetic role in international and multilateral organisations and fora. At various times over the past decade, it has chaired the African Union, Non-Aligned Movement, New Partnership for Africa's Development, Commonwealth Heads of Government Summit, World Conference Against Racism, Southern African Development Community, and others. It also hosts the Pan-African Parliament.

- Empowerment
  Empowerment in the workplace is continuing, albeit slowly. By 2001, 13% of top management and 16% of senior management were black people. Black ownership of public companies was 9,4% in 2002 compared with virtually nothing in 1994. The Broad-Based Economic Empowerment Act, 2003 will further promote participation of black people and women in the economy.

Justice, crime prevention and security

South Africa's justice and police resources have, since 1994, concentrated on stabilising crime. Government has identified and prioritised 169 police stations that register the highest levels of contact crime.

Except for robbery and malicious damage to property, most of the 20 categories of serious crime have either stabilised or decreased in the last 10 years. Murder rates are down by 40% since 1994.

By May 2005, all of the top 200 wanted criminals identified earlier in the year had been arrested.

The socio-demographic profiling for 148 priority police-station areas had been completed by June 2005. Action plans aimed at addressing the social causes of crime were developed for 116 priority police stations responsible for 50% of all contact crime in South Africa.

International relations

South Africa's post-1994 success in defining its place in the world is remarkable given its size.

After being shunned by much of the world for decades, South Africa is now actively promoting its own interests and those of the South in all significant regional, continental and multilateral institutions.

Challenges of the next decade

The next decade's challenges arise from lessons learnt in the First Decade of Freedom and new challenges created by the first stage of transformation.

Key challenges will be creating jobs for the millions seeking work, and equipping them for a changing economy in which higher skills are required.

After a decade of freedom and transformation, the Government, elected in April 2004, has embarked on a programme of action to consolidate democracy in South Africa and to put the country on a faster growth and development path.

History

Modern humans have lived in what is today South Africa for over 100 000 years, and their ancestors for some 3,3 million years.

One site which is particularly rich in fossil remains, the area around the Sterkfontein caves near Johannesburg, is justifiably called the Cradle of Humankind.

Rock paintings

More recent evidence of early humans is the many vivid rock paintings which were created by small groups of Stone Age hunter-gatherers, the ancestors of the Khoekhoen and San.

Some 2 000 years ago, the Khoekhoen (the Hottentots of early European terminology) were pastoralists who had settled mostly along the coast, while the San (the Bushmen) were hunter-gatherers spread across the region. At this time, Bantu-speaking agro-pastoralists began arriving in southern Africa, spreading from the eastern lowlands to the Highveld.

At several archaeological sites there is evidence of sophisticated political and material cultures.

European contact

The first European settlement in southern Africa was established by the Dutch East India Company in Table Bay (Cape Town) in 1652. Created to supply passing ships, the colony grew quickly as Dutch farmers settled to grow produce. Shortly after the establishment of the colony, slaves were imported from East Africa, Madagascar and the East Indies.

Conflict

From the 1770s, colonists came into contact and inevitable conflict with Bantu-speaking chiefdoms some 800 km east of Cape Town. A century of intermittent warfare ensued during which the colonists gained ascendancy over the isiXhosa-speaking chiefdoms.

At approximately this time, in the areas beyond the reach of the colonists, a spate of state-building was being launched. The old order was upset and the Zulu kingdom emerged as a highly centralised state.

In the 1820s, the celebrated Zulu leader Shaka established sway over a vast area of south-east Africa.

As splinter groups from Shaka's Zulu nation conquered and absorbed communities in their path, the region experienced a fundamental disruption. Substantial states, such as Moshoeshoe's Lesotho and other Sotho-Tswana chiefdoms were established, partly for reasons of defence. This temporary disruption of life on the Highveld served to facilitate the expansion northwards of the original Dutch settlers' descendants, the Boer Voortrekkers, from the 1830s.

Occupation

In 1806, Britain reoccupied the Cape. As the colony prospered, the political rights of the various races were guaranteed, with slavery being abolished in 1838.

Throughout the 1800s, the boundaries of European influence spread eastwards. From the port of Durban, Natal settlers pushed northwards, further and further into the land of the Zulu.

From the mid-1800s, the Voortrekkers coalesced in two land-locked white-ruled republics, the South African Republic (Transvaal) and the Orange Free State.

The mineral revolution

The discovery of diamonds north of the Cape in the 1860s brought tens of thousands of people to the area around Kimberley. In 1871, Britain annexed the diamond fields. Independent African chiefdoms were systematically subjugated and incorporated. The most dramatic example was the Zulu War of 1879, which saw the Zulu State brought under imperial control, but only after King Cetshwayo's soldiers inflicted a celebrated defeat on British forces at Isandlwana.

Gold

The discovery of the Witwatersrand goldfields in 1886 was a turning point in the history of South Africa. The demand for franchise rights for English-speaking immigrants working on the new goldfields was the pretext Britain used to go to war with the Transvaal and Orange Free State in 1899.

The Boers initially inflicted some heavy defeats on the British but eventually the might of imperial Britain proved too strong for the guerilla bands and the war ended in 1902. Britain's scorched-earth policy included farm burnings and the setting up of concentration camps for non-combatants in which some 26 000 Boer women and children died.

The incarceration of black (including coloured) people in racially segregated camps has only recently been acknowledged in historical accounts of the war.

Union and opposition

In 1910, the Union of South Africa was created out of the Cape, Natal, Transvaal and Free State. It was to be essentially a white union.

Black opposition was inevitable, the African National Congress (ANC) being founded in 1912 to protest the exclusion of blacks from power. In 1921, the Communist Party came into being at a time of heightened militancy.

In the face of a groundswell of opposition to racially defined government, the seminal Natives Land Act was legislated in 1913. This defined the remnants of blacks' ancestral lands for African occupation. The homelands, as they were subsequently called, eventually comprised about 13% of South Africa's land. More discriminatory legislation – particularly relating to job reservation favouring whites, and the disenfranchisement of coloured voters in the Cape – was enacted. Meanwhile, Afrikaner nationalism, fuelled by job losses arising from worldwide recession, was on the march.

The rise of apartheid

After the Second World War, in 1948, the pro-Afrikaner National Party (NP) came to power with the ideology of apartheid, an even more rigorous and authoritarian approach than the previous segregationist policies.

While white South Africa was cementing its power, black opposition politics were evolving. In 1943, a younger, more determined political grouping came to the fore with the launch of the ANC Youth League, a development which was to foster the leadership of figures such as Nelson Mandela, Oliver Tambo and Walter Sisulu.

On 26 June 2005, President Thabo Mbeki addressed thousands of people gathered at the Walter Sisulu Square of Dedication in Kliptown, Soweto, to mark the 50th anniversary of the Freedom Charter.

The following day, national Parliament and the nine provincial legislatures held a people's assembly to mark the 50th anniversary of the Congress of the People at the Walter Sisulu Square of Dedication.

The charter was adapted by the Congress of the People in 1955.

Repression

In 1961, the NP Government under Prime Minister H.F. Verwoerd declared South Africa a republic after winning a whites-only referendum.

A new concern with racial purity was apparent in laws prohibiting interracial sex and in provisions for population registration requiring that every South African be assigned to one discrete racial category or another.

Residential segregation was enforced, with whole communities being uprooted and forced into coloured and black 'group areas'.

Separate development

At a time when much of Africa was on the verge of independence, the South African Government was devising its policy of separate development, dividing the African population into artificial ethnic 'nations', each with its own 'homeland' and the prospect of 'independence'. The truth was that the rural reserves were by this time thoroughly degraded by overpopulation and soil erosion.

Forced removals from 'white' areas affected some 3,5 million people, and vast rural slums were created in the homelands. The pass laws and influx control were extended and harshly enforced.

The introduction of apartheid policies coincided with the adoption by the ANC in 1949 of its Programme of Action, expressing the renewed militancy of the 1940s.

The programme embodied a rejection of white domination and a call for action in the form of protests, strikes and demonstrations.

Defiance

The Defiance Campaign of the early 1950s carried mass mobilisation to new heights under the banner of non-violent resistance to the pass laws. In 1955, the Freedom Charter was drawn up at the Congress of the People in

Soweto. The charter enunciated the principles of the struggle, binding the movement to a culture of human rights and non-racialism.

Soon the mass-based organisations, including the ANC and the Pan-Africanist Congress (PAC), were banned. Matters came to a head at Sharpeville in March 1960 when 69 PAC anti-pass demonstrators were killed. A state of emergency was imposed, and detention without trial was introduced.

Struggle days

Leaders of the black political organisations at this time either went into exile or were arrested. In this climate, the ANC and PAC abandoned their long-standing commitment to non-violent resistance and turned to armed struggle, waged from the independent countries to the north.

Top leaders still inside the country, including members of the ANC's newly formed military wing, Umkhonto we Sizwe (Spear of the Nation), were arrested in 1963. At the 'Rivonia Trial', eight ANC leaders, including Mandela, convicted of sabotage (instead of treason, the original charge), were sentenced to life imprisonment.

While draconian measures kept the lid on activism for much of the 1960s, the resurgence of resistance politics in the early 1970s was dramatic.

The year 1976 marked the beginning of a sustained anti-apartheid revolt. In June, school pupils in Soweto rose up against apartheid education, followed by youth uprisings all around the country. Strong, legal vehicles for the democratic forces tested the State, whose response until then had been invariably heavy-handed repression.

Reform

Shaken by the scale of protest and opposition, the Government embarked on a series of limited reforms in the early 1980s, an early example being the recognition of black trade unions.

In 1983, the Constitution was reformed to allow the coloured and Indian minorities limited participation in separate and subordinate houses of parliament, which enjoyed limited support.

In 1986, the hated pass laws were scrapped. At this time, the international community strengthened its support for the anti-apartheid cause.

However, these steps fell far short of the democratic aspirations of the majority of South Africans. Mass resistance increasingly challenged the apartheid State, which resorted to intensified repression accompanied, however, by eventual recognition that apartheid could not be sustained.

Apartheid's last days

In February 1990, newly elected President F.W. de Klerk announced the unbanning of the liberation movements and the release of political prisoners, notably Mandela.

Democracy at last

After a difficult negotiation process, South Africa held its first democratic election in April 1994 under an interim Constitution.

The ANC emerged with a 62% majority. South Africa, now welcomed back into the international community, was divided into nine new provinces in place of the four provinces and 10 'homelands' that existed previously. In terms of the interim Constitution, the NP and Inkatha Freedom Party participated in a government of national unity under Mandela, South Africa's first democratically elected president.

The ANC-led Government embarked on a programme to promote the reconstruction and development of the country and its institutions.

The second democratic election, in 1999, saw the ANC increasing its majority to a point just short of two-thirds of the total vote. South Africa was launched into the post-Mandela era under the presidency of Thabo Mbeki.

In the election on 14 April 2004, the ANC won the national vote with 69,68%. The inauguration of South Africa's third democratically elected president on 27 April 2004 was combined with the celebration of 10 Years of Freedom and attended by heads of state and government delegations from across the world. In his speech, President Mbeki vowed to fight poverty as a central part of the national effort to build the new South Africa.

In the First Decade of Freedom, much progress was made in improving the lives of ordinary people. This commitment continues.

South Africa's people

South Africa is a country where various cultures form a unique nation, proud of their heritage and of their unity in diversity.

People

According to the 2001 Census, there were 44 819 778 people in South Africa on the night of 10 October 2001. They classified themselves as follows:

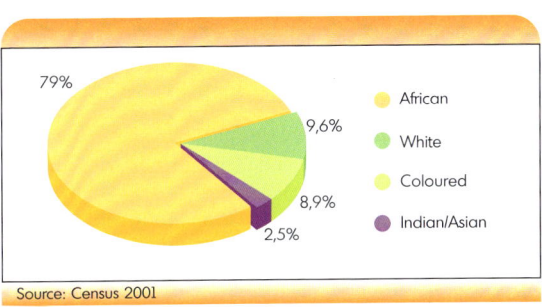

Source: Census 2001

The South African population is made up of the following groups:
- Nguni people (the Zulu, Xhosa, Ndebele and Swazi)
- Sotho-Tswana people (including the Southern, Northern and Western Sotho [Tswana])
- Tsonga
- Venda
- Afrikaners
- English-speakers

Pocket Guide to South Africa 2005/06

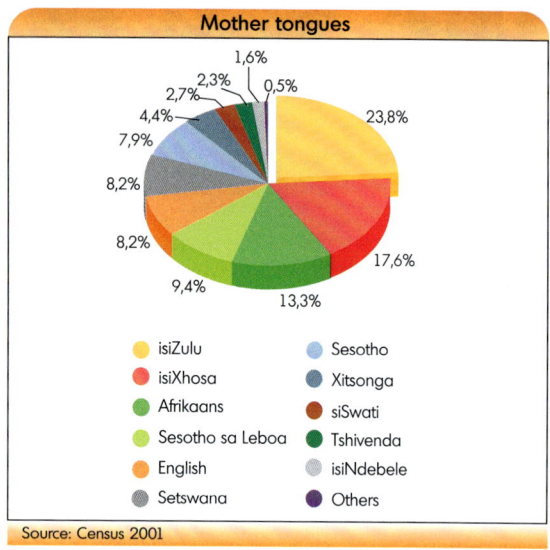

- coloureds
- Indians
- those who have immigrated to South Africa from the rest of Africa, Europe and Asia and maintain their own strong cultural identities
- a few members of the Khoi and the San.

The mid-2005 population was estimated at 46,9 million people.

Languages

The Constitution of the Republic of South Africa, 1996 states that everyone has the right to use the language and to participate in the cultural life of his/her choice, but no one may do so in a manner inconsistent with any provision of the Bill of Rights. Each person also has the right to instruction in the language of his/her choice where this is reasonably practicable.

South Africa's people

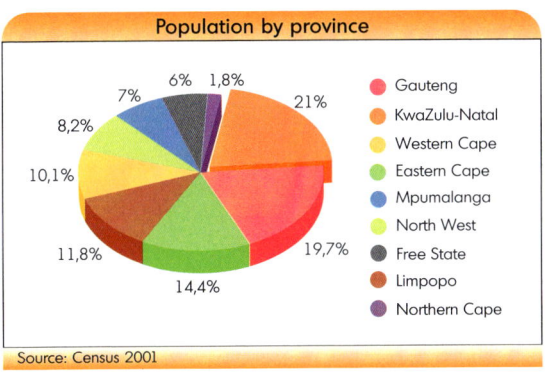

Population by province

- Gauteng 21%
- KwaZulu-Natal 19,7%
- Western Cape 14,4%
- Eastern Cape 11,8%
- Mpumalanga 10,1%
- North West 8,2%
- Free State 7%
- Limpopo 6%
- Northern Cape 1,8%

Source: Census 2001

Official languages

To cater for South Africa's diverse peoples, the Constitution provides for 11 official languages, namely Afrikaans, English, isiNdebele, isiXhosa, isiZulu, Sesotho sa Leboa, Sesotho, Setswana, siSwati, Tshivenda and Xitsonga.

Recognising the historically diminished use and status of the indigenous languages, the Constitution expects government to implement positive measures to elevate the status, and advance the use of these languages.

National and provincial governments may use any two or more official languages. While communication with the public tends to be produced in more than one language, internal communication takes place mostly in English.

According to a report of the University of South Africa's Bureau of Market Research on *National Personal Income of South Africans by Population Group, Income Group, Life Stage and Lifeplane 1960 – 2007*, in 2001, 4,1 million out of 11,2 million households in South Africa lived on an income of R9 600 or less per year. This decreased to 3,6 million households in 2004, even after taking the negative effect of price increases on spending power into account. On the other hand, the number of households receiving a real income of R153 601 or more per year rose from 721 000 in 1998 to more than 1,2 million in 2004.

South Africa's people

In 2003, Cabinet approved the National Language Policy Framework to promote the equitable use of the 11 official languages and to ensure redress for previously marginalised indigenous languages.

In March 2004, the Department of Arts and Culture launched the Language Initiatives Programme. Of particular importance to provinces is the setting up of nine language research and development centres, one for each of South Africa's nine indigenous languages, at tertiary institutions situated among communities where those languages are spoken.

The centres are the implementation agencies of the National Language Policy. In 2004/05, government spent R9 million establishing these centres. During 2004/05, the department spent over R10 million rolling out the Telephone Interpreting Service for South Africa. The project employs about 60 full-time personnel, who include interpreters, project managers and call-centre operators.

About R2 million has been dedicated to a pilot project aimed at developing literature in indigenous African languages.

Religion

Religious groups in South Africa

Almost 80% of South Africa's population is Christian. Other religious groups include Hindus, Muslims and Jews. A minority of South Africa's population do not belong to any of the major religions, but regard themselves as traditionalists or of no specific religious affiliation.

Freedom of worship is guaranteed by the Constitution.

Christian churches

Churches continue to play a critical role as agents of social change and transformation in pursuit of equality and the creation of a human-rights culture.

Pocket Guide to South Africa 2005/06

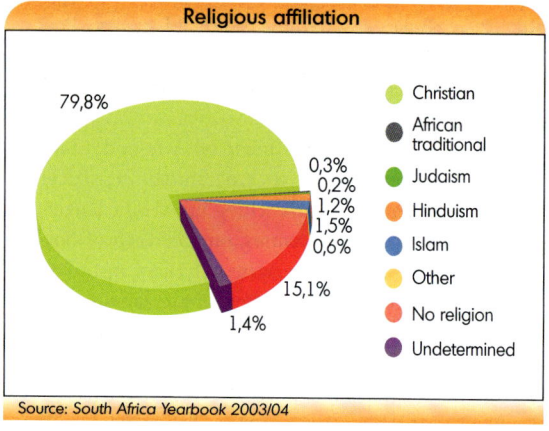

Source: *South Africa Yearbook 2003/04*

African independent churches (AICs)
The largest grouping of Christian churches is the AICs, and one of the most dramatic aspects of religious affiliation has been the rise of this movement.

There are 4 000 or more independent churches with a combined membership of more than 10 million.

Most are regarded as Zionist or Apostolic churches.

The Zion Christian Church is the largest of these churches in South Africa and the largest church overall, with over four million members.

Afrikaans churches
The Dutch Reformed family of churches represents some 3,5 million people. The Nederduits Gereformeerde Kerk has about 1 200 congregations countrywide. The other churches are the Uniting Reformed Church of South Africa and the smaller Reformed Church in Africa, with predominantly Indian members. The Nederduitsch Hervormde Kerk and the Gereformeerde Kerk are regarded as sister churches.

The Roman Catholic Church
In recent years, the Roman Catholic Church has grown strongly in numbers and influence, even though South Africa is predominantly Protestant. It works closely with other churches on the socio-political front.

Other Christian churches
Established churches in South Africa include the Methodist Church, the Church of the Province of Southern Africa (Anglican Church), and various Lutheran, Presbyterian, Congregational and Baptist churches. Together, these churches form the nucleus of the South African Council of Churches.

The largest traditional Pentecostal churches are the Apostolic Faith Mission, the Assemblies of God and the Full Gospel Church, but there are numerous others.

A number of charismatic churches have been established in recent years. Also active in South Africa, among the smaller groups, are the Greek Orthodox and Seventh Day Adventist churches.

African traditionalists
Because the traditional religion of the African people has a strong cultural base, the various groups have different rituals, but there are certain common features.

A supreme being is generally recognised, but ancestors are of great significance. As a result of close contact with Christianity, many people find themselves in a transitional phase somewhere between traditional African religion and Christianity.

Other religions
Two-thirds of South Africa's Indians are Hindus.

The Muslim community in South Africa is small, but is growing strongly. The major components of this community are the Cape Malays, who are mainly descendants of Indonesian slaves, as well as 20% of people of Indian descent.

The Jewish population is less than 100 000. Of these, the majority are Orthodox Jews.

Commission for the Promotion and Protection of the Rights of Cultural, Religious and Linguistic Communities

The Commission for the Promotion and Protection of the Rights of Cultural, Religious and Linguistic Communities is a constitutional body, which became active in January 2004 after 18 commissioners were sworn in during November 2003.

The commission is funded through transfers from the Department of Provincial and Local Government. Its mission is to develop and promote peace, friendship, humanity, tolerance and national unity among cultural, religious and linguistic communities.

This will be achieved by facilitating the development of programmes to foster sensitivity, respect and understanding for cultural, religious and linguistic diversity and also by mediating in intercommunity conflict situations and facilitating harmonious co-existence.

Local lexicon

bakkie (pronounced bucky) – refers to a small pick-up truck/van
dumpie – South African beer served in a brown 340 ml bottle
howzit – a greeting that translates roughly as 'How are you?' or 'How are things?'
sawubona – good day/hello
voetsek – go away/beat it
hamba kahle – a farewell greeting meaning go gently/go well
kunjani? – how are you?
indaba – a meeting/debate
lekker – nice/pretty/good.

Source: *Annual Report*, International Marketing Council

Government

The Constitution of the Republic of South Africa took effect in February 1997. The Constitution is the supreme law of the land. No other law or government action may supersede its provisions. South Africa's Constitution is one of the most progressive in the world and has been acclaimed internationally.

The Preamble to the Constitution states that its aims are to:
- heal the divisions of the past and establish a society based on democratic values, social justice and fundamental human rights
- improve the quality of life of all citizens and free the potential of each person
- lay the foundations for a democratic and open society in which government is based on the will of the people and every citizen is equally protected by law
- build a united and democratic South Africa able to take its rightful place as a sovereign state in the family of nations.

Government

Government consists of national, provincial and local spheres. The powers of the legislature, executive and courts are separate.

Parliament

Parliament consists of the National Assembly and the National Council of Provinces (NCOP). Parliamentary sittings are open to the public. Several measures have been implemented to make Parliament more accessible and accountable.

The National Assembly consists of no fewer than 350 and no more than 400 members elected through a system of proportional representation for a term of five years. It elects the President and scrutinises the executive.

Seats by party

Party	Votes	% of votes in 2004 election	Seats in National Assembly after 1999 election	Seats in National Assembly after floor crossing 15/09/05
African Christian Democratic Party	250,272	1,6%	6	4
African National Congress	10 880 915	69,69%	279	293
Democratic Alliance	1 931 201	12,37%	50	47
Independent Democrats	269 765	1,73%	7	5
Inkatha Freedom Party	1 088 664	6,97%	28	23
New National Party	257 824	1,65%	7	-
Pan Africanist Congress of Azania	113 512	0,73%	3	3
United Christian Democratic Party	117 792	0,75%	3	3
United Democratic Movement	355 717	2,28%	9	6
Freedom Front Plus	139 465	0,89%	4	4
National Democratic Convention	-	-	-	4
Progressive Independent Movement	-	-	-	1
Others	210 204	1,36%	4	8

Source: Independent Electoral Commission

National Council of Provinces

The NCOP consists of 54 permanent members and 36 special delegates, and aims to represent provincial interests in the national sphere of government.

The Presidency

The President is the head of state and leads the Cabinet. He or she is elected by the National Assembly from among its members, and leads the country in the interest of national unity, in accordance with the Constitution and the law.

The President of South Africa is Mr Thabo Mbeki.

Cabinet ministers, 1 November 2005		
Portfolio	Minister	Deputy Minister
The Presidency	Essop Pahad	
Agriculture & Land Affairs	Thoko Didiza	Dirk du Toit
Arts & Culture	Pallo Jordan	Ntombazana Botha
Communications	Ivy Matsepe-Casaburri	Radhakrishna Padayachie
Correctional Services	Ngconde Balfour	Cheryl Gillwald
Defence	Mosiuoa Lekota	Mluleki George
Education	Naledi Pandor	Enver Surty
Environmental Affairs & Tourism	Marthinus van Schalkwyk	Joyce Mabudafhasi
Finance	Trevor Manuel	Jabu Moleketi
Foreign Affairs	Nkosazana Dlamini-Zuma	Aziz Pahad and Sue van der Merwe
Health	Manto Tshabalala-Msimang	Nozizwe Madlala-Routledge
Home Affairs	Nosiviwe Mapisa-Nqakula	Malusi Gigaba
Housing	Lindiwe Sisulu	
Intelligence Services	Ronnie Kasrils	
Justice & Constitutional Development	Brigitte Mabandla	Johnny de Lange
Labour	Membathisi Mdladlana	
Minerals & Energy	Lindiwe Hendricks	Lulama Xingwana
Provincial & Local Government	Sydney Mufamadi	Nomatyala Hangana

Pocket Guide to South Africa 2005/06

Portfolio	Minister	Deputy Minister
Public Enterprises	Alec Erwin	
Public Service & Administration	Geraldine Fraser-Moleketi	
Public Works	Stella Sigcau	Ntopile Kganyago
Safety & Security	Charles Nqakula	Susan Shabangu
Science & Technology	Mosibudi Mangena	Derek Hanekom
Social Development	Zola Skweyiya	Jean Benjamin
Sport & Recreation	Makhenkesi Stofile	Gert Oosthuizen
Trade & Industry	Mandisi Mpahlwa	Rob Davies and Elizabeth Thabethe
Transport	Jeff Radebe	
Water Affairs & Forestry	Buyelwa Sonjica	

The Deputy President

The President appoints the Deputy President from among the members of the National Assembly. The Deputy President is Ms Phumzile Mlambo-Ngcuka.

Cabinet

Cabinet consists of the President, as head of the Cabinet, the Deputy President and ministers. The President appoints the Deputy President and ministers, assigns their powers and functions and may dismiss them. No more than two ministers may be appointed from outside the National Assembly.

Provincial government

Each of the nine provinces has its own legislature of 30 to 80 members. They elect the Premier who heads the Executive Council.

Provinces may have legislative and executive powers concurrently with the national sphere, over:

It was announced in May 2005 that Parliament would be establishing nine regional offices in the remotest areas of the country. It is part of a broader plan to make the legislature relevant, effective and responsive to the needs of South Africans.

Government

- agriculture
- casinos, horse racing and gambling
- cultural affairs
- education at all levels, except university and university of technology education
- environment and nature conservation
- health, housing and welfare
- language policy
- police services, public transport, traffic regulation and vehicle licensing
- regional planning and development and urban and rural development.

Provinces are also responsible for promoting trade, investment and tourism.

Provinces have exclusive competency over:

- abattoirs
- ambulance services
- liquor licences
- museums other than national museums
- provincial planning
- provincial cultural matters
- provincial recreation
- provincial roads and traffic.

Local government

Local governments are not merely instruments of service

Premiers, 1 November 2005	
Province	**Premier**
Eastern Cape	Nosimo Balindlela
Free State	Beatrice Marshoff
Gauteng	Mbhazima Shilowa
KwaZulu-Natal	S'bu Ndebele
Limpopo	Sello Moloto
Mpumalanga	Thabang Makwetla
North West	Ednah Molewa
Northern Cape	Dipuo Peters
Western Cape	Ebrahim Rasool

delivery, but are expected to act as key agents for economic development.

Municipalities

The Constitution provides for three categories of municipalities:
- metropolitan municipalities
- local municipalities
- district areas or municipalities.

Johannesburg, Durban, Cape Town, Pretoria, East Rand and Port Elizabeth are metropolitan areas. There are 231 local municipalities and 47 district municipalities.

Municipalities enjoy significant powers to corporatise their services. Legislation provides for them to report on their performance, and for residents to compare this performance with that of other municipalities.

After the new system of local government was introduced in 2000, total national transfers to local government amounted to only R6,5 billion in the 2001/02 financial year. These have been increased to R19,7 billion and R21,4 billion in the 2006/07 and 2007/08 financial years, respectively.

Over the next three years, from 2005 to 2008, local government will receive total transfers of about R58,3 billion from national government.

Municipal Infrastructure Grant (MIG)

The MIG has been allocated R15 billion in the Medium Term Expenditure Framework, which is in line with government's commitment to allocate more resources to accelerate the delivery of services, particularly to the poor, while simultaneously creating conditions for economic development.

The MIG replaces all existing capital grants for municipal infrastructure and incorporates the following seven local government programmes:
- Consolidated Municipal Infrastructure Programme
- Local Economic Development Fund

Government

- Water Services Project
- Community-Based Public Works Programme
- Municipal Sports and Recreation Programme
- National Electrification Programme to local government
- Urban Transport Fund.

At the end of June 2005, 97,2% of the 2004/05 MIG allocation and 7,4% of the 2005/06 allocation had been spent. Households had benefited from the MIG in respect of water (212 828), sanitation (74 245), roads (122 582), stormwater (83 593) and solid waste (55 880). A total of 287 655 person days of employment had been created specifically through the use of labour-intensive methods, in relation to the 2004/05 MIG allocation. Some R135 million was spent on urban nodes and R992 million was spent on rural nodes in the implementation of MIG 2004/05.

Project Consolidate

Project Consolidate, a hands-on local government engagement programme allows national and provincial government, with private-sector partners, to find new ways of working with local government. It gives targeted focus and capacity-building to 136 municipalities identified for assistance. A pool of 38 service-delivery facilitators has been mobilised.

Communicating with the people

The Government Communication and Information System (GCIS) is primarily responsible for facilitating communication between government and the people. A high premium is placed on communication that emphasises direct dialogue, especially with people in disadvantaged areas.

The GCIS is responsible for maintaining the Government's website (*www.gov.za*), which includes both an information portal for general information about government, and a services portal that is a source of information about all the services offered by national government.

GCIS leads or is involved in various communication partnerships and joint processes, including:

- An intersectoral programme to set up multi-purpose community centres (MPCCs), providing information about accessing government services, as well as some government services at the centres themselves. In September 2005, there were 66 MPCCs in operation. A strategy for setting up one MPCC in each of the country's 284 municipalities by 2014 has been approved.
- Institutional support to the Media Development and Diversity Agency (MDDA), established in terms of the MDDA Act, 2002, for which the Minister in The Presidency is the responsible minister.
- The development of the new Coat of Arms, launched on Freedom Day, 27 April 2000, and the redesign of the national orders.
- The process towards the transformation of the advertising and marketing industry.
- The Academy of Government Communication and Marketing, in collaboration with the School of Public and Development Management, Unilever and the Mandela-Rhodes Foundation.
- The international marketing campaign led by the International Marketing Council (IMC).
- The *Imbizo* Campaign of direct interaction between government and the public.

The GCIS publishes, among others, the *South Africa Yearbook* and *Pocket Guide to South Africa*.

In 2004, President Thabo Mbeki announced that the Government's Programme of Action (POA) would be posted on the Government website (www.gov.za), together with reports on progress made in the implementation of the POA. Accordingly, reports of the Governance and Administration Cluster; Social Cluster; Economic Cluster; Justice, Crime Prevention and Security Cluster; and International Relations, Peace and Security Cluster are posted bimonthly.

Government

International Marketing Council

The IMC of South Africa was established in 2000 as a public-private partnership aimed at creating a positive, united image for South Africa to give the country a strategic advantage in an increasingly competitive marketplace.

The IMC's mission is three-fold:
- to articulate a brand for South Africa, which positions the country to attract tourism, trade and investment, as well as realise international relations objectives
- to establish an integrated approach within government and the private sector towards the international marketing of South Africa
- to build national support for Brand South Africa.

The Public Service

On 31 December 2004, the Public Service had 1 043 698 people in its employ, 62% of whom were attached to the Social Services Sector (health, social development and

---

The Presidential Municipal Imbizo Programme was initiated in 2005 to align Project Consolidate and government's imbizo programmes. In May 2005, the first Presidential Municipal Imbizo was held in the Bojanala District Municipality in North West. Several others followed.

The National Imbizo Focus Week, held in October 2005, focused on the implementation of Project Consolidate. Attention was paid to practical work in assisting the 136 municipalities identified, as well as others that may be prioritised by provinces, to improve their capacity and to implement projects aimed at reducing poverty and improving services to the people.

Members of the executive from all spheres of government interacted directly with the public and communities regarding programmes that require partnerships of local, provincial and national government with communities.

South Africa, your road to
UNLIMITED OPPORTUNITIE

Trade and Investment South Africa, a division of **the dti**, is responsible for attracting foreign and domestic investment into all sectors of the South African economy.

Agro-processing, Automotive, Marine, Rail and Aerospace, Business Process Outsourcing, and I Enabled Services, Capital Equipment, Chemical Clothing, Textiles and Footwear, Cultural Industrie (including Film), Electrotechnical Industries, Minin and Mineral Beneficiation, and Tourism have bee identified for them to have high potential and achieve the national objectives of economic growth employment creation and the redistribution of th ownership base in the country.

Trade and Investment South Africa offers an arra of services to potential, new and existing investor These include the following:

- Information Services

- Facilitation services

- Customised Sector Programmes (CSP)

- Foreign Economic Representation

- Exports

For more information contact

The Department of Trade and Industry (**the dti** 77 Meintjies Street, Pretoria, 0002
the dti Customer Contact Centre
0861 843 384 (South African)
+ 27 12 394 9500 (International)
Website: www.thedti.gov.za

the dti
Department:
Trade and Industry
REPUBLIC OF SOUTH AFRICA

Government

Public servants by race on 31 March 2005

- African: 73,9%
- Asian: 3,7%
- Coloured: 8,9%
- White: 13,5%

Source: *South Africa Yearbook 2005/06*

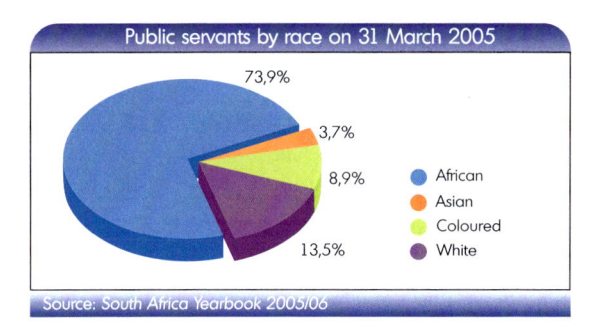

education), followed by 19% in the Criminal Justice Sector, and 7% in the Defence Sector.

The Public Service has been restructured extensively, with employees being deployed particularly in service-delivery positions.

A public service that serves the public

Government believes that the Public Service exists to create a better life for all.

Community development workers (CDWs) are part of government's drive to ensure that service delivery reaches poor and marginalised communities. CDWs act as a bridge between government and citizens, providing information on services, benefits and economic opportunities. They are in a position to inform the Government of the needs of the people.

By September 2005, 2 238 full-time CDWs and CDW learners had been recruited and were active in the programme. Of this number, 1 329 had completed their yearlong learnership programme.

Provinces were involved in the process of recruiting a further 920 CDW learners, which will bring the total of CDWs to 3 158. Progress made indicated that the initial target of 2 840 CDWs countrywide will be exceeded by March 2006.

The Batho Pele (People First) policy promotes integrated and seamless service delivery.

Various projects are being delivered through Batho Pele. These include:
- the electronic e-Gateway project to facilitate access to all government services and information, and which is maintained by the GCIS
- modernising government, for example, through the Centre for Public-Service Innovation
- creating new service-delivery mechanisms such as MPCCs and one-stop centres
- the Government Information Technology Officers' Council to alert government when and how to intervene to improve service delivery
- active auditing of national and provincial departments' anti-corruption capabilities by the Public Service Commission.

Affirmative action

On 31 March 2005, 73,9% of the Public Service was African; 3,7% Asian; 8,9% coloured; and 13,5% white. With regard to

Fighting corruption

The National Anti-Corruption Forum (NACF) convened the second National Anti-Corruption Summit in March 2005 in Pretoria, Gauteng. Attended by 396 representatives from the public, civil society and business sectors, the summit recognised the progress that South Africa had made in fighting corruption and generally expressed the need for a greater emphasis on implementation of the existing anti-corruption framework, policies and legislation.

Several resolutions were adopted to form the basis of a national programme to fight corruption. These resolutions pertain to ethics, awareness, prevention, combating corruption, oversight, transparency, accountability and the NACF. An implementation committee was established to develop the National Anti-Corruption Programme that will be implemented within sectors and as cross-sectoral plans.

Government

Between April and November 2004, missions abroad and provincial offices processed 51 376 applications for permits. Of these, 10 503 were permanent permits, 2 529 were business permits, 8 822 were work permits and 29 522 were visitors' permits.

gender, 53,3% was female and 46,7% male. However, at senior management level, 54% was African; 7,5% Asian; 7,7% coloured; and 30% white. The gender breakdown for senior management was 28,5% female and 71,5% male.

Home affairs

The Department of Home Affairs has a network of offices in all the provinces. Where the establishment of fixed offices is not warranted, mobile offices or units service such areas regularly.

The Population Register is being rewritten, and an associated document-management system will be developed and rolled out gradually. This will consist of a large database, an online document-storage system, and a query interface for the retrieval and viewing of electronically stored documentation. The system will reduce processing time for each business transaction, while enhancing information integrity.

The rewriting of the Population Register is closely aligned with the implementation of the Home Affairs National Identification System (HANIS).

HANIS is a key pillar of government's e-government programme. Through this system, the Department of Home Affairs seeks to create and maintain an integrated biometric database of all people – citizens and visitors – that it deals with. As part of the department's Turnaround Strategy, it plans to computerise all application processes to enable a quick, reliable and secure system of identification and service delivery.

Pocket Guide to South Africa 2005/06

Permanent residence

The department is responsible for admitting people suitable for immigration, such as skilled workers who are in short supply locally.

Applications are particularly encouraged from industrialists and other entrepreneurs who wish to relocate their existing concerns or establish new concerns in South Africa.

Those wishing to enter the country as work seekers or for study purposes must have the relevant permit, which is issued outside the country.

Independent Electoral Commission (IEC)

The IEC is a permanent body created by the Constitution to promote and safeguard democracy in South Africa. Although publicly funded and accountable to Parliament, the commission is independent of government. Its immediate task is the impartial management of free and fair elections at all levels of government.

> **fact**
> A total of 154 808 illegal foreigners were deported in 2003, and 141 722 were deported from January to October 2004. A small percentage of detainees are released due to logistical or legal hindrances to deportation. Of roughly 18 889 asylum applications received during 2003/04, 2 045 were processed by the Department of Home Affairs' refugee-status determination officers.

Provinces

South Africa's surface area covers 1 219 090 km^2, divided into nine provinces, each with its own unique landscape, economic activities, people and attractions. Few, if any, other countries offer the visitor as much breathtaking beauty and astonishing variety.

Each province has its own legislature, premier and executive council. The provinces are: Western Cape, Eastern Cape, KwaZulu-Natal, Northern Cape, Free State, North West, Gauteng, Mpumalanga and Limpopo.

Western Cape

This is a region of majestic mountains; well-watered valleys; wide, sandy beaches; and breathtaking scenery.

Cape Town, the legislative capital, is one of the world's most beautiful cities and is a must-see for every tourist.

WESTERN CAPE

Capital: Cape Town
Principal languages: Afrikaans 55,3%
isiXhosa 23,7%
English 19,3%
Population: 4 645 600 (*Mid-year estimates, 2005*)
Area (km^2): 129 370
% of total area: 10,6%
GDPR* at current prices (2003): R181,069 billion
% of total GDP**: 14,5%
* GDPR (Gross Domestic Product by Region)
** GDP (Gross Domestic Product)
Source: Statistics South Africa

Pocket Guide to South Africa 2005/06

Other important towns in the province include Worcester and Stellenbosch for their winelands; George, renowned for indigenous timber and vegetable produce (and, nowadays, for world-class golf courses); and Oudtshoorn, known for its ostrich products and the celebrated Cango caves.

Provincial economy

The agricultural sector accounts for over 55% of all South African agricultural exports; fruit and wine from the Cape are enjoyed around the world, as is seafood from the province.

The Western Cape's share of the national economy grew to 14,5% in 2003. Financial and business services are strong contributors to the provincial economy, while Information Technology is set to become an important source of growth.

Some tourist attractions:
- Robben Island, where former President Nelson Mandela was imprisoned for a number of years, in Table Bay off Cape Town
- Table Mountain, with its modern cableway, which takes visitors to the top, providing breathtaking views
- the National Botanical Gardens at Kirstenbosch
- whale-watching at Hermanus
- a wine-tasting tour of the spectacular winelands
- the Cape Floral Region, a World Heritage Site.

Eastern Cape

The Eastern Cape, a land of undulating hills, endless sandy beaches, majestic mountain ranges and deep green forests, is the second-largest of the nine provinces. The region ranges from the dry, desolate Great Karoo to the lush forests

The Western Cape's fynbos is one of six floral kingdoms worldwide, with more plant species than the whole of Europe.

Provinces

EASTERN CAPE

Capital: Bisho
Principal languages: isiXhosa 83,4%
Afrikaans 9,3%
English 3,6%
Population: 7 039 300 (*Mid-year estimates, 2005*)
Area (km²): 169 580
% of total area: 13,9%
GDPR at current prices (2003): R88,032 billion
% of total GDP: 8,1%
Source: Statistics South Africa

of the Wild Coast and the Keiskamma Valley, and the mountainous southern Drakensberg region.

Provincial economy

The Eastern Cape has excellent agricultural and forestry potential. The fertile Langkloof Valley has enormous deciduous fruit orchards, while the Karoo interior is an important sheep-farming area.

The metropolitan economies of Port Elizabeth and East London are based primarily on manufacturing, the most important being motor manufacturing. The Coega Industrial Development Zone near Port Elizabeth is one of the biggest initiatives ever undertaken in South Africa.

Some tourist attractions:

- Grahamstown, the City of the Saints, a historical, educational and religious centre
- the endless golden beaches of Port Alfred and Kenton-on-Sea
- a walking tour of the Wild Coast
- the pachyderms of the Addo Elephant National Park.

KwaZulu-Natal

South Africa's garden province boasts a lush subtropical coastline, sweeping savanna in the east, and the magnificent

Pocket Guide to South Africa 2005/06

KWAZULU-NATAL

Capital: Pietermaritzburg
Principal languages: isiZulu 80,9%
English 13,6%
Afrikaans 1,5%
Population: 9 651 100 (Mid-year estimates, 2005)
Area (km²): 92 100
% of total area: 7,6%
GDPR at current prices (2003): R206,766 billion
% of total GDP: 16,5%
Source: Statistics South Africa

Drakensberg mountains in the west. The warm Indian Ocean washing its beaches makes KwaZulu-Natal one of the country's most popular holiday destinations. Some of South Africa's best-protected indigenous coastal forests are found along the subtropical coastline.

The bustling metropolis of Durban has the busiest port in Africa.

Provincial economy

KwaZulu-Natal was the second-highest contributor to the South African economy in 2003, at 16,5% of gross domestic product (GDP). Sugar-cane plantations form the mainstay of the agricultural economy. Other important agricultural contributors are dairy, fruit and vegetables, and forestry.

Tourist attractions:

- the 19th-century battlefields where imperial Britain clashed with the Zulu nation
- Durban's fascinating mix of eastern and western cultures
- dolphin-spotting on the coast between the Umdloti and Tugela rivers
- experiencing Zulu traditions and culture at authentic villages
- deep-sea fishing off Sodwana Bay

KwaZulu-Natal is the only province with a monarchy provided for in its legislation.

Provinces

NORTHERN CAPE

Capital: Kimberley
Principal languages: Afrikaans   68%
                         Setswana   20,8%
                         isiXhosa   2,5%
Population: 902 300 (*Mid-year estimates, 2005*)
Area (km²): 361 830
% of total area: 29,7%
GDPR at current prices (2003): R29,659 billion
% of total GDP: 2,4%
Source: Statistics South Africa

- the Greater St Lucia and Ukhahlamba-Drakensberg World Heritage Sites.

Northern Cape

The Northern Cape lies to the south of the mighty Orange River, which provides the basis for a healthy agricultural industry. Away from the Orange, the landscape is characterised by vast arid plains with outcroppings of haphazard rock piles.

The province is renowned for its spectacular display of spring flowers which, for a short period every year, attracts thousands of tourists.

Provincial economy

Mining, particularly the production of diamonds and iron ore, dominates the economy. The province is also rich in asbestos, manganese, fluorspar and marble. Strong growth areas include game farming and food production.

Tourist attractions:
- the Kalahari Gemsbok National Park, which, together with the Gemsbok National Park in Botswana, forms Africa's first transfrontier conservation area, the Kgalagadi Transfrontier Park
- the Augrabies Falls, among the world's greatest cataracts
- the Sol Plaatje Museum in Kimberley.

Free State

The Free State lies in the heart of South Africa. Between the Vaal River in the north and the Orange River in the south, this immense rolling prairie stretches as far as the eye can see.

The capital, Bloemfontein, houses the Supreme Court of Appeal, a leading university and some top schools.

FREE STATE

Capital: Bloemfontein
Principal languages: Sesotho   64,4%
                           Afrikaans 11,9%
                           isiXhosa   9,1%
Population: 2 953 100 (Mid-year estimates, 2005)
Area (km^2): 129 480
% of total area: 10,6%
GDPR at current prices (2003): R69,094 billion
% of total GDP: 5,5%
Source: Statistics South Africa

Provincial economy

Mining, particularly gold, is the biggest employer, followed by manufacturing. A gold reef of over 400 km stretches across Gauteng and the Free State. The province accounts for 30% of South Africa's total gold production, and contributes significant amounts of silver, bituminous coal and diamonds. The Free State has cultivated land covering 3,2 million ha. Field crops yield almost two-thirds of the province's agricultural income, with most of the balance being contributed by animal products.

Tourist attractions:
- the sandstone formations at Golden Gate
- the spectacular scenery of the town of Clarens

> The Free State is the third-biggest province but has the second-smallest population.

- the King's Park Rose Garden in Bloemfontein
- the Basotho Cultural Village in the QwaQwa National Park
- the desolate beauty – and watersports – of Sterkfontein Dam.

North West

North West borders Botswana, fringed by the Kalahari Desert in the west, and the Witwatersrand in the east. A province of varied attractions, North West is home to some of South Africa's most visited national parks, the celebrated Sun City and Lost City resorts, picturesque dams and dense bush.

NORTH WEST

Capital: Mafikeng
Principal languages: Setswana 65,4%
Afrikaans 7,5%
isiXhosa 5,8%
Population: 3 823 900 (Mid-year estimates, 2005)
Area (km^2): 116 320
% of total area: 9,5%
GDPR at current prices (2003): R81,442 billion
% of total GDP: 6,5%
Source: Statistics South Africa

Provincial economy

North West is, thanks to platinum in particular, the dominant province in terms of mineral sales, which contribute 25,6% to the provincial economy. Diamonds are also mined here. Manufacturing activities include fabricated metals, food and non-metals. North West is South Africa's leading producer of white maize. Some of the world's largest cattle herds are found in the area around Vryburg.

> The Rustenburg-Brits region is the largest single platinum-production area in the world.

Pocket Guide to South Africa 2005/06

Tourist attractions:
- Mafikeng, site of the Anglo-Boer/South African War siege
- the mampoer (moonshine) country of Groot Marico
- entertainment, gaming and sports at Sun City and the Palace of the Lost City
- a game drive or walk in Madikwe Game Reserve, home to 10 000 animals
- spotting the Big Five in the Pilanesberg National Park
- Vredefort Dome World Heritage Site.

Gauteng

Although geographically the smallest of the nine provinces, Gauteng (Sotho word for 'the place of gold') contributes more than a third of South Africa's GDP.

The main cities are Johannesburg, the biggest city in southern Africa, and Pretoria, the administrative capital of the country.

Provincial economy

Manufacturing, financial and business services and logistics make Gauteng the economic powerhouse of southern Africa. Success in attracting value-added new-economy investment is borne out by the burgeoning high-tech corridor in Midrand.

GAUTENG

Capital: Johannesburg
Principal languages:
- isiZulu 21,5%
- Afrikaans 14,4%
- SeSotho 13,1%
- English 12,5%

Population: 9 415 231 (*Mid-year estimates, 2005*)
Area (km^2): 17 010
% of total area: 1,4%
GDPR at current prices (2003): R413,554 billion
% of total GDP: 33%
Source: Statistics South Africa

Provinces

Gauteng has a greater proportion of its labour force in professional, technical, managerial and executive positions than any other province. Johannesburg houses the JSE Limited, the largest securities exchange in Africa. Hundreds of leading local companies have their head offices here, as do the regional operations of many multinationals.

> Gauteng is the wealthiest province in South Africa, generating 33% of South Africa's GDP.

Tourist attractions:
- Soweto, home to two million people and the site of much of the anti-apartheid struggle
- Pretoria in spring when some 50 000 jacaranda trees turn the city purple
- the Cradle of Humankind, the richest source of pre-hominid fossils on the planet, and a World Heritage Site
- bustling, funky downtown Johannesburg, city of gold.

Mpumalanga

Mpumalanga (place where the sun rises) is bordered by Mozambique and Swaziland in the east, and Gauteng in the west. It is situated mainly on high plateau grasslands which roll eastwards for hundreds of kilometres. In the north-east, the province rises towards mountain peaks

MPUMALANGA

Capital: Nelspruit
Principal languages: siSwati 30,8%
  isiZulu 26,4%
  isiNdebele 12,1%
Population: 3 219 900 (*Mid-year estimates, 2005*)
Area (km^2): 79 490
% of total area: 6,5%
GDPR at current prices (2003): R87,461 billion
% of total GDP: 7%
Source: Statistics South Africa

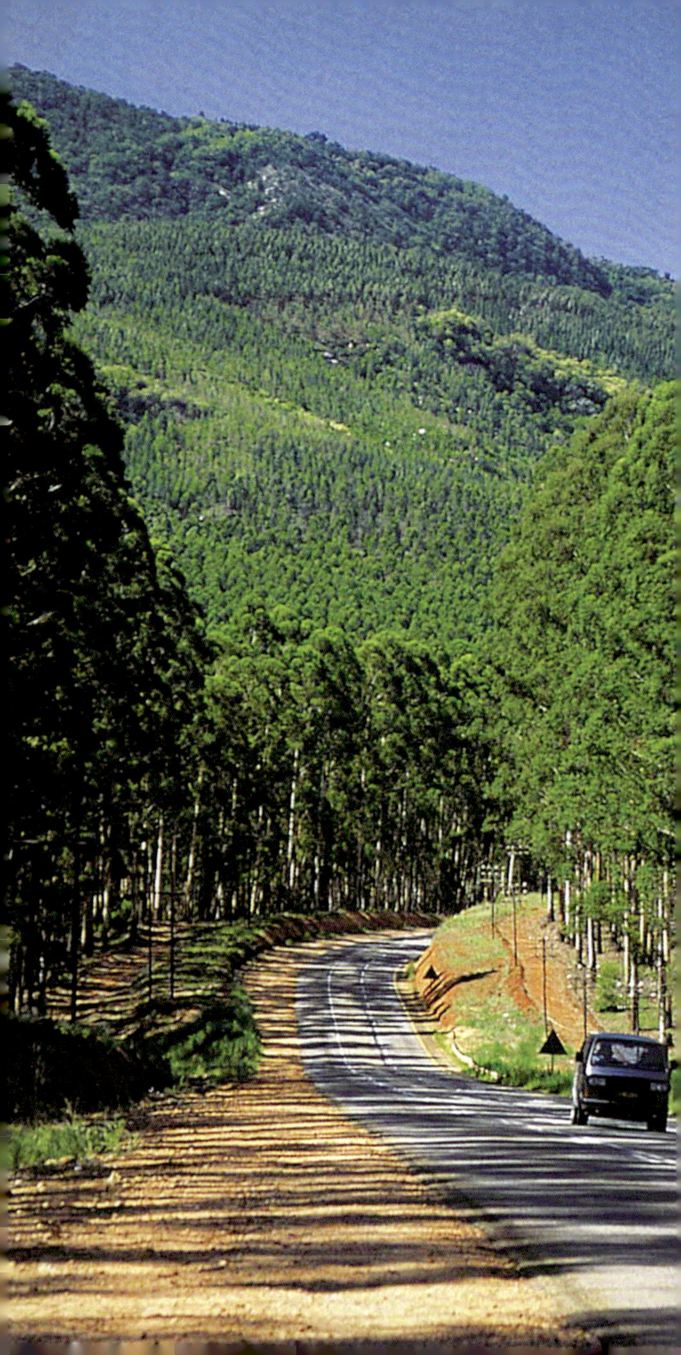

Provinces

> The southern hemisphere's three biggest power stations are located in Mpumalanga.

and then terminates in an immense escarpment. In some places, this escarpment plunges hundreds of metres down to the low-lying Lowveld, home to the Kruger National Park.

Provincial economy

Mpumalanga combines mining and heavy industry with the cultivation of citrus, tropical and subtropical fruits and extensive forests. The southern hemisphere's three biggest power stations are located in the province, supplied by the Witbank coalfields which are among the most extensive in the world. Middelburg is a major steel producer and Secunda has a key oil-from-coal installation.

Tourist attractions:
- Kruger National Park and its ultra-luxurious, privately owned adjoining lodges
- the spectacular Mac Mac Falls outside Sabie
- the well-preserved historical gold-rush towns of Pilgrim's Rest and Barberton
- the stunning scenery of the Blyde River Canyon
- spectacular scenery at God's Window
- the historic train ride between Waterval-Boven and Waterval-Onder.

Limpopo

In the extreme north of South Africa, Limpopo is a province of dramatic contrasts: bush, mountains, indigenous forests and plantations. Well-situated for economic growth and trade with other parts of southern Africa, between 1995 and 2001 the province recorded the highest real economic growth rate in South Africa. The greater part of the Kruger National Park is located within Limpopo.

Pocket Guide to South Africa 2005/06

LIMPOPO

Capital: Polokwane
Principal languages:
Sesotho sa Leboa 52,1%
Xitsonga 22,4%
Tshivenda 15,9%
Population: 5 635 000 (*Mid-year estimates, 2005*)
Area (km^2): 123 910
% of total area: 10,2%
GDPR at current prices (2003): R81,295 billion
% of total GDP: 6,5%
Source: Statistics South Africa

Provincial economy

Limpopo is rich in minerals, including copper, asbestos, coal, iron ore, platinum, chrome, diamonds and gold. While exports are mostly primary products, the province is rich in resources, particularly in tourism, agriculture and minerals. Cattle ranching is frequently combined with hunting. Tropical and citrus fruits are extensively cultivated while tea, coffee and forestry are important economic contributors.

About 60% of South Africa's tomatoes, 33% of its oranges and 70% of its mangoes come from Limpopo. More than 45% of the R2-billion annual turnover of the Johannesburg Fresh Produce Market is from the province.

Tourist attractions:
- the unforgettable bushveld scenery of the Waterberg
- fun and relaxation in the mineral baths of Bela-Bela
- the Big Tree (the biggest baobab in southern Africa) near Tzaneen
- the springs of Tshipise, which attract a million visitors a year
- the Modjadji Nature Reserve
- the Mapungubwe iron age site.

Economy

South Africa has experienced strong economic growth since the end of apartheid in the early 1990s. A profound restructuring of the economy has borne fruit in the form of macro-economic stability, booming exports and improved productivity in both capital and labour.

The performance of the South African economy in 2004 was encouraging, with growth accelerating above 5% in the second half of the year. By February 2005, the economy was growing more strongly than at any time in the previous 20 years.

South Africa's fiscal deficit was reduced from 46% of gross domestic product (GDP) in 1996 to 1,5% in 2005.

Not surprisingly, South Africa's global competitiveness has soared. Manufactured value-added products are now increasingly eating into commodities' traditionally dominant share of exports.

South African vehicle exports

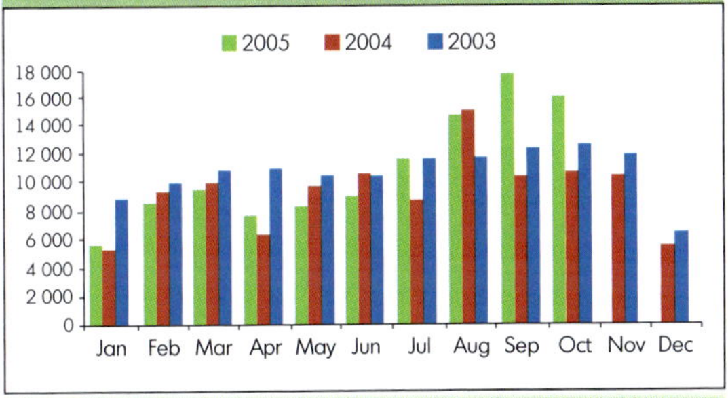

Source: National Association of Automobile Manufacturers of South Africa

Pocket Guide to South Africa 2005/06

Domestic output

Real economic activity in South Africa improved in 2004. Real GDP, which increased by 2,8% in 2003, rose a further 3,7% in 2004. It was expected to accelerate to 4,3% in 2005 and to average 4,2% a year over the next three years.

The enhanced performance was particularly evident in the middle quarters of 2004 when quarter-to-quarter growth accelerated from an annualised rate of 4% in the first quarter to 4% and 5% in the second and third quarters, respectively.

In 2004, the level of real output in the primary sector rose by 3% compared with an increase of only 1% in 2003, mainly as a recovery in the real value added by the agricultural sector.

Following a decline of 6% in 2003, the real value added by the agricultural sector increased by 1% in 2004 mainly on account of higher field crop production, particularly maize.

Growth in the real value added by the mining sector amounted to 4%, which is comparable to the rate of 4% recorded in 2003.

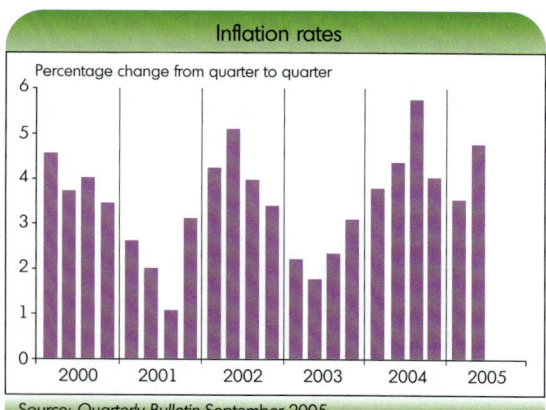

Inflation rates

Percentage change from quarter to quarter

Source: *Quarterly Bulletin* September 2005

Economy

In October 2005, Cabinet received a report of the task team headed by the Deputy President dealing with the Accelerated and Shared Growth Initiative for South Africa. The initiative deals with challenges of ensuring that the country raises the trajectory of growth to average at least 4,5% in the next five years and about 6% between 2010 and 2014.

Domestic expenditure

All the major components of real domestic final demand rose strongly in 2004, which impacted on the accelerated growth in real gross domestic expenditure for 2004 as a whole.

Growth in aggregate real gross domestic expenditure increased from an annualised rate of 2% in the third quarter of 2004 to 4% in the fourth quarter.

The level of real gross domestic expenditure was 6% higher in 2004 than in 2003.

The buoyancy in consumer spending was also reflected in a year-on-year growth rate of 6% in 2004 compared with a growth rate of 3% in 2003.

The strong household spending was underpinned by several factors, including:
- An increase of 5% in real household disposable income in 2004, partly due to wage settlements which remained above the contemporaneous inflation rate and income tax rates which were lowered marginally.
- The steady decline in bank lending rates in 2003 and 2004, culminating in the lowest nominal short-term interest rates since 1998. This reduced the debt-servicing cost of households as a percentage of disposable income from 8% in 2003 to 6% in 2004.
- The high levels of consumer confidence recorded in 2004, previously observed in 1997.
- The wealth effects arising from the exceptional increase in property and other asset prices.

Price inflation

The rate of increase in the consumer price index for metropolitan and other urban areas less mortgage interest cost (CPIX) has remained within the mandated target range of 3% to 6% since September 2003. Year-on-year CPIX inflation rose from the February 2005 low of 3,1% to 3,6% and 3,8% in March and April 2005, respectively. This upward trend was due almost entirely to consecutive increases in the petrol price totalling 82 cents per litre in March and April. Most of the short-term volatility in the inflation rate can be attributed to petrol price developments. If petrol and diesel prices are excluded, annual CPIX inflation increased marginally from 3,2% in February 2005 to 3,3% in March and April 2005. The annualised quarter-on-quarter seasonally adjusted rate of increase of CPIX in the first quarter of 2005 amounted to 2,1% compared with 5% in the fourth quarter of 2004.

Exchange rates

The weighted exchange rate of the Rand, which appreciated by 16,2% between the end of December 2002 and the end of December 2003, improved by a further 11,7% between the end of December 2003 and the end of December 2004.

The net average daily turnover in the domestic market for foreign exchange, which decreased to US$10,8 billion in the third quarter of 2004, rose to US$12,4 billion in the fourth quarter of 2004 – its highest level to date.

The average monthly real effective exchange rate of the Rand increased by 4,3% from December 2003 to December 2004.

Foreign trade and payments

Growth in the global economy accelerated to nearly 4% in 2004, from 2,4% in 2003.

Economy

The deficit on the current account of the balance of payments widened considerably from R18,9 billion in 2003 to R44,4 billion in 2004. As a ratio of GDP, the deficit rose to 3,2%.

The significant widening of the deficit on the current account in 2004 resulted mainly from the sustained high level of real economic activity and concomitant strong increase in merchandise imports.

Robust domestic demand and the strengthening of the exchange rate of the Rand were reflected in the physical quantity of imported goods, which advanced by no less than 16,5% over the period.

As could be expected against the background of a vigorous upturn in economic activity, South Africa's trade balance with the rest of the world deteriorated considerably from a surplus of R25,6 billion recorded in 2003 to a deficit of R0,2 billion in 2004.

The value of merchandise exports increased throughout 2004. For the year as a whole, export values were 8,8% higher at R278,9 billion, from R256,3 billion in 2003. In particular, mining export values increased by no less than 13,5% in 2004, while manufactured goods increased by only 3% over the period.

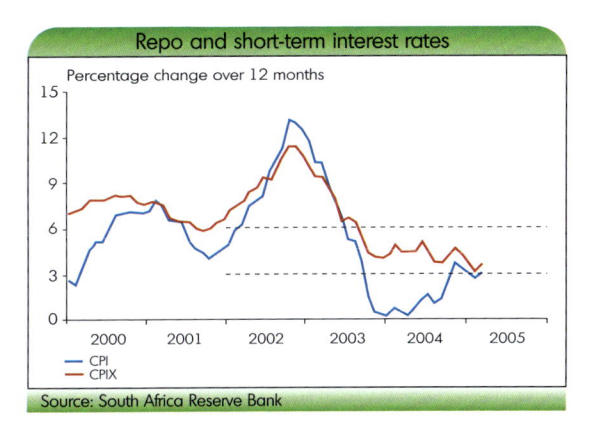

Repo and short-term interest rates

Percentage change over 12 months

Source: South Africa Reserve Bank

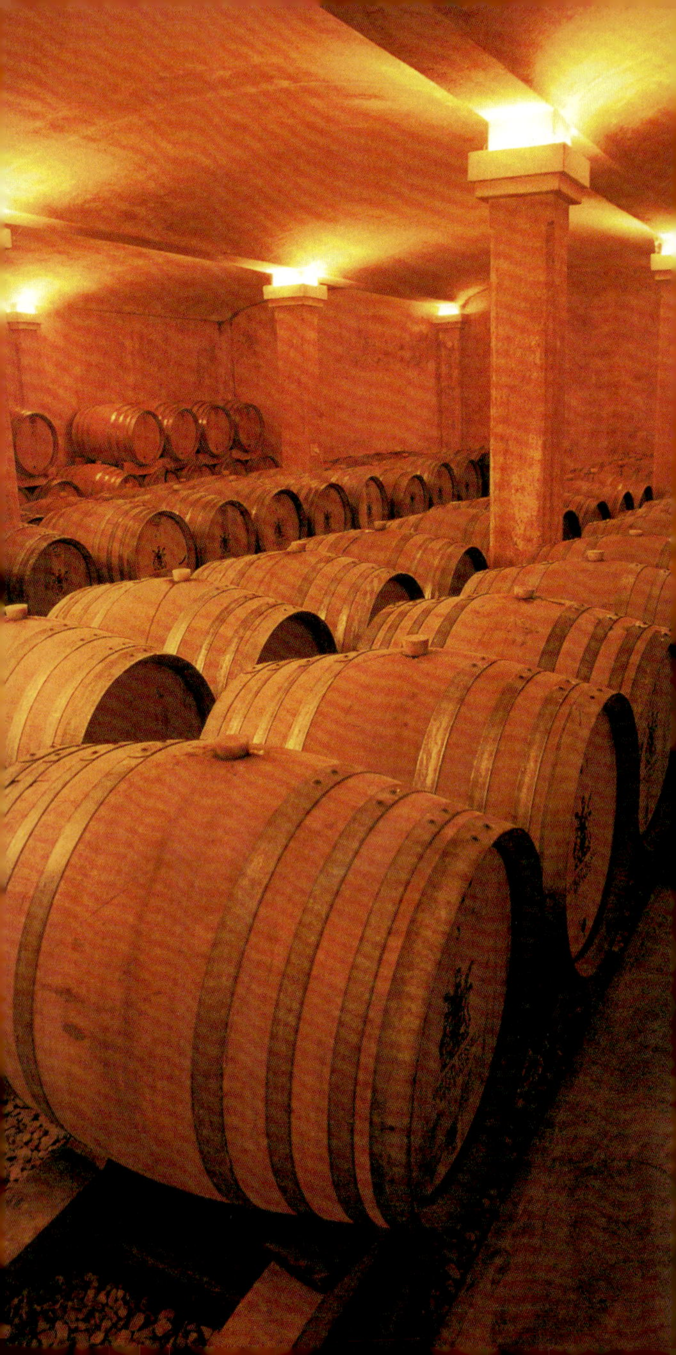

Economy

The Rand prices of goods exported from South Africa in 2004 increased by about 3%, while the Rand prices of commodity exports increased by about 5%.

The further widening of the current account deficit in 2004 was also brought about by a decrease of 4% in the value of net gold exports from R34,2 billion in 2003 to R32,8 billion in 2004.

Trade relations

Africa

South Africa's economy is inextricably linked to that of the southern African region, and its continued growth to the

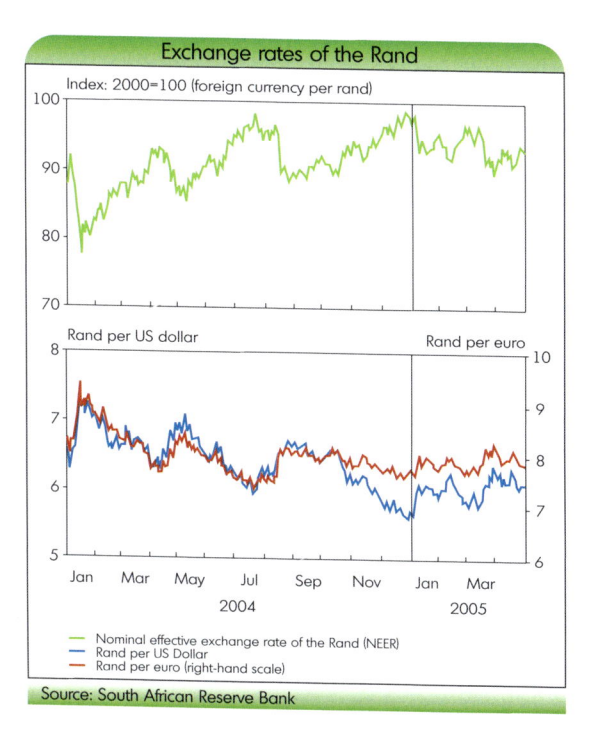

Exchange rates of the Rand

- Nominal effective exchange rate of the Rand (NEER)
- Rand per US Dollar
- Rand per euro (right-hand scale)

Source: South African Reserve Bank

economic recovery of the continent through the New Partnership for Africa's Development. Most of South Africa's investment into the rest of Africa is aimed at infrastructural development.

Africa is an important market for South African exports. In 2003, about 23% of South Africa's exports were destined for the continent. There was a huge increase in imports from the continent. In 2003, only 4% of total imports came from Africa. However, this increased to 40% in 2004.

Southern African Development Community (SADC)

The centrepiece of South Africa's foreign economic policy is the SADC. Within the SADC, South Africa, Botswana, Lesotho, Namibia and Swaziland have organised themselves into the Southern African Customs Union (SACU). SACU shares a common tariff regime without any internal barriers.

Two-way trade between South Africa and the rest of the SADC member states is characterised by the prevailing trade imbalance in terms of exports, versus imports from the region.

A sizeable share of South Africa's exports (estimated at over R38,5 billion at the end of 2004) is destined for SACU and other SADC countries. South African trade with this region increased significantly between 2002 and 2004, from R15 billion to R38,8 billion. Trade with SADC countries

---

New research by the South African Advertising Research Foundation shows that between 1998 and 2004 more than two million people moved out of the poorer end of the scale of living standards measures (LSMs), which ranks the poorest at one and the richest at 10.
- In 1998, the poorest four categories represented 48% of the population. In 2004, the figure was 42%.
- LSM 5 grew by 1,4 million adults with virtually all the newcomers moving up from poor groups.
- LSM 6 grew by 1,6 million adults, including those who had moved up from LSM 5.

Source: *BuaBriefs Issue 69*

Economy

also increased from R32 billion to about R38 billion between 2002 and 2004.

Europe

Europe is the largest source of investment for South Africa and accounts for almost half of South Africa's total foreign trade. In 2003, Europe accounted for 40% (R92 billion) of South Africa's total exports, and 45,8% (R116,59 billion) of its total imports.

The historic Trade, Development and Co-operation Agreement, which was provisionally implemented in January 2000, established a free trade agreement between South Africa and the European Union (EU). South Africa will grant duty-free access to 86% of EU imports over a period of 12 years, while the EU will liberalise 95% of South Africa's imports over 10 years.

The agreement provides a legal framework for ongoing EU financial assistance for development co-operation, which amounts to R900 million per year.

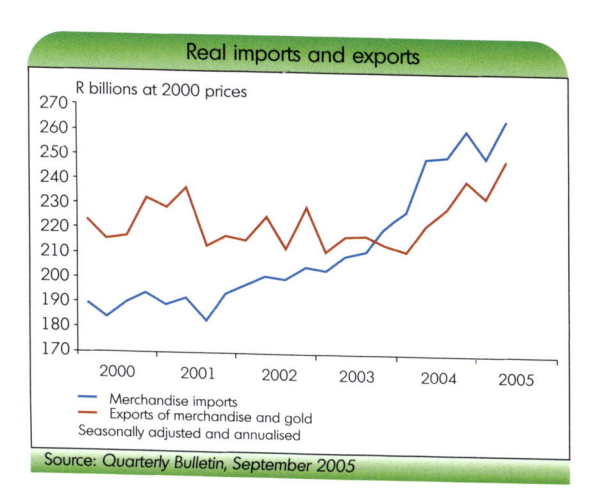

Real imports and exports

R billions at 2000 prices

— Merchandise imports
— Exports of merchandise and gold
Seasonally adjusted and annualised

Source: *Quarterly Bulletin, September 2005*

United States of America (USA)

The USA is South Africa's number one trading partner in terms of total trade. Exports to the USA rose in nominal terms from R29 billion in 2003 to R30 billion in 2004. Imports from the USA recorded a paltry increase in nominal terms from R25 billion in 2003 to R26 billion in 2004. South Africa is a beneficiary of the USA's Generalised System of Preferences (GSP), which grants duty-free treatment for more than 4 650 products, and of the Africa Growth and Opportunity Act, in terms of which an additional 1 783 products were added to the existing GSP products.

Latin America

South Africa's major trading partners in South America are Brazil, Argentina, Chile, Mexico and Peru. South Africa and the Mercosur states signed a framework agreement in 2000, which commits them to working towards a free trade agreement. Trade between South Africa and Mercosur grew from R2,7 billion in 1994 to R12,7 billion in 2004. About 62,5% of total trade between South Africa and Mercosur is with Brazil.

Asia

Between 1995 and 2002, trade with the Indian Ocean Rim Association for Regional Co-operation accounted for 14% of South Africa's global trade.

Trade with India has grown particularly rapidly. Total two-way trade between South Africa and India reached R8,26 billion in 2004.

Japan is South Africa's biggest trading partner in Asia and was its third-largest export destination during 2004, with total trade between the two countries reaching R47,5 billion.

From March to September 2005, South Africa participated in the World Exposition in Aichi, Japan. South Africa showcased itself as a trading nation whose sophisticated infrastructure, natural environment, rich

Economy

cultural heritage and history make it one of the world's top investment and travel destinations.

Total trade between South Africa and the People's Republic of China grew from R5,3 billion in 1998 to R29,6 billion in 2004.

South African trade with the Association of South-East Asian Nations region totalled R1,64 billion in 2004, and is set for continued growth.

Economic transformation

Small is big

The Government's National Strategy for Small Business aims to boost small enterprises, equalise income and wealth and create long-term jobs. Fostering entrepreneurship among women is a particular focus.

The development of small, medium and micro enterprises has attracted more and more attention in South Africa during recent years, as an engine for general economic growth as well as for employment creation and equity acceleration.

The Department of Trade and Industry launched the Small Enterprise Development Agency (SEDA) in December 2004.

SEDA, which provides non-financial support to small and medium enterprises (SMEs), was formed through the merger of Ntsika Enterprise Promotion Agency and the National Manufacturing Advisory Centre.

National Empowerment Fund (NEF)

The NEF was launched in May 2004 to finance Black Economic Empowerment (BEE) businesses and reduce the real risk by developing creative and unique products that respond appropriately to the circumstances faced by black businesses.

The fund received its first boost of R150 million during the 2004/05 financial year and was allocated a further R400 million in 2005/06.

I pose a question: what is different about a company that carries the Proudly South African symbol?

Yes, it meets the standards set by the campaign with regard to the level of loca content, quality and labour practices. But perhaps there is a deeper and more significant difference. Such a company is not necessarily bigger, better or more successful. But it is making a statement that is at once a statement of origin, a statement of purpose and a statement of optimism. The symbol imbues such

Proudly South African Founder Sponsors

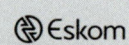

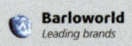

SOUTH AFRICAN AIRWAYS — Eskom — Barloworld Leading brands — PetroSA — Telkom

Proudly South African   Tel: (011) 327 7778   Fax: (011) 32

BLUEPRINT 341

Picture supplied by Matube Publishing

Support your country. Buy Proudly South African.

ompany with a unique and uplifting national identity:
rands its products with the same sense, and provides
e people in that company with a motivation and
fying principle that ties their work to a larger purpose
he building of our country.

y Proudly South African and help build the pride
d prosperity of our nation.

African Strategic Partners | Founder Broadcast Partner

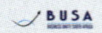

BUSA · FEDUSA · SABS · SABC

ers@proudlysa.co.za   Website: www.proudlysa.co.za

The fund has also introduced new products and services such as the Group Entrepreneurial Schemes (loans and equity finance to BEE SMEs) and Market Making (larger BEE transactions finance in capital markets, warehousing and strategic projects).

The fundamental difference between the NEF and the existing finance institutions is its approach to evaluating businesses, the scope of business sizes that it will be financing, and its range of products.

Industrial Development Corporation (IDC)

During 2004, the IDC approved projects worth R6,2 billion, representing a growth of 26% from 2003.

More than 17 000 job opportunities created by IDC financing during 2004, and 74% of the number of approvals, were directed to SMEs.

Some 46% of the number and 33% of the value of approvals were allocated to historically disadvantaged people.

For the first time in history, the IDC received the investment grade rating of Baa2 awarded by Moody's Investor Service, which was in line with South Africa's sovereign debt rating.

Business Partners Ltd

Business Partners Ltd is a specialist investment group, providing customised investment, mentorship and property-management services to SMEs in South Africa.

In 2004/05, it boasted an investment portfolio of R1,066 billion, with equity-based investments amounting to 42% of the portfolio. A total of 538 investments valued at

> According to Ernst & Young, the number of Black Economic Empowerment (BEE) transactions in South Africa in 2004 increased by 29% to 244 from 189 in 2003. BEE deal value increased from R42,2 billion in 2003 to R52,9 billion in 2004.

R660,5 million were approved in 2004/05. Of these, 213 investments to the value of R265,9 million were approved for historically disadvantaged entrepreneurs, and 159 investments amounting to R154,4 million were approved for female entrepreneurs.

State-owned enterprises (SOEs)

The Department of Public Enterprises ensures that SOEs play an upliftment and development role.

In June 2005, government announced a major investment drive which includes a R40-billion and R95-billion investment plan over five years for Transnet and Eskom, respectively.

The money will be used for construction, renovation and expansion, including:
- R15 million for the rehabilitation of the three Eskom power stations – Camden, Grootvlei and Komati
- R2,9 billion for the expansion and redesign of Pier 1 and the widening of the entrance at the Durban Harbour
- R2,6 billion for the container terminal at Ngqura/Coega
- R1,4 billion for the expansion of the Cape Town container terminal.

Expanded Public Works Programme (EPWP)

The EPWP celebrated its first anniversary in April 2005. It is the largest job-creating initiative to be undertaken by government. The EPWP is expected to create over 300 000 work opportunities by April 2007.

The EPWP is operational in all nine provinces. Projects include the construction of rural or low-volume roads, water and sanitation trenches and sidewalks.

In addition, government will increase spending on the maintenance of schools, clinics and other government buildings. EPWP projects will also be launched in the area of home-based care for people affected by HIV and AIDS, childcare projects, and in environmental projects like LandCare and clearing alien vegetation from river banks.

> Global car-makers and aerospace companies view South Africa as one of the most attractive destinations worldwide for foreign direct investment (FDI), according to a survey, the *Annual FDI Confidence Index*, by global management consulting firm AT Kearney. South Africa ranked seventh-most attractive destination globally for investment in the transportation equipment sector. This was partly the result ofw government assistance in the form of the Motor Industry Development Programme, which has helped global car-makers operating in South Africa to grow car exports nine-fold over the past decade.

While most of the jobs created will be for a limited period, people employed will receive basic training that will allow them to find jobs in future. Government will be spending almost R20 billion on this programme over the next five years.

The EPWP is on course to reach its target of one million job opportunities in five years. By September 2005, some 223 400 gross work opportunities had been created from 3 400 EPWP projects nationwide in the first year of the EPWP, yielding at least R823 million in total wages paid. Of those who benefited from these projects in the first year of the programme, 38% were women, 41% youth, and 0,5% people with disabilities.

National finances

South Africa's debt, both domestic rand-denominated bonds and foreign debt issues, enjoys increasing recognition on international capital markets. The South African economy grew by 3,7% in 2004, and is set to grow by over 4% a year for the next three years. The economy is growing more strongly than at any time in the past 20 years.

This reflects:
- the country's macro-economic success
- sustainable fiscal and macro-economic policies
- a sound and transparent approach to debt management
- a healthy balance-of-payments position
- the maturity of South Africa's financial markets.

South African foreign debt continues to trade at tighter spreads than the Emerging Market Bond Index.

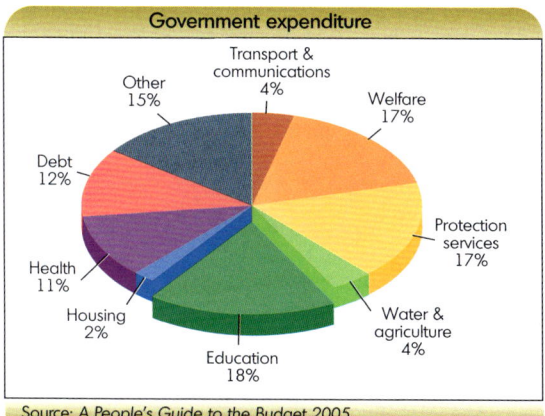

Government expenditure

- Transport & communications 4%
- Welfare 17%
- Protection services 17%
- Water & agriculture 4%
- Education 18%
- Housing 2%
- Health 11%
- Debt 12%
- Other 15%

Source: A People's Guide to the Budget 2005

The primary objective of domestic debt management has in recent years shifted to reducing the cost of debt to within acceptable risk limits, with diversification of funding instruments and ensuring flexible government access to markets as secondary goals. Recourse to foreign borrowing has been stepped up, allowing the fiscus to contribute to reducing the foreign currency exposure of the South African Reserve Bank in its forward market portfolio.

State debt costs continue to fall as a share of government expenditure. It was expected to be 2,3% of gross domestic product (GDP) in 2005/06, while debt service costs were expected to total 3,5% of GDP according to the Budget speech delivered early in 2005. Debt service accounted for 5,6% of GDP in 1999. The liquidity in the domestic government bond market, measured by the increase in nominal trades, has improved substantially in recent years.

Financial markets

Primary capital market
Although primarily a government-bond market, the Bond

Emerging-market bond indices

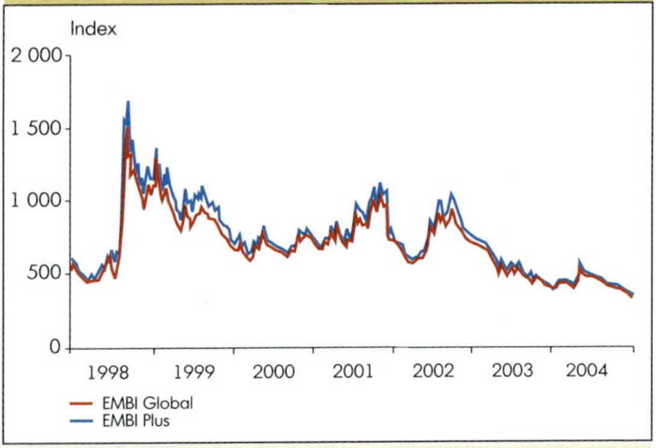

Source: South African Reserve Bank

National finances

Exchange of South Africa (BESA) also lists rand-denominated debt securities issued by local government, public enterprises and major corporates. At 31 December 2004, BESA had 378 fixed-income securities outstanding, issued by 65 borrowers, with a total nominal value of R572 billion. Just over 70% of this debt had been issued by central and municipal government, with a further 11% issued by parastatal and utility organisations. The remaining listed debt had been issued by companies in a wide range of sectors: banking, gold mining, chemical, food, household goods and textiles, telecommunications and transport. Securitisation issues include vehicle, credit card, loan receivables, equipment receivables and mortgage products.

Market performance

The South African bond market is one of the most liquid emerging bond markets in the world. Turnover in listed debt declined in 2004, with volumes decreasing from R10,7 trillion nominal in 2003 to R8,4 trillion nominal, representing a drop of 21%. The decrease in nominal turnover was also reflected in the lower number of matched

Non-financial public-sector borrowing requirement

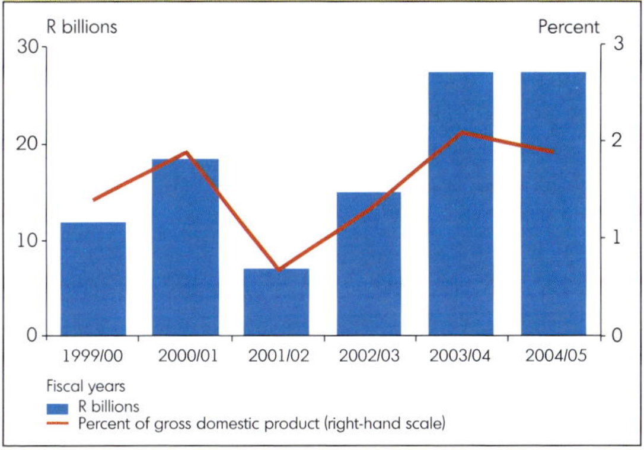

Source: South African Reserve Bank

Pocket Guide to South Africa 2005/06

Tax revenue

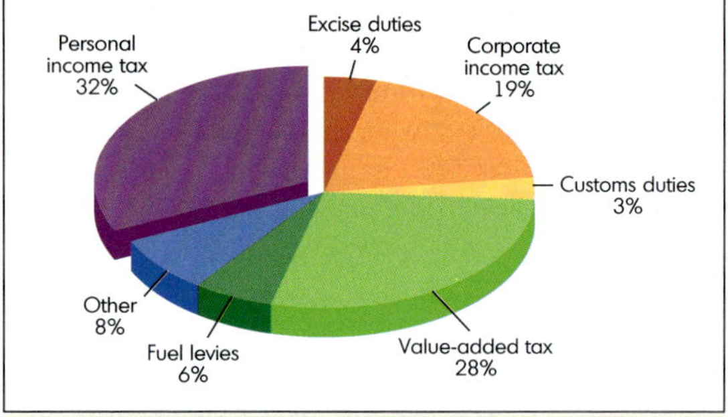

- Personal income tax 32%
- Excise duties 4%
- Corporate income tax 19%
- Customs duties 3%
- Value-added tax 28%
- Fuel levies 6%
- Other 8%

Source: A People's Guide to the Budget 2005

trades for the year, which decreased from 356 000 in 2003 to 328 000 in 2004. Turnover in the spot market increased from 33,6% of total turnover in 2003 to 34,1% in 2004.

Although turnover figures for 2004 dropped significantly, the turnover velocity of listed debt instruments remained healthy at 14 times the market capitalisation for 2004.

While 94% of market turnover in 2004 was in government and utilities stock, there has been an ever-increasing amount of listings and turnover in corporate issuances and securitisations which together, in 2004, accounted for 6% of total turnover.

Offshore turnover in listed debt that was settled locally amounted to R2 trillion, or 23,6% of total turnover, indicating that South Africa's local debt has significant attraction for international investors.

Secondary capital-market activity

South African bond yields declined considerably from May 2004 until February 2005. The yields on government bonds declined to historically low levels, with the yields on two-year R194, five-year R153 and 20-year R186 government bonds declining to 7,22%, 7,40% and 6,98%, respectively, by 28 February 2005.

National finances

Factors that contributed to this decline in local yields include the firmer Rand-Dollar exchange rate, reductions in the repo rate, low yields in the developed countries, and a ratings upgrade by Moody's in January 2005. In addition, the inflation outlook has remained promising, with CPIX moving to historically low levels, and not expected to breach the upper band of the Reserve Bank's 3% to 6% guideline range over the forecast period. Improved investor sentiment towards the country's political and economic policies also contributed to the decline in bond yields, as reflected by non-resident interest in the local bond market. After being net sellers of South African bonds to the value of R8,1 billion in 2003, foreigners were net purchasers of bonds to the value of R450 million in 2004.

During March 2005, bond yields increased by an average of 80 basis points, in reaction to external factors, such as increasing United States (US) Treasury yields.

Managing public finances

The Public Finance Management Act, 1999 holds heads of departments accountable for the use of resources and emphasises regular financial reporting, independent auditing and measuring output and performance.

State departments are closely monitored by the National Treasury and any deviations are referred to the Auditor-General for investigation.

Taxation

The South African Revenue Service (SARS) collected

The Auditor-General has a budget of more than R712 million and 1 598 employees. These are divided into various centres of excellence that provide auditing services, corporate services and specialised audit work, namely performance, forensic auditing, computer auditing and technical support. It also boasts an impressive international auditing complement.

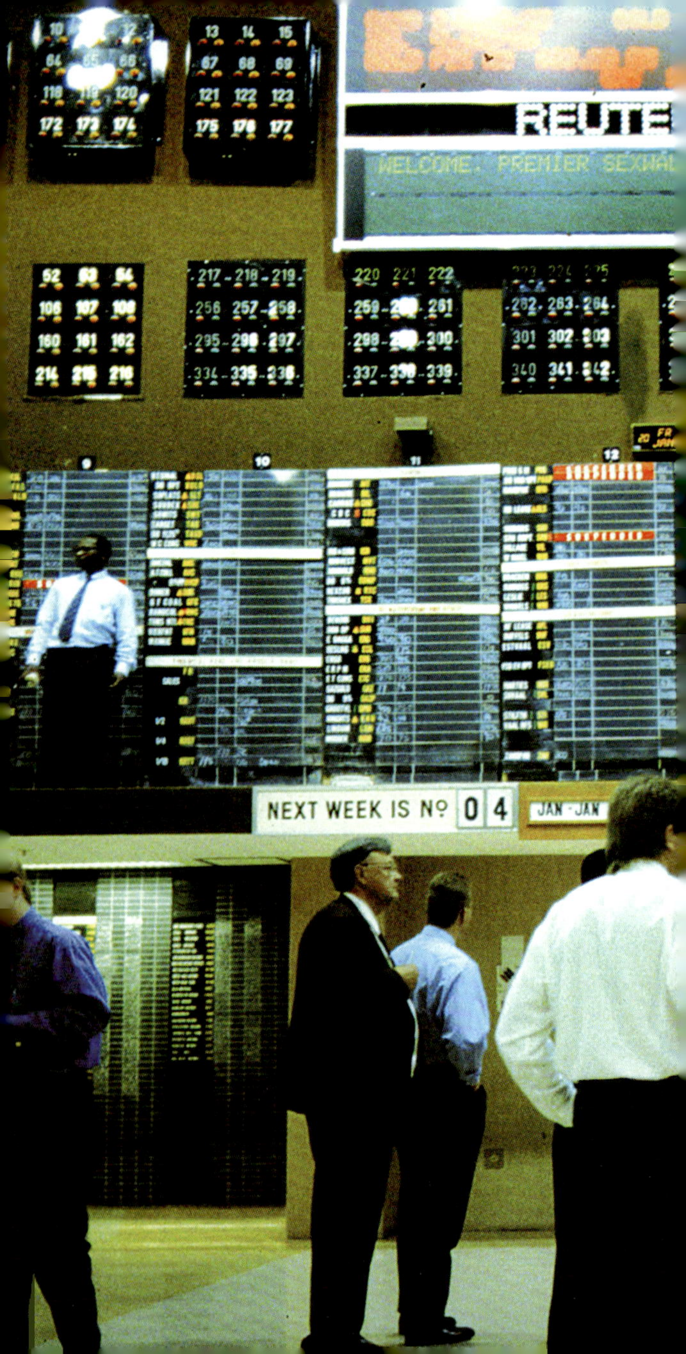
REUTE
WELCOME. PREMIER SEXWAL
NEXT WEEK IS Nº 04
JAN - JAN

National finances

Yields on long-term government bonds

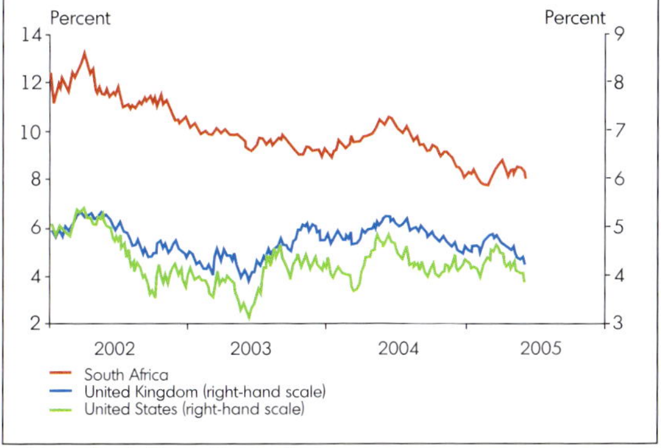

- South Africa
- United Kingdom (right-hand scale)
- United States (right-hand scale)

Source: South African Reserve Bank

R354,9 billion in taxes during 2004/05, exceeding its revised target of R333,7 billion by almost R10 billion and its original target of R345,3 billion by R21 billion. The revenue haul will help trim South Africa's budget deficit for 2004/05 from 2,3% to 1,6% of GDP.

South African residents are (subject to certain exclusions) taxed on their worldwide income.

Companies are taxed at a rate of 29% after a 1% reduction for 2005/06 to stimulate investment and job creation. In addition, secondary tax on companies is levied on companies at a rate of 12,5% on dividend distributions. A formula tax applies to gold-mining companies. A number of administrative interventions as well as tax-relief measures were announced in the Budget to regularise and to stimulate growth for small businesses. Small business corporations (annual turnover limit increased to R6 million) benefit from a revised graduated tax rate of 0% on the first R35 000 of taxable income and 10% up to R250 000 of taxable income. They are eligible for accelerated depreciation allowances, and can write off investments in manufacturing plant and equipment in the year in which it is incurred.

Value-added tax is levied at a standard rate of 14%. Transfer duty, estate duty, stamp duty, marketable securities tax, customs duty and excise duty are also levied. Local governments levy rates on the value of fixed property.

A skills development levy applies at the rate of 1% of payroll, for employers with an annual payroll of more than R250 000.

The Minister of Finance, Mr Trevor Manuel, presented the Budget for 2005/06 on 23 February 2005.

Highlights included:
- R6,8 billion in tax relief for individuals and households, directed mostly at those earning below R200 000 a year
- people earning below R35 000 a year (R60 000 for over 65s) would not pay personal income tax
- a change in the tax treatment of medical scheme contributions to reduce costs of membership for lower-income families
- scrapping of transaction tax on debit entries to credit card and bank accounts, to keep banking services affordable
- beer went up 11c a bottle, and 5c a can, while a packet of 20 cigarettes cost 52c more
- levies on petrol and diesel increased by 10c a litre
- tax relief of R1,4 billion for small business, to free up resources for growth
- measures to reduce tax-compliance costs and red tape for small business
- a drop in the company tax rate from 30% to 29%
- changes to the tax on travel allowances to remove unwarranted benefits for higher-income earners
- a R40 increase in the maximum monthly old age, disability and care dependency grants to R780, and a R10 increase in the monthly Child Support Grant to R180
- a R6-billion allocation to allow the land restitution programme to complete its work over the next three years
- eliminating regional services council levies in 2006

National finances

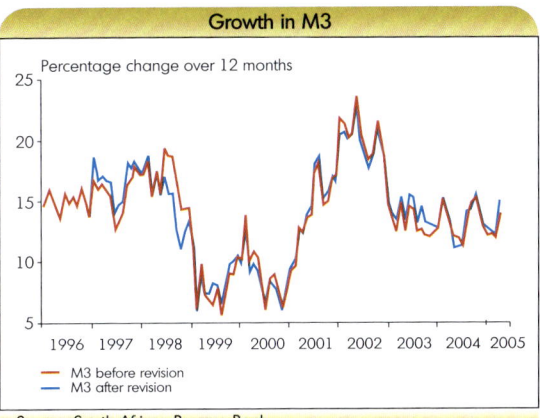

Growth in M3

Percentage change over 12 months

- M3 before revision
- M3 after revision

Source: South African Reserve Bank

- R2 billion for the new comprehensive housing strategy and R3 billion for related community infrastructure
- R1,7 billion for water, sanitation and other municipal infrastructure investment
- R6,9 billion for improving teachers' salaries
- R5 billion to allow for pay progression in police salaries and an increase in police numbers
- R3 billion for public transport investments and roads, including for the 2010 Soccer World Cup
- R3,7 billion for the delivery of municipal services
- R776 million for the National Student Financial Aid Scheme
- R1 billion to revitalise Further Education and Training colleges
- R1,4 billion for South Africa's African development agenda, including peacekeeping operations, the African Union and the Pan-African Parliament
- a new micro-agricultural finance scheme, with funding of R1 billion.

Auditor-General

The Constitution guarantees the independence of the

Auditor-General. The office audits national, provincial and local government. The Auditor-General has the power to audit the activities of public entities without the approval of the CEO or directors.

South African Reserve Bank

The bank, which is independent, formulates and implements monetary policy and regulates the supply of money by influencing its cost.

An important responsibility of the bank is to ensure that the banking system as a whole is sound and meets the requirements of the community.

The bank acts as a banker to other banking institutions. It is also the custodian of the statutory cash reserves and provides facilities for the clearing and settlement of interbank obligations.

Monetary policy

The main objective of monetary policy is to secure a stable financial environment. Policy is therefore not applied to address short-term cyclical events.

Growth in broad monetary aggregated M3 exceeded 11% throughout 2004, registering the highest value for the year of 14,9% in October.

South African Revenue Service's 'volumetrics' as at May 2005:
- 14 600 employees
- 14 million returns processed
- 1,4 million corporate taxpayers
- 4,3 million individual taxpayers
- 573 876 value-added tax vendors
- 300 268 pay-as-you-earn employers
- 14 million passengers moving through customs
- 68 775 consignments stopped
- 1,4 million Southern African Customs Union movements
- 1 851 total seizures
- 998 221 export transactions and 1,7 million import transactions
- R21 billion collections over budget.

Source: Finance Ministry, Budget Vote, 2005

National finances

The banking industry

At the end of December 2004, 35 banks, including 15 branches of foreign banks and two mutual banks, were registered with the Office of the Registrar of Banks. Furthermore, 45 foreign banks had authorised representative offices in South Africa. By the end of December 2004, the banking institutions collectively employed 116 940 workers.

Four major groups dominated the South African banking sector, holding 82% of its assets:
- Amalgamated Banks of South Africa (Absa) Group Limited
- Standard Bank Investment Corporation Limited
- FirstRand Holdings Limited
- Nedcor Limited.

Industry-wide net income after tax declined to 0,4% of total assets in 2002. As a percentage of equity, industry-wide net income after tax decreased from 9,2% in 2001 to 5,4% in 2002.

In July 2005, Barclays, the third-largest British bank, paid R30 billion for a 53,9% stake in Absa. At the time, it was the biggest foreign direct investment yet in post-apartheid South Africa.

Insurance companies

As at 31 March 2004, 78 long-term insurers were registered. The total net premiums received and outstanding for 2003 (unaudited figures) amounted to R156,8 billion, while total assets amounted to R822,1 billion.

Online banking accounts reached the one million mark in South Africa for the first time at the end of 2003. According to the World Wide Worx research report, *Online Banking in South Africa 2004*, the number of online bank accounts in South African grew by 28% in 2003. The number of online bank accounts reached 1,04 million and was expected to increase by more than 30% during 2004.

Pocket Guide to South Africa 2005/06

Banknotes with improved security features went into circulation from 1 February 2005.

The upgraded banknotes retain the Big Five animal motif on the front and the economic sector themes on the back. There are, however, some design changes. Celebrating South Africa's democracy, the upgraded banknotes were the first to show the South African Coat of Arms and to use all 11 languages across the denominations.

The improved security features make it easier for the public to distinguish between good banknotes and counterfeit ones and further give the upgraded banknotes a distinct look. Examples are the shimmering gold band, visible on the back of the banknote when it is tilted, as well as the colour-changing ink on the number value on the front bottom right of the R50, R100 and R200 banknotes.

Development Bank of Southern Africa (DBSA)

The primary purpose of the bank is to promote economic development and growth, human resource development and institutional capacity-building. The bank's mandate is focused on infrastructure.

The DBSA estimates the scale of the impact of its funding operations using economic modelling techniques. According to these, the level of DBSA loan approvals in South Africa and the Southern African Development Community is projected to grow to R6 billion per year by 2013/14. This in turn should have an impact of creating a 127 000 jobs in South Africa, connecting 2,4 million households to one or more basic services and contributing R22,2 billion to the local economy. Toward this end, it plans to invest R45,6 billion (loans and equity finance) in infrastructure development and well over R1 billion in technical assistance, capacity-building grants and knowledge development/networking.

Doing business in South Africa

The South African economy is firmly on a higher economic growth range, emphasising the economic turnaround that has been achieved over the past 10 years.

This has created a strong platform for accelerated growth in the next decade, with an emphasis on achieving higher levels of productive investment, employment creation, exports and productivity.

Fiscal deficit has been reduced from 4,6% in 1996 to just 1,5% of gross domestic product (GDP) in 2005.

Excellent investment opportunities exist in a number of sectors, including tourism, mining and mineral beneficiation, hi-tech industries and communications, manufacturing, transport and agriculture. By April 2005, South Africa's investment rate had increased from 14% to 17% of GDP. Business confidence was at a record high.

Policy

To reinforce and sustain economic growth, government is focusing on three key areas of intervention, namely, increasing the rate of investment, improving levels of competitiveness and broadening economic participation.

Over the past few years, government has initiated various measures to speed up economic growth and job creation. These include the Micro-Economic Reform Strategy, which is government's primary strategy for addressing constraints, economic growth and employment creation, decisions of the Growth and Development Summit, new infrastructure projects, initiatives to lower the cost of production,

SACOB business confidence index

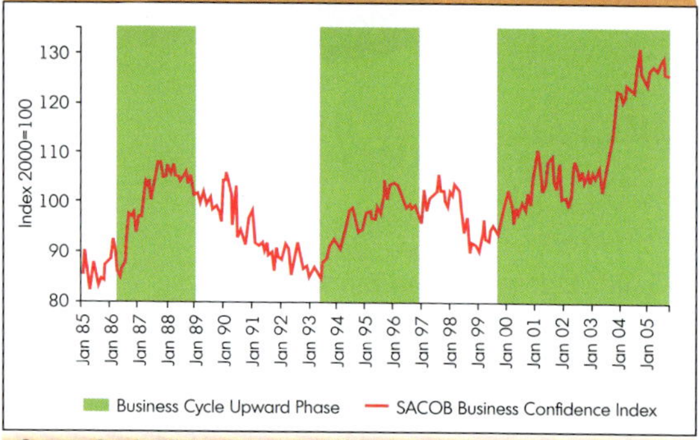

Source: South African Chamber of Business

including telecommunications and other input costs, and programmes in respect of the Second Economy.

In recent years, South Africa has made great strides in opening the domestic economy to international competition.

Achievements include:
- a market-related and competitive exchange rate
- no restrictions on the type or extent of foreign investments
- strengthening competition policy
- abolishing exchange control for non-residents, and a reduction in that applicable to residents
- a significant reduction in tariff barriers, ahead of the World Trade Organisation timetable
- providing world-class investment incentives.

Attracting investment

In line with promoting foreign investment in South Africa and positioning the country as a financial centre for Africa, government announced in February 2004 that foreign companies, governments and institutions may list on South Africa's bond and securities exchanges.

Government aims to facilitate an increase in the rate of investment – gross fixed capital formation in both the public and private sectors – from 16% of GDP by October 2004 to 25% by 2014.

Increasing competitiveness

A number of incentives are being offered to both large and small businesses to improve their competitiveness, including those under the:

- Small and Medium Enterprise Development Programme, which has benefited over 12 000 enterprises
- Competitiveness Fund, which supported over 1 200 enterprises
- Sector Partnership Fund, which has assisted over 85 successful partnerships consisting of over 600 individual enterprises
- Black Business Supplier Development Programme, which has assisted over 600 small, black-owned enterprises to improve systems, quality, skills and marketability.

To improve access to affordable finance as a key element to broadening economic participation, the National Empowerment Fund was relaunched in May 2004 and allocated R150 million during 2004/05, which has been committed to Black Economic Empowerment (BEE) transactions.

The South African Micro-Finance Apex Fund, launched in April 2005, provides loans of up to R10 000 to micro businesses and some small businesses.

Broadening economic participation

The Broad-Based BEE Strategy is the overarching framework to broaden economic participation. In 2004, the National Small Business Act, 1996 was amended to provide for the merging of Ntsika and the National Manufacturing Advisory Centre, and the birth of the integrated Small Enterprise Development Agency.

2010 and

At ACSA, we are proud to be the largest airports authority in Africa with many flagship airports in our portfolio. We provide world-class infrastructure and services for airlines to move people and goods to desired destinations.

We are innovative in designing new ways to provide efficient, safe and secure airport infrastructure and services to meet the future demands of airlines across the world. We are also proactively promoting tourism, the facilitation of economic growth, job creation and the protection of the environment.

Towards that end, we will be investing R5,2 billion in infrastructure and service improvement at our network of airports over the period to 2009 in order to enable us to manage world-class airports that contribute to the economic growth of our country.

Beyond

MAPPING THE FUTURE

ACSA
AIRPORTS COMPANY SOUTH AFRICA

www.acsa.co.za

Pocket Guide to South Africa 2005/06

The Small Enterprise Development Strategy was unveiled in 2005.

Trade and Investment South Africa (TISA)

TISA, a division of the Department of Trade and Industry, aims to develop the South African economy by focusing on investment development and promotion, export development and promotion, and sector policy development.

TISA is responsible for developing the following priority sectors:
- agroprocessing
- chemical and allied industries
- clothing, textiles, leather and footwear
- cultural industries
- exportable services (business process outsourcing)
- Information and Communications Technology (ICT) and electronics
- metals and mineral-based industries
- tourism
- transport industries.

During 2004/05, outward-bound missions that had been financially assisted by TISA considerably increased market access for at least 123 companies.

National Industrial Participation Programme (NIPP)

The NIPP became obligatory on 1 September 1996, focusing on purchases arising mainly from the transport, energy and ICT sectors.

Since 2000, there has been a major increase in the size of obligations as a result of purchases from South African

> The automotive sector is the leading manufacturing sector and the third-largest sector in the South African economy. The sector's contribution to gross domestic product in 2003 amounted to 6,4%, up from 5,7% in 2002 and 5,4% in 1999.

Airways and the Strategic Defence Procurement package. By November 2004, the size of obligations being monitored was in excess of US$14,5 billion.

By November 2004, the programme had facilitated over 125 projects, resulting in investments and sales credits worth US$2 billion, consisting of investments of US$677 million, export sales of US$1 billion, and local sales, including BEE and small and medium enterprise (SME) promotion of US$457 million.

These projects have created and/or sustained 7 000 direct jobs, increased international markets for South African value-added products, developed whole new ranges of products in emerging, higher opportunity industrial sectors, and brought in millions of rands in new investment, mostly to the poorest and most neglected parts of the country.

Spatial development

To encourage investment in geographic areas of greatest poverty and economic potential, 11 spatial development initiatives (SDIs) and four industrial development zones

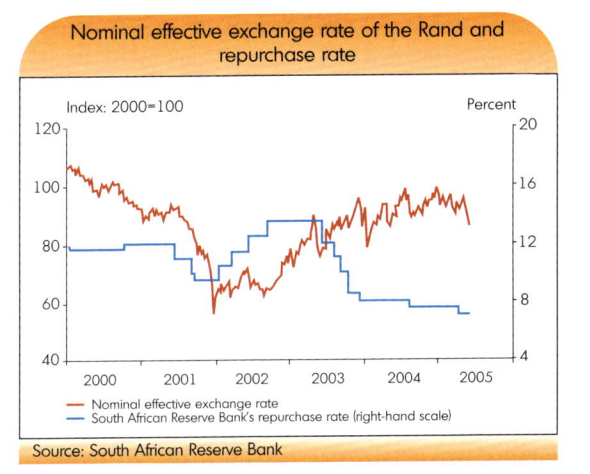

Nominal effective exchange rate of the Rand and repurchase rate

- Nominal effective exchange rate
- South African Reserve Bank's repurchase rate (right-hand scale)

Source: South African Reserve Bank

(IDZs) have been created and are at varying stages of delivery.

Those created are:
- SDIs: Maputo Development Corridor; Lubombo SDI; Richards Bay SDI, including the Durban and Pietermaritzburg nodes; Wild Coast SDI; Fish River SDI; West Coast Investment Initiative; Platinum SDI; Phalaborwa SDI; and Coast-2-Coast Corridor
- IDZs: Gauteng, Coega, East London, Saldanha and Richards Bay.

The SDI concept may have a variety of focuses, such as:
- industrial – KwaZulu-Natal and Fish River SDIs
- agritourism – Lubombo and Wild Coast SDIs
- sectoral mix – Maputo Development Corridor
- IDZs – Coega, Saldanha and East London.

IDZs are located near major transport notes such as ports or airports. The benefits of IDZs are support to investing companies, especially for greenfields development projects; access to transport for export; waiver of import duties for export products; and subsidised skills training.

In 2001, work started on the Coega Deep Water Harbour and IDZ near Port Elizabeth.

Investments committed for the Coega Project – both the IDZ and the deep water port of Ngqura – amount to R5 billion. The French aluminium group Pechiney selected Coega over other sites in Canada and Australia for the first of a new generation of smelters.

The Enterprise Organisation (TEO)

TEO's purpose is to stimulate and facilitate the development of sustainable competitive enterprises through the

---

fact: An incentive scheme for the film industry was launched in June 2004. Thirteen approvals were granted in this sector in 2004/05.

efficient provision of effective and accessible supply-side incentive measures.

It contributes to the realisation of the Department of Trade and Industry's strategic objectives by:
- developing incentives in support of identified policies and sector strategies
- efficiently administering the department's incentive programmes
- facilitating access to and impact of products and services rendered by TEO through a focused business-development effort.

Help for exporters

A draft export development strategy was developed in 2004/05. Eleven trade bulletins were published containing over 613 unified business opportunities. It is estimated that the bulletins are distributed monthly to over 4 000 exporters.

Non-financial assistance in the form of information and general advice was provided to over 857 exporters. Some 1 500 copies of the *Export Answer Book* were also distributed. The export-readiness of 15 enterprises in the cosmetics sector was improved by facilitating training in supply-chain management for export delivery.

For export promotion, 28 national pavilions across eight sectors were organised and managed. Some 375 companies were financially supported in national pavilions. The value of the orders taken from these companies at these events was R330 million.

In addition, 87 companies were trained in maximising their participation in trade fairs, and 14 companies and five export councils were trained in intelligence-gathering techniques at trade fairs. A total of 22 inward-buying missions were facilitated from 26 countries across nine sectors. Fourteen outward-bound trade missions were facilitated. Outward-bound missions financially assisted by

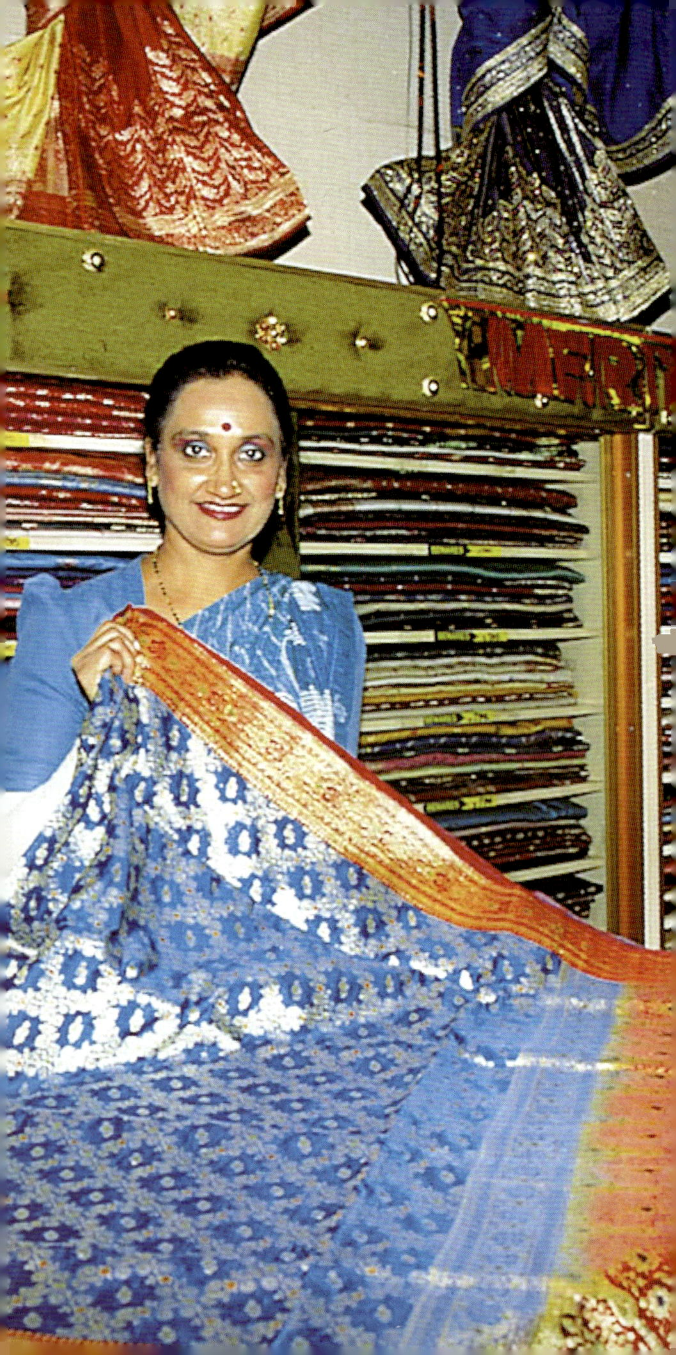

TISA have considerably increased market access for at least 123 companies.

Employment and skills development

At the June 2003 Growth and Development Summit, government, business, trade unions and community leaders recommitted themselves to creating jobs and boosting training. Employers and unions agreed to strengthen the 25 sector education and training authorities (SETAs). These government-business-labour organisations were established in March 2000 to identify and meet skills needs in each sector.

The amalgamation of several SETAs, which began in March 2005, resulted in the formation of three new SETAs. One of the country's largest SETAs, the Safety and Security Education and Training Authority, came into effect on 1 July.

By April 2005, at least 107 000 youth were being trained through learnerships and apprenticeships. In addition, 5 562 174 workers had participated in structured learning programmes, of which 4 641 810 had successfully completed their programmes.

A total R65,3 million was allocated to the National Students Financial Aid Scheme and the National Research Foundation, of which R15,8 million benefited post-graduate bursary holders in scarce skills.

During the last three-and-a-half years, the National Skills Fund (NSF) disbursed more than R2,3 million (75%) of its total income of R3,12 billion to fund various projects in provinces and with SETAs. Some R1 billion was allocated towards strategic projects that represent a single biggest investment in skills development funded under the NSF.

By March 2005, the NSF had achieved the following:
- R883 million (74%) of the total R1 billion strategic project had been spent
- 44 838 learners had benefited from Adult Basic Education and Training or other programmes at National Qualifications Framework level 1

> The Companies and Intellectual Property Registration Office became a trading entity in July 2002 and has registered over 100 000 close corporations in the past three financial years. In 2002, 10 408 patents were registered.
>
> Highlights for the Competition Commission in 2004/05 included its 284 mergers and acquisitions cases. Of these, 278 were finalised, 262 approved and seven approved with conditions. A total of 82 complaints on prohibited restrictive business practices were completed.
>
> In 2004/05, the National Lotteries Board paid out R262 million in lottery funds, of which 61% went to charitable organisations, 22% to beneficiaries in the sport and recreation sector, and 14% to beneficiaries in the arts, culture and heritage sector.

- 35 943 people completed structured learning programmes
- a total of 21 107 SMEs benefited from learnerships funded through strategic projects
- under the NSF Social Development Funding Window, R700 million was spent between 1999 and 2004 to train about 400 000 unemployed people in skills development projects managed by the Department of Labour's provincial offices.

Taxation

Companies are taxed at a rate of 29% after a 1% reduction in 2005/06 to stimulate investment and job creation. In addition, secondary tax on companies is levied at a rate of 12,5% on dividend distributions.

A formula tax applies to gold-mining companies. A number of administrative interventions as well as tax-relief measures were announced in the 2005 Budget to regularise and stimulate growth for small businesses.

Small business corporations (annual turnover limit increased to R6 million) benefit from a revised graduated tax rate of 0% on the first R35 000 of taxable income, and 10% up to R250 000 of taxable income; are eligible for accelerated depreciation allowances; and can write off

Doing business in South Africa

investments in manufacturing plant and equipment in the year in which it is incurred.

Additional measures to reduce the administrative and compliance burden on small business were announced in the Budget.

Exchange control

National Treasury has followed and continues to follow a policy of gradual relaxation of exchange controls since 1995. The following major reforms were announced by the Minister of Finance and implemented in 2004 in relation to resident and non-resident corporates, and South African individuals:

- Foreign-owned South African companies were able to borrow locally up to 300% of the total shareholders' investment. This debt capital would be used to finance investment in South Africa or as domestic working capital.
- Foreign entities (including foreign governments and multilateral institutions) were allowed to list their securities, both bonds and equities, on South African exchanges (i.e. inward listings). South African institutional investors are allowed to invest an additional 5% of their total retail assets in 'African'-classified inward-listed securities, while South African individuals can invest freely in such African and non-African inward-listed securities.
- Exchange control limits on outward foreign direct investment by South African corporates have been

---

The 2005–2010 National Skills Development Strategy (NSDS) has been finalised and R21,9 billion in funding allocated to it over five years.

The new NSDS is expected to play a key role in realising government's goal of halving the country's unemployment by 2014.

abolished. Yet, South African corporates are still required to lodge an application with the South African Reserve Bank. As part of further relaxation on corporates, South African companies are no longer compelled to repatriate foreign-earned dividends to South Africa. Government is working towards the transition from exchange controls to a system of prudential regulation for institutional investors.

Currently, South African long-term insurers, investment managers and pension funds can invest up to 15% of their total retail assets offshore, while collective investment schemes can invest 20% of their total retail assets offshore.

JSE Limited (JSE)

Founded on 8 November 1887, the JSE is the sole licensed securities exchange in South Africa. In July 2005, after 188 years as a mutual association, the JSE celebrated its demutualisation and is now known as JSE Limited, a public unlisted company.

In 2001, the JSE incorporated the South African Futures Exchange, presenting two new divisions – the Financial Derivatives Division, which covers the equity and interest-rate futures and options markets, and the Agricultural Products Division, which covers commodities futures and options.

Foreign affairs

The role of the Department of Foreign Affairs is to realise South Africa's foreign policy objectives. These are guided by a commitment to promoting human rights, democracy, justice and international law; international peace and internationally agreed mechanisms for resolving conflicts; Africa in world affairs; and economic development through regional and international co-operation.

South Africa and Africa

The South African Government firmly believes that the future of the country is inextricably linked to the future of

Representation, July 2005

South African representation abroad	Total
Embassies/high commissions	83
Consulates/consulates-general	16
Honorary consulates	46
Other (e.g. liaison offices)	4
Non-resident accreditation	106
International organisations	7

Foreign representation in South Africa	Total
Embassies/high commissions	113
Consulates/consulates-general	53
Honorary consuls/honorary consular agencies	73
Other (e.g. liaison offices)	1
Non-resident accreditation	16
International organisations	22

Source: Department of Foreign Affairs

Pocket Guide to South Africa 2005/06

the African continent and that of its neighbours in southern Africa. The national vision of building a united, non-racial, non-sexist and prosperous society is also relevant to the vision for Africa.

Coupled with this is the understanding that socio-economic development cannot take place without political peace and stability. South Africa's efforts are directed at creating an environment in which all states on the continent will achieve their full potential. Africa therefore remains the central area of focus in the conduct of the country's foreign policy.

Through the Department of Foreign Affairs, South Africa played an active role in setting up the African Union (AU) and making it work. Key AU structures include the AU Commission, which is responsible for the day-to-day running of the AU, and the Pan-African Parliament, which was inaugurated in 2004 and is hosted by South Africa.

In July 2004, South Africa was elected a member of the Peace and Security Council for three years. Its role is to prevent, manage and resolve conflicts.

Through active interventions in the Democratic Republic of Congo (DRC), Burundi, Ethiopia/Eritrea, Côte d'Ivoire and Sudan, South Africa supports peace and security efforts in Africa.

The AU appointed South Africa to spearhead the resolution of the political crisis in Côte d'Ivoire and to chair the committee on the post-conflict reconstruction of the Sudan, respectively.

---

fact

African Union (AU) financial institutions that will be set up to provide funding for projects and programmes are the:
- African Central Bank, assigned to the western region of the AU
- African Monetary Fund, assigned to the central region of the AU
- African Investment Bank, assigned to the northern region of the AU.

Foreign affairs

In July 2005, President Thabo Mbeki attended the inauguration of the new Sudanese President Omar Hassan Ahmed el-Mashir and his two deputies.

New Partnership for Africa's Development (NEPAD)

South Africa is a key driver of NEPAD, a socio-economic initiative to promote good governance, eradicate poverty and create sustainable economic growth.

The Department of Foreign Affairs will continue to facilitate implementing NEPAD's priority sectors, namely infrastructure, agriculture, environment, tourism, Information and Communications technology, health, human resources, and science and technology. Attention will increasingly be paid to establishing structures in South Africa to enable the country to maximise the increased trade and investment benefits arising from NEPAD.

By the end of 2005/06, South Africa was preparing for its review by NEPAD's African Peer Review Mechanism, an instrument voluntarily agreed to by AU member states for African self-monitoring. South Africa held its first consultative conference in September 2005.

The country's representatives sit on the Heads of State and Government Implementation Committee and its Steering Committee. The NEPAD Secretariat's full-time core staff are located in Midrand, near Johannesburg.

South Africa and the Southern African Development Community (SADC)

The SADC is a critical vehicle for southern African regional development.

The SADC provides for regional peace and security, sectoral co-operation and an integrated regional economy. The SADC member states are Angola, Botswana, the DRC, Lesotho, Malawi, Mauritius, Mozambique, Namibia, the Seychelles, South Africa, Swaziland, Tanzania, Zambia and Zimbabwe.

South Africa has been engaged in restructuring the SADC to enable it to execute evolving AU mandates and respond to changing development challenges. Considerable work has gone into setting up new institutions, as well as reviewing existing ones. From August 2004, the focus has been on chairing the SADC Organ on Politics, Defence and Security.

One of the organ's main functions is to ensure that the regional peace and security arrangements are linked to continental arrangements. Another challenge is finalising the Memorandum of Understanding between the AU Commission and Africa's regional economic communities to ensure a co-ordinated interface for addressing AU themes and activities.

Asia and Australasia

South Africa continues to strengthen its relations with the region through increases in two-way trade; personal exchanges between high-level dignitaries; and the finalisation of new instruments of co-operation in the scientific and technological fields, through technology transfer, investments and overseas development assistance in capacity-building.

By June 2005, South Africa had 17 residential diplomatic missions in 15 of the 30 countries or territories in Asia, Australasia and Central Asia. Eighteen countries from this region maintained 30 diplomatic missions in South Africa.

While Japan, Malaysia and Taiwan already rank among the foremost sources of foreign direct investment (FDI) in South Africa, the significance of China and India, as future sources of investment, is expected to grow. South Africa's multinational companies are finding attractive investment opportunities in Australia, China, Indonesia and Thailand in diverse fields such as mining, minerals processing, electronic media and the petrochemical industry.

South Africa also plays a leading role in the Indian Ocean Rim Association for Regional Co-operation, which creates an opportunity for countries of the South to serve their economic interests.

As a result of South Africa's participation in the Association of South East Asian Nations Summit in November 2002, a decision was taken to launch the Asia-Africa Sub-Regional Organisations Conference (AASROC I) in Bandung, Indonesia, in April 2003. South Africa and Indonesia co-host AASROC.

The AASROC II Conference, held in August 2004 in Durban, identified three broad areas of co-operation between Asia and Africa, namely: political, economic, social and cultural.

The India/Brazil/South Africa (IBSA) Dialogue Forum remains of strategic importance to all three countries as a powerful global forum to drive South-South co-operation and the agenda of the South, and to champion the needs of the developing world.

The second IBSA Ministerial Trilateral Commission meeting, held in Cape Town in March 2005, provided an opportunity for the further strengthening of trilateral co-operation among the three countries. The highlight of the commission was the launch of the IBSA Business Council, which will pave the way for closer co-operation.

The Middle East

The Department of Foreign Affairs distinguishes between two clearly identifiable subregions in the Middle East. There is the Levant, which comprises Israel, Iraq, Jordan, Lebanon, Palestine and Syria, and on the other hand, the Arabian/Persian Gulf Region, consisting of the member

The Asia-Africa Summit held in Bandung, Indonesia, in April 2005, saw the launch of a new Asian-African strategic partnership focusing on economic issues, trade, investment, health and human resources development.

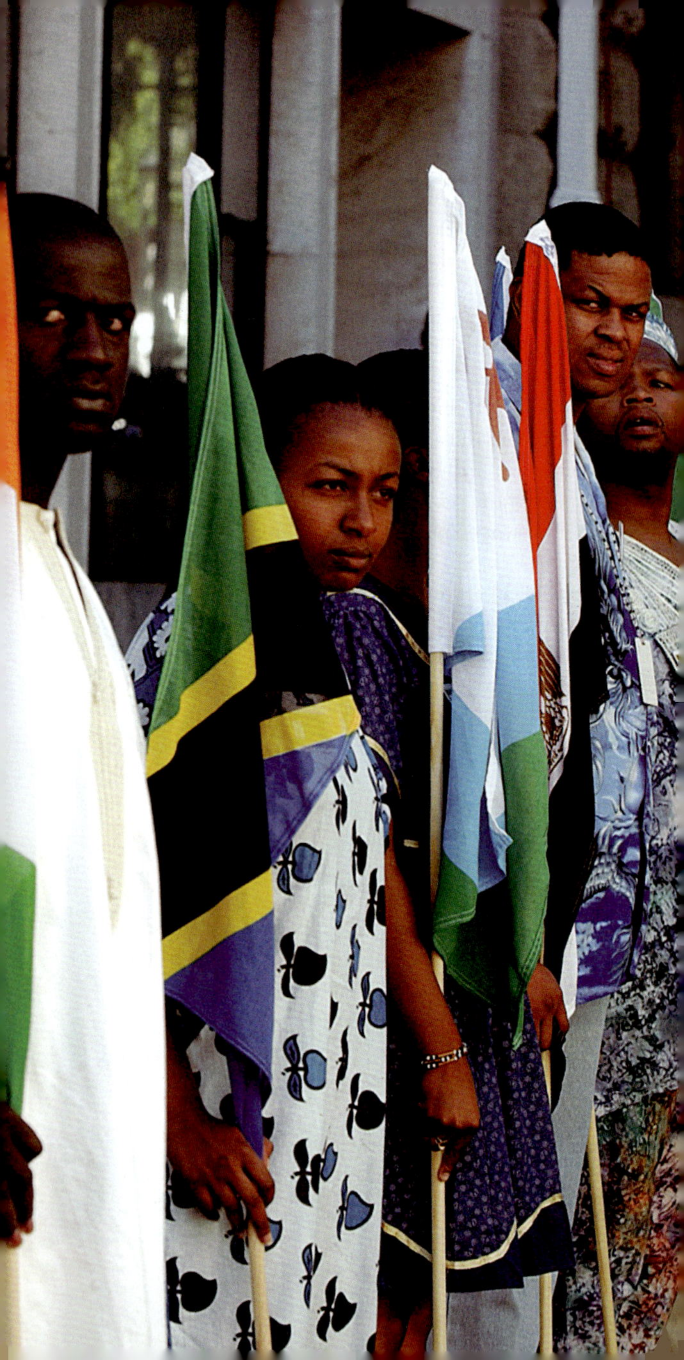

states of the Gulf Co-operation Council, namely Bahrain, Kuwait, Oman, Qatar, Saudi Arabia, the United Arab Emirates (UAE), Iran and Yemen.

The Middle East is an important economic region as it occupies a unique geopolitical position in the tri-continental hub of Europe, Asia and Africa.

South Africa's leading trade partners in the region are Saudi Arabia, Iran, Kuwait, Qatar, Israel and the UAE.

In June 2004, South Africa hosted the annual United Nations (UN) African Meeting in Support of the Inalienable Rights of the Palestinian People, in an attempt to give impetus to initiatives to bring peace to the region.

South Africa supports a just, equitable and comprehensive peace process in the Middle East and an end to the illegal occupation of land that has led to conflict and violence between the peoples of the region.

In August 2005, South Africa welcomed the withdrawal of Israel from Gaza, effectively ending 38 years of occupation.

The Americas

The bilateral relationship with the United States of America (USA) remains strong. Since 1994, business, civilian and governmental links with the USA have expanded exponentially, and a strong and long-term South Africa-USA working partnership has been established.

The USA remains one of the largest single foreign investors in the South African economy since 1994 and the largest tradings partner, as well as the largest donor of official development assistance.

The USA Administration has identified Africa as a foreign policy priority, and among other things, has further identified South Africa as an anchor state in the region in terms of the US National Security Strategy.

The USA Agency for International Development (USAID) programmes in South Africa focus, among other things, on strengthening the capacity of educational institutions; improving primary healthcare delivery, providing technical assistance and scholarships to improve economic capacity in the country; and improving quality and access to housing in South Africa.

Under the current co-operation agreement, R234 million will be geared directly towards South African government initiatives. This amount represents 56% of USAID's total annual budget of R546 million to South Africa.

South Africa has, in the past two years, been the top recipient of development assistance from among the 27 African countries supported by USAID.

Canada remains a strong supporter of the African Agenda and NEPAD, also in a G8 context. Canada is actively seeking closer co-operation with South Africa on peace-keeping on the continent.

Canada reconfirmed its commitment to development co-operation with South Africa by making available R100 million per year over the next five years. Its technical assistance programme is aimed at social upliftment, policy development and human resource development.

South Africa maintains formal diplomatic relations with all the Latin American countries.

Europe

The advent of a new democratic political dispensation more than 10 years ago marked the dawn of a new era in South Africa-European Union (EU) relations. The legal framework that governs South Africa's relationship with the EU is the Trade, Development and Co-operation Agreement (TDCA), which is premised on three main areas of co-operation, namely, political dialogue, trade and economic co-operation, and development assistance.

In terms of the South Africa-EU TDCA, which provisionally came into force in 2000, South Africa will eliminate tariffs on 86% of EU exports within 12 years, while the EU will phase out tariffs on 95% of South African

Foreign affairs

Top sources of imports (2005)	
Germany	12,21%
China	6,81%
United States of America (USA)	6,48%
Japan	5,45%
United Kingdom (UK)	5,01%
Top export destinations (2005)	
UK	8,19%
Japan	7,94%
USA	7,43%
Germany	5,23%
Netherlands	3,81%

Source: Department of Foreign Affairs

exports over 10 years. The TDCA is expected to increase substantially South Africa's trade with Europe.

In November 2004, the Minister of Foreign Affairs, Dr Nkosazana Dlamini-Zuma, and a top-level delegation, attended the South Africa-EU Joint Co-operation Council meeting in Brussels, Belgium.

The meeting reviewed South Africa-EU co-operation within the framework of the TDCA, with specific reference to political dialogue and trade and development.

The EU accounts for 44% of the total FDI flows to South Africa. Six out of the top 10 foreign investors in South Africa are member states of the EU.

Since 2000, South Africa exported an annual average of R80,6 billion worth of goods to the EU, and annually imported an average of R120,2 billion worth of products from the EU.

In January 2005, the EU donated R80 million to South Africa's Parliament and the nine legislatures to help strengthen democracy and promote accountability.

The European Programme for Reconstruction and Development, which is funded directly from the EU Commission at 127,5 million euro a year, is the largest single development programme in South Africa financed by foreign donors.

South Africa is Germany's largest trading partner on the African continent. Germany ranks with the United Kingdom (UK) and USA among the three largest economic role-players in South Africa regarding trade, investment, finance and tourism. More than 370 German companies have invested in South Africa and collectively employ more than 65 000 people here.

Relations with the UK were strengthened during the 6th meeting of the South Africa-UK Bilateral Forum in Cape Town in August 2004.

President Thabo Mbeki visited Italy in May 2005, where he met his counterparts as well as the newly selected Pope Benedict XVI.

United Nations

South Africa remains an active participant in ongoing discussions on the reform of the UN and believes that the multilateral system should be fully engaged in the endeavour for human development and poverty eradication, starting with the achievement of the millennium development goals; the common struggle to address environmental degradation; the pursuit of an overarching human rights agenda; the promotion of democracy and good governance; and all efforts to combat terrorism and the proliferation of weapons of mass destruction and small arms.

President Mbeki used the General Debate of the UN General Assembly in September 2005 as a platform to expand on the above-mentioned national priorities. He also reviewed progress made in the implementation of the millennium development goals and deliberated on the reform of the UN, including the Security Council.

During 2004/05, an additional amount of R8,5 million was transferred to various UN agencies in support of

> Various multilateral economic fora, such as the World Trade Organisation, the Organisation of Economic Co-operation and Development, the G8 and the World Economic Forum serve as focal points for South Africa to engage in dialogue with the countries of the North on key global economic issues, ensuring that the Africa and development agendas remain part of the focus of such fora.
>
> The 2005 G8 Summit in Gleneagles, Scotland, provided an important platform for engagement on the New Partnership for Africa's Development.
>
> The G8 announced adopted measures to combat global warming and African poverty, by boosting aid to poor countries in Africa and elsewhere by R170 billion a year by 2010, and cutting farm subsidies.

projects alleviating the plight of vulnerable groups such as women, children, internally displaced persons and refugees.

In recognition of its active participation in this regard, South Africa was elected to chair the 43rd session of the Commission for Social Development in New York, USA, during February 2005.

As party to the UN conventions on climate change, desertification and biodiversity, South Africa is committed to reducing poverty and the loss of biodiversity by 2010. South Africa is also firmly committed to the protection of the oceans and the sustainable management of its marine resources.

United Nations Development Programme (UNDP)

The first agreement South Africa signed with the UN was the Standard Basic Assistance Agreement with the UNDP. The Comprehensive Country Co-operation Framework (CCF) to cover the period 1997 to 2001 followed this basic agreement. The current CCF covers 2002 to 2006.

In terms of the CCF, the UNDP seeks to implement programmes that are relevant to government's transformation and development imperatives. Programmes focus on priority areas such as the eradication of poverty and underdevelopment, strengthening local government, building civil society co-operation, and addressing the challenges of globalisation.

South Africa's voluntary contribution to the UNDP for 2004/05 was R950 000, which was used for the UNDP operational costs of development programmes in South Africa.

The UNDP has a country office in Pretoria, which is headed by the resident representative, who is also the UN resident co-ordinator for all UN operational activities for development in South Africa.

Commonwealth

South Africa rejoined the Commonwealth in 1994 after an absence of 33 years. South Africa actively participates in all meetings of the Commonwealth and has played a leading role, also as a voice of the South, in supporting the Commonwealth's commitment to further the millennium development goals, relations with NEPAD, poverty relief, debt relief for heavily indebted poor countries, a human rights agenda, assistance to small and island states, Information Technology, and human and administrative capacity-building.

Non-Aligned Movement (NAM)

South Africa joined the 115-member NAM in 1994, and chaired the organisation from 1998 to 2003.

In August 2004, South Africa hosted the XIV Ministerial Conference of the NAM in Durban. South Africa initiated the Durban Declaration on Multilateralism, which was adopted by ministers attending the conference.

Communications

South Africa boasts an outstanding telecommunications infrastructure and a diversity of print and broadcast media. Telecommunications is the fastest growing industry in South Africa.

Access

In recent years, the Department of Communications has established policy and regulatory frameworks to create a sound and enabling environment that promotes business and the sharing of information.

The Telecommunications Amendment Act, 2001 provides for operators, especially black- and women-owned operators, to be licensed in areas with teledensities of less than 5%.

A second national operator was licensed in December 2005, to operate a publicly switched telephone network..

Mobile communications

Over the past years, South Africa has witnessed tremendous growth in the cellular phone industry, with over 20 million subscribers. South Africa has three operators, namely Vodacom, MTN and Cell C.

Internet

A World Wide Worx survey, entitled *The Goldstuck Report: Internet Access in South Africa 2005*, showed that an

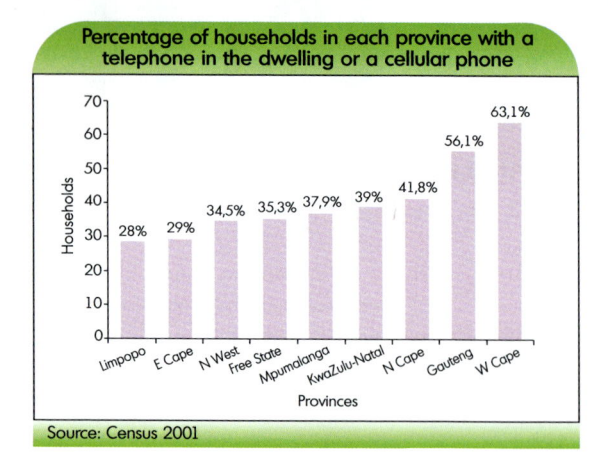

Percentage of households in each province with a telephone in the dwelling or a cellular phone

Province	Percentage
Limpopo	28%
E Cape	29%
N West	34,5%
Free State	35,3%
Mpumalanga	37,9%
KwaZulu-Natal	39%
N Cape	41,8%
Gauteng	56,1%
W Cape	63,1%

Source: Census 2001

estimated 3,6 million South Africans had access to the Internet at the end of 2005.

The Telecommunications Business Unit in the Department of Communications has established a specialist unit to develop a national strategy and to focus on the development and expansion of the Internet.

Bringing communications and services to all the people

During 2004, 600 public information terminals (PITs) were installed throughout the country. This brought the total number of PITs rolled out to 700. Some 575 of the newly installed PITs were operational by mid-2005.

By September 2005, there were 66 multi-purpose community centres in operation, and an approved strategy for setting up a centre in each of the country's 284 municipalities by 2014.

These centres offer one-stop government services, as well as telephony and PITs.

Communications

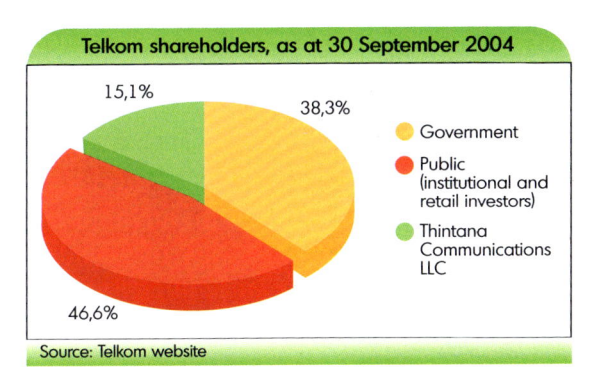

Telkom shareholders, as at 30 September 2004

- Government: 38,3%
- Public (institutional and retail investors): 46,6%
- Thintana Communications LLC: 15,1%

Source: Telkom website

Telkom

Telkom provides total communications solutions in the Information and Communications Technology (ICT) sector.

On 5 March 2003, Telkom listed on the JSE Securities Exchange (JSE) and the New York Stock Exchange. The first day of the listing raised R3,9 billion, making it the biggest initiative that far on government's programme to restructure state-owned enterprises, and the second-biggest global initial public offering in 2003.

Group financial highlights for 2005 included:
- 6,5% growth in operating revenue to R43,117 million (2004: R40,484 million)
- 21,4% growth in operating profit to R11,222 million (2004: R9,245 million)
- basic earnings per share up 52,9% to 1 241,8 cents per share.

South Africa ranks 34th out of 104 countries surveyed in the World Economic Forum's *Global Information Technology Report 2004/05* – up from 37th place overall in 2003/04, and ahead of China, Greece, Hungary, Italy and India.
The report, in its fourth year, assessed countries' readiness to participate in and benefit from global developments in Information and Communications Technology.

Art says far more than mere words. It voices everything that science and pure fact can not. It is the record of an adventure into a different world. It is a way of saying what it means to be alive and, importantly, it is an individual's expression of culture.

For these reasons and many more, the Arts and Culture Department plays a pivotal role on the stage of South Africa. Over the last few years South African artists, unleashed by the new freedom, have become a force to be reckoned with. They have enjoyed much success and recognition in crafts, music, literature, film, theatre, dance, the visual arts and more. Much of the credit for this creative explosion is due to the Arts and Culture Department. By its encouragement and practical funding it has fostered artistic expression in its rich and varied forms, and established the platform for creative energy to thrive. The power of this sector to transform lives both economically and spiritually is almost unlimited and we remain committed to the preservation of our country's wonderful cultures and the growth of South African artists.

Tel: (012) 441-3000 • Fax: (012) 441-3699
Private Bag X897, Pretoria, 0001, South Africa
Kingsley Centre, 481 Church Street, Arcadia, Pretoria • www.dac.gov.za

Reflecting a nation's soul

arts and culture
Department:
Arts and Culture
REPUBLIC OF SOUTH AFRICA

Vutha Advertising 1450

Pocket Guide to South Africa 2005/06

Postal sector

The Government-subsidised South African Post Office (SAPO) is required to provide a basic letter service that is reasonably accessible to all.

With more than 2 000 outlets and 5 500 service points, the Post Office is one of the largest business undertakings in the country. It delivers some eight million mail items to almost 6,5 million addresses. Of these, 3,4 million are street addresses and three million are postboxes.

Speed Services Couriers moves 37 tons of mail each night.

To distribute mail in South Africa, about 70 50-ton container vehicles ply the nation's major routes. Between them they cover 19 million kilometres each year.

Annually, the SAPO prints more than 384 million stamps and serves stamp collectors and dealers throughout the world.

The media

The freedom of the press and other media is guaranteed by South Africa's Bill of Rights.

Broadcasting
The independence of the public broadcaster, the South African Broadcasting Corporation (SABC), is guaranteed by legislation. The SABC is being corporatised and restructured to better fulfil its mandate.

Radio
In 2005, the SABC's national radio network comprised 15

> The South African web attracted a combined local and overseas audience of 4,38 million readers or unique browsers in April 2005, generating 111,6 million page impressions.

Communications

> In May 2005, the Meraka Institute, also known as the African Advanced Institute for Information and Communications Technology (AAIICT), was launched in Pretoria.
> The institute will contribute towards stimulating the development of the local ICT industry through the provision of intellectual human capital.
> Meraka is a Sesotho word meaning 'common grazing' denoting sharing, mutual benefit and the potential for prosperity.
> The institute will encourage the use of technology in communications and various other activities.

stations broadcasting in 11 languages, which, collectively, reached an average daily adult audience of 19 million.

For its internal coverage, Radio News uses about 13 editorial offices, a countrywide network of 1 300 correspondents and more than 2 000 news contacts.

Channel Africa Network comprises four language services, reaching millions of listeners throughout Africa. Broadcasts are in English, French, Kiswahili and Portuguese. It targets audiences in Africa and the Indian Ocean islands, and concentrates on providing programmes with a specific African content.

The following private radio stations have been granted licences by the Independent Communications Authority of South Africa (ICASA):

- Radio Algoa (ex-SABC)
- Classic FM (greenfield)
- Kaya FM (greenfield)
- YFM (greenfield)
- Highveld Stereo (ex-SABC)
- Radio 702
- Radio Jacaranda (ex-SABC)
- Radio Oranje (ex-SABC)
- East Coast Radio (ex-SABC)
- P4 (greenfield)
- Cape Talk MW (greenfield)
- Radio KFM (ex-SABC).

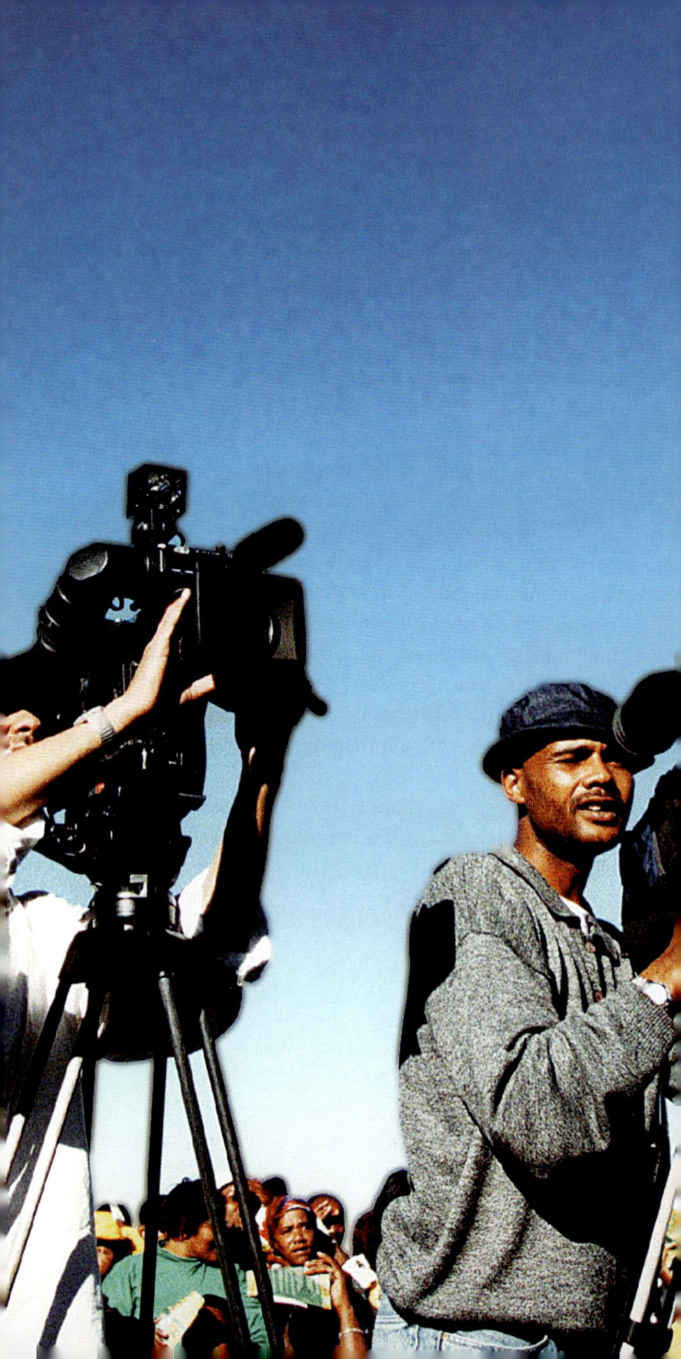

Community radio stations have a huge potential for the support of, among other things, cultural and educational information exchange. These radio stations use all indigenous languages, ensuring that people receive information in languages they understand.

By February 2005, 92 licences had been issued. ICASA has called for applications for a further 18 in the nodal points.

Television

South Africa has by far the largest television audience in Africa. There are more than four million licensed television households.

The SABC's national television network comprises three full-spectrum free-to-air channels and one satellite pay-TV channel aimed at audiences in Africa. Combined, the free-to-air sound broadcasting stations broadcast in 11 languages and reach a daily adult audience of almost 18 million people via the terrestrial signal distribution network and a satellite signal.

In October 1998, the country's first privately owned free-to-air television channel, e.tv, started operations.

M-Net became South Africa's first private subscription television service when it launched in 1986. Today, it broadcasts its array of general entertainment and niche channels to more than 1,3 million subscribers in more than 50 countries across the African continent and adjacent Indian Ocean islands.

MultiChoice Africa (MCA) was formed in 1995 to manage the subscriber services of its sister company, M-Net. It became the first African company on the continent to offer digital satellite broadcasting.

Operations include subscriber-management services and digital satellite television platforms broadcasting 55 video and 48 audio channels, 24 hours a day. Included are six data channels, which were the first interactive television offerings on the continent.

MCA is 100% owned by the MIH Group, which is listed on the JSE, NASDAQ in New York, and AEX in Amsterdam.

Print

Technically, the local print media rate among the best in the world. However, the recent juniorisation of the newsroom has had a negative effect on most major publications.

South African newspapers and magazines are mainly organised into press groups, which have burgeoned as a result of take-overs. The major press groups are Independent Newspapers (Pty) Ltd, Media24 Ltd, CTP/Caxton Publishers and Printers Ltd, and Johnnic Communications.

Other important media players include Primedia, New Africa Investments Limited (Nail) and Kagiso Media. Nail has unbundled into a commercial company (New Africa Capital) and a media company (New Africa Media).

Since 1994, the major press groups have embarked on programmes to boost black empowerment in media ownership.

Biggest weekly and daily newspapers

Paper	Audited circulation: Jul – Dec 2004
Weekly papers	
Sunday Times	505 402
Rapport	322 731
Soccer-Laduma	244 509
City Press	173 992
Die Son	199 959
Daily papers	
Daily Sun	364 356
The Star	166 461
Sowetan	122 825
Beeld	102 070
The Citizen	76 183

Source: Audit Bureau of Circulation

Communications

Newspapers

By mid-2005, the newspaper market consisted of:
- 21 dailies
- eight Sunday newspapers
- 150 local or country newspapers, most of them weeklies.

Daily newspapers showed an upward trend in readership from 20,2% in 2003 to 21% in 2004 with 6,357 million readers. Weekly newspapers remained stable at 31,2% or 9,422 million readers. In general, newspapers saw a decline in readership among 16- to 24-year-olds.

The only truly national newspapers are the *Sunday Times, Rapport, Sunday Independent, Sunday Sun* and *City Press,* and *Sowetan Sunday World*.

Magazines

The magazine industry in South Africa is fiercely competitive with new titles appearing all the time, despite the worldwide challenge from electronic and interactive media. Judging from the proliferation of titles on the shelves in supermarkets and bookstores, it seems that many readers are still attracted to print. However, there is evidence to suggest the overall magazine reading population in South Africa is shrinking, which is a concern for the industry.

A positive development has been the segmentation of the market into niche publications that provide opportunities for advertisers to reach target markets.

Weeklies *Huisgenoot* and *You* are the two biggest money-making magazines in South Africa, and gossip and celebrity titles are the biggest over-the-counter sellers. *FHM* and *Heat* are in the top five.

The major magazine publishers are Media24, Caxton, Johnnic, Associated Magazines and Ramsay Son & Parker.

The *Daily Sun* remains the biggest selling daily newspaper in South Africa and showed an increase in circulation from 235 386 (July to December) in 2003 to 364 356 for the same period in 2004.

News agencies

The national news agency, the South African Press Association, is a co-operative, non-profit organisation.

The main foreign news agencies operating in South Africa are Reuters, Agence France-Presse, Associated Press, Deutsche Presse-Agentur and United Press International.

Media diversity

The independent Media Development and Diversity Agency (MDDA) is jointly funded by government, the media and other donors.

Headed by a nine-member board, the MDDA works to foster diversity, particularly in community and small commercial media, and to redress imbalances in the industry.

The MDDA awarded its first grants to community and small commercial media projects in January 2004.

By the end of March 2005, the MDDA had provided support to close to 60 different media and research projects around South Africa.

Advertising

Several South African agencies are active in Africa. Among the top three are McCann-Erickson Africa, Ogilvy Africa and FCB Africa.

The industry is self-regulated through the Advertising Standards Authority.

> **fact**
> Total advertising spend on all media (print, TV, cinema, radio, outdoor, direct mail and Internet) increased to an estimated R9 billion between July and December 2004. This is compared with R7 billion for the previous six-month period. The total advertising expenditure across all media for 2004 was an estimated R16 billion.

Transport

The Department of Transport's overarching objective is the sustainable and efficient movement of people and goods, locally, in the Southern African Development Community region and internationally, in a transport system that responds to the needs of both the first and second economies.

Agencies

The four bodies tasked with commercialising certain elements of government's operational activities are the South African National Roads Agency Ltd, the South African Maritime Safety Authority, the Cross-Border Road Transport Agency and the Civil Aviation Authority.

Transnet Limited

Transnet is a public company wholly owned by the Government. It is a dominant player in southern Africa's transport infrastructure.

Transnet consists of the following divisions – Spoornet, the National Ports Authority (NPA), South Africa Port Operations, Freight Dynamics, Petronet, Metrorail, Propnet, Transtel, Transwerk and South African Airways (SAA).

> By March 2005, about R9 million was being spent on a multimedia road-safety project involving the training of 116 000 primary school educators in 2 300 workshops throughout the country.

Road transport

South Africa has the longest road network of any country in Africa. The Department of Transport continues to integrate and improve the road network, ensuring that it is well developed, well maintained and safe.

Expenditure on national roads has grown steadily in recent years, increasing by 10,6% annually from R1,1 billion in 2001/02 to R1,5 billion in 2004/05.

Minibus taxis are responsible for 65% of the 2,5 billion annual passenger trips in urban areas, as well as a high percentage of rural and intercity transport.

Buses and trains respectively account for 21% and 14% of all public transport. By May 2005, there were 34 interim bus contracts in the country that accounted for 67% of the total subsidy allocation of R2,28 billion. There was R2,5 billion in subsidies a year for train commuters.

By March 2005, the Operator Code of Practice for the bus industry was being implemented on a voluntary basis. The code requires improved quality management systems for the productivity and effectiveness of bus operations. This should lead to reduced operating costs and fewer accidents.

According to the National Household Travel Survey, 2003, about 26% of households in South Africa have access to a motor car. At 108 cars per 1 000 of the population, car ownership in South Africa remains in its infancy.

fact: Transnet annually handles 176 million tons of rail freight, 2,8 million tons of road freight, 2,5 million passengers by road and 194 million tons of freight through the ports. At the same time, 15,3 billion litres of liquid fuels and 466 million cubic metres of gas are pumped through its pipelines. Annually the group flies more than 6,5 million domestic, international and regional passengers and provides 467 million rail-commuter trips. Transnet has R68,766 billion worth of assets and a workforce numbering some 76 000.

Vehicle sales continued to grow year-on-year, with March 2005 sales up 12,2% compared with the same month in 2004. By March 2005, some 43 651 new vehicles were sold, compared with 38 892 sold in March 2004. These comprised new cars, light commercial vehicles, bakkies and minibuses, and medium and heavy trucks.

In the new-car category, a record 28 722 units were sold in March 2005, representing the highest number of new cars ever sold in March.

Sales of new light commercial vehicles, bakkies and minibuses improved by 6,3% compared with March 2004, from 12 099 vehicles to 12 868 vehicles sold.

Medium-sized truck sales improved by 22,7% to 887 units in March 2005, compared with the corresponding month in 2004.

Sales of heavy trucks and buses also increased, with 18,6% more vehicles sold to bring the total to 1 174 units.

Taxi Recapitalisation Programme (TRP)

In 2005, Cabinet approved the detailed strategy for the roll-out of the TRP, which aims to replace the current ageing minibus taxi fleet with new, safer, purpose-built 18- and 35-seater vehicles which will be locally built.

Government intends to remove 10 000 old and unroadworthy vehicles from the roads by December 2006. The payment of a scrapping allowance of R50 000 to taxi operators who voluntarily hand in their vehicles will only take place after operating licensing boards have registered applications, evaluated them and verified the validity of permit/operating licences linked to the vehicle.

Total market sales		
Total market sales	Year	Sales
Total sales October	2005	50 697
Total sales October	2004	42 441
Total sales September	2005	54 560
Total sales September	2004	43 146
Total sales January-October	2005	468 717
Total sales January-October	2004	371 976

Source: National Association of Automobile Manufacturers of South Africa

Pocket Guide to South Africa 2005/06

> **fact:** Government has committed R2,5 billion over the next five years to increase its capacity to enforce public transport laws.

The TRP roll-out strategy comprises the:
- introduction of safety requirements for the new vehicles
- scrapping of existing vehicles
- effective regulation of the taxi industry
- effective law enforcement in respect of public transport
- empowerment of the taxi industry.

On 22 February 2005, the South African National Taxi Council signed a memorandum of understanding (MoU) with Absa, Nedbank, Standard Bank, Wesbank and Daimler Chrysler Services in Pretoria.

In terms of the MoU, taxi operators may receive finance from any of the participating institutions to replace their old fleet with the newly approved vehicles.

Goods transport

Eighty percent of all freight in South Africa is transported by road. Nearly 7% of gross domestic product is spent on freight transport.

About 69% of road-freight tonnage is carried by firms or operators transporting freight in the course of their business, and 29% by road haulage firms.

Rail transport

Spoornet is the largest division of Transnet. It operates in 18 African countries, and has interests in other parts of the world.

> **fact:** On 17 March 2005, the Minister of Transport, Mr Jeff Radebe, launched the Arrive Alive Patrol Car Project, which will provide provincial and metropolitan/local traffic authorities with additional patrol vehicles.
> During the first phase, 60 vehicles worth R6,29 million were distributed.

Transport

The Department of Transport has begun developing Broad-Based Black Economic Empowerment (BBBEE) strategies and charters for eight of the transport sectors. These will make a significant contribution towards economic growth, job creation, skills development and poverty alleviation.

The strategy is expected to ensure representivity for people with disabilities and women across most of the BBBEE indicators, such as ownership, management and employment equity. The strategy was expected to be implemented from 2005 to 2010.

Some 246 locomotives were overhauled or upgraded in 2004, compared with 204 in 2003 and 171 in 2002. In 2004, Spoornet announced a R14-billion, five-year programme to upgrade ageing assets and infrastructure, and procure new locomotives and wagons.

Sub-Saharan Africa boasts about 83% of all Africa's railways, and South Africa's share of the African total is some 35% or 42% of Sub-Saharan Africa's system.

South Africa accounts for about 47% of the total number of locomotives of all types in sub-Saharan Africa or 32% of the African total. However, South Africa's dominance of electric locomotives is nearly complete, with about 96% of sub-Saharan locomotives and 92% of the continent's total number of electric locomotives.

The African freight wagon fleet is small by international standards. However, South Africa dominates with about 62% of the total African fleet and 74% of the sub-Saharan total. The amount of rail freight tonnes moved also occurs mostly in the South African system, with about 71% of the African total and some 91% of sub-Saharan traffic.

Specialist Spoornet divisions

COALlink – transports export coal from Mpumalanga to the Richards Bay Coal Terminal.

Orex – hauls iron ore over the 861-km track from Sishen in the Northern Cape to Saldanha Bay.

Shosholoza Meyl – offers daily intercity passenger rail services.

Pocket Guide to South Africa 2005/06

> The newly developed electronic national road traffic information system (e-NaTIS) was expected to replace the NaTIS (paper-based) by December 2005. NaTIS administers driver and vehicle registration and deregistration. By May 2005, the new system was 65% complete.
>
> A new state-of-the-art data centre has been created to host the centralised e-NaTIS database, which is linked to a back-up site. During 2004/05, four e-NaTIS pilot sites were launched in Benoni and Akasia in Gauteng, and in the Western Cape and KwaZulu-Natal.

Metrorail – provides commuter rail services in the Witwatersrand, Pretoria, Western Cape, Durban, Port Elizabeth and Cape Town. Metrorail transports some 1,5 million commuters to and from work daily.

AFB Commercial – handles some 52% of its freight tonnage.

Luxrail – operates the Blue Train.

Spoornet International Joint Ventures – plans to be a global leader in operations on the 1 000 mm and 1 067 mm rail networks.

Civil aviation

The Airports Company of South Africa (ACSA) owns and operates the 10 principal airports, including the three major international airports in Johannesburg, Cape Town and Durban. The others are domestic airports in Bloemfontein, Port Elizabeth, East London, George, Kimberley, Upington and Pilanesberg. Other airports in South Africa

> The expansion and redesign of Pier 1 and the widening of the entrance at the Durban Harbour will cost about R2,9 billion. The construction of the container terminal at Ngqura and the expansion of the Cape Town Container Terminal will cost about R2,6 billion and R1,4 billion, respectively. The new multi-purpose pipeline from Durban to Gauteng will be a R3-billion investment.

Transport

By June 2005, there were 9 063 aircraft on the South African Civil Aircraft Register. A total of 4 810 (53%) of these aircraft represented aeroplanes, helicopters and agricultural aircraft. The other 4 253 (47%) represented sport and recreational aircraft. Micro-light aircraft (2 284) represented 25% of the total aircraft and 54% of the sport and recreational aircraft. At 2 459 (27%), aeroplanes with one-piston engines were by far the largest group of aircraft on the register. This group and the micro-lights have grown faster than all the other aircraft on the register. Helicopter aircraft (722) represented 8% of the register.

include Lanseria (Midrand), Gateway (Polokwane), Nelspruit and Kruger (Mpumalanga).

In 2003/04, ACSA upgraded the Port Elizabeth terminal, constructed new security gates and landside access roads at Johannesburg International Airport (JIA), opened a new R44-million domestic to international passenger transfer facility at JIA, completed a new R14,9-million access control facility at JIA, completed the first phase of a programme for the replacement of screening equipment, and invested R53 million in security infrastructure.

Revenue increased by 13,5%, from R1,7 billion in 2003/04 to R1,9 billion in 2004/05.

In 2003/04, ACSA recorded a 7,4% rise in total departing passenger traffic to 11,9 million. This was mainly due to an increase of 7,9% in domestic passenger volumes and 6,4% in international passenger volumes.

As part of preparations for the 2010 Soccer World Cup, ACSA has pledged about R3,58 billion over the next five years to increase capacity and efficiency at all airports.

Major plans include a multistorey parkade at Cape Town International with in-house check-in counters and an international passenger-transfer facility in the JIA terminal, which will be integrated with the Gautrain Rapid Rail Link between JIA, Sandton and Johannesburg to be constructed by the Gauteng Provincial Government. The JIA's capacity will be increased to accommodate the

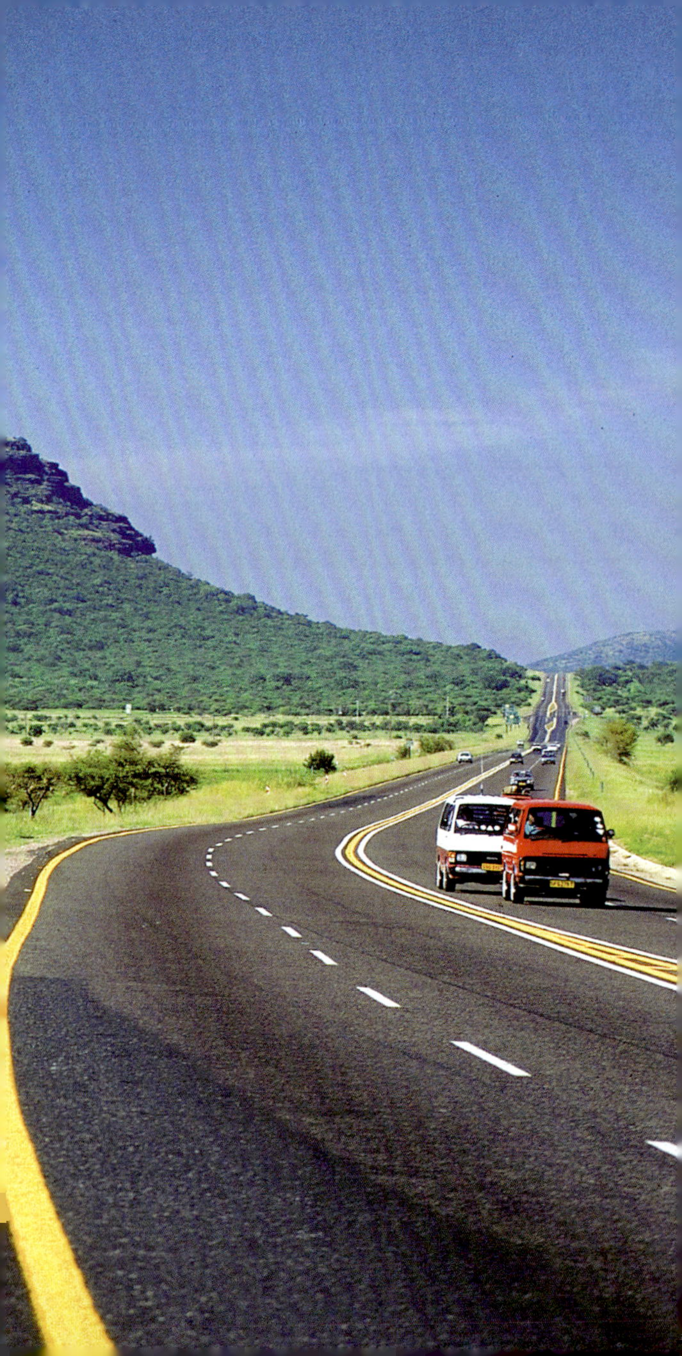

Transport

new wide-body long-haul aircraft such as the A380 at connecting stands.

The number of airlines operating in South African airspace increased from nine in 1994 to more than 50 in 2004.

SAA

SAA is Africa's leading airline and serves more than 40 cities across the world, in 30 countries on six continents.

The SAA:
- carries more than 6,5 million passengers each year
- employs close to 12 000 people worldwide
- undertakes maintenance for more than 40 major airlines
- flies more than 20 domestic routes
- serves more than 700 destinations throughout the world.

Ports

The NPA manages South Africa's biggest ports: Richards Bay, Durban, East London, Port Elizabeth, Mossel Bay, Cape Town and Saldanha, as well as Ngqura, which was set to become operational in 2005.

Handling 55 Mt of cargo through five cargo terminals annually, Durban is the busiest port in southern Africa.

The draft Maritime Agenda 2010 identifies 20 interventions required to develop the industry. The Department

---

Some of the South African Maritime Safety Authority's (SAMSA) recent achievements include:
- 1 011 ships with a gross tonnage of 238 196 tons were registered under the South African flag
- 219 foreign flagged ships were inspected and four detained
- 19 oil-pollution incidents were investigated
- 277 candidates passed various examinations conducted by SAMSA
- 3 082 safety certificates were issued out of 3 530 ship surveys
- 930 dry-dock certificates were issued out of 1 023 surveys.

of Transport continues to provide maritime information services to the seafaring community and has established an improved pollution prevention response.

The adoption and implementation of measures to enhance maritime security has resulted in South Africa being fully compliant with the International Ships and Ports Security Code since July 2004.

Petronet owns, maintains and operates a network of 3 000 km of high-pressure pipelines.

Agriculture, forestry and land

South Africa has a dual agricultural economy: a well-developed commercial sector and a predominant subsistence sector. About 13% of the country can be used for crop production. High-potential arable land comprises only 22% of total arable land. Some 1,3 million ha are under irrigation.

Agricultural activities range from intensive crop production and mixed farming to cattle-ranching in the bushveld, and sheep farming in the more arid regions.

Economic contribution

Primary agriculture contributes about 3,3% to the gross domestic product (GDP) of South Africa and about 7,2% to formal employment. However, there are strong linkages

---

The estimated value of agriculture imports during 2004 came to about R15,847 billion, compared with R13,921 billion in 2003. The estimated value of exports decreased from R23,453 billion in 2003 to about R22,662 billion in 2004. According to the 2004 export values, citrus fruit, wine, grapes, apples, pears, quinces and sugar were the most important export products. Rice, wheat, oil cake, undenatured ethyl alcohol and palm oil were the most important import products.

During 2004, the United Kingdom, the Netherlands, Germany, Mozambique and the United States of America (USA) were South Africa's five largest trading partners in terms of export destinations. The five largest trading partners from whom South Africa imported agricultural products during 2004 were Argentina, Brazil, USA, Thailand and Australia.

Source: AgriNews, April 2005

into the economy, so that the agro-industrial sector actually comprises 15% of GDP.

South Africa is self-sufficient in virtually all major agricultural products, and in a normal year is a net food exporter. However, the country remains vulnerable to drought. In 2004, government spent R100 million on fodder and water to help drought-affected farmers. In anticipation of a predicted continued drought, a further

Gross value of agricultural production, 2004 (R'000)

Field crops	
Maize	8 318 266
Wheat	2 000 529
Hay	2 257 501
Grain sorghum	404 228
Sugar cane	2 730 628
Ground-nuts	367 307
Tobacco	581 999
Sunflower seed	1 235 948
Cotton	215 102
Other	1 318 057
Total	19 428 565
Horticulture	
Viticulture	2 623 417
Citrus fruit	3 670 562
Subtropical fruit	1 336 969
Deciduous and other fruit	5 743 251
Vegetables	3 870 485
Potatoes	2 364 441
Other	1 171 116
Total	20 780 241
Animal products	
Wool	936 607
Poultry and poultry products	13 389 903
Cattle and cattle products	6 991 676
Sheep and goats slaughtered	1 760 828
Pigs slaughtered	1 276 595
Fresh milk	3 776 064
Milk for dairy products	1 171 814
Other	1 766 442
Total	31 069 939
Grand total	**71 279 745**

Source: Agricultural Statistics, Department of Agriculture

Agriculture, forestry and land

Price of maize, wheat and sunflowers per ton		
	End Sept 2004	End Sept 2005
White maize	R904	R823
Yellow maize	R942	R755
Wheat	R1 436	R1 440
Sunflower	R2 130	R2 185

Source: South African Futures Exchange

R120 million was requested in 2005/06 to buy fodder and prepare for the drilling of boreholes.

Production

Overall, prices of agricultural products increased by 2,3% from 2003 to 2004. During 2004, the producer price of field crops was 18,1% higher than during 2003. In 2004, producer prices of horticultural products decreased by 3,4% compared with 2003.

Prices of field crops increased by 35%, and horticultural and livestock products both increased by 23%. In 2005/06, government transferred R100 million to provinces for the implementation of the farmer-support programme.

Field crops and horticulture
- Maize is the largest crop, followed by wheat, sugar cane and sunflowers. South Africa is the main maize producer in the Southern African Development Community region. A total of 9,7 million tons (mt) of maize was produced in 2003/04 on 3,2 million ha of land. An estimated 3 mt maize surplus was carried over to 2004/05. This carry-over contributed to the slump in maize prices to four-year lows in the first quarter of 2005.

The Micro-Agricultural Finance Institutions of South Africa, the first state-owned scheme to provide micro and retail agricultural financial services on a large, accessible, cost-effective and sustainable basis in the rural areas, was launched in May 2005.

Pocket Guide to South Africa 2005/06

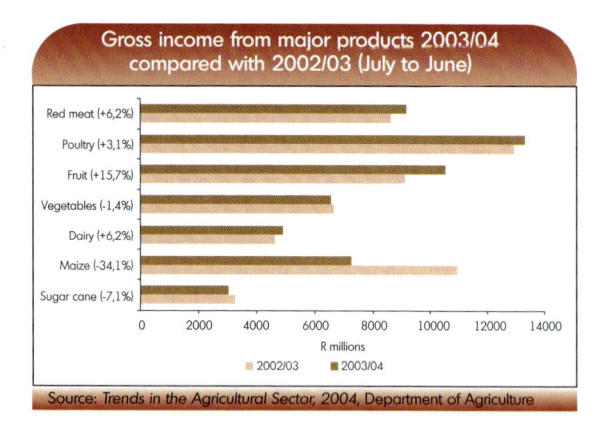

Gross income from major products 2003/04 compared with 2002/03 (July to June)

Product	2002/03	2003/04
Red meat (+6,2%)		
Poultry (+3,1%)		
Fruit (+15,7%)		
Vegetables (-1,4%)		
Dairy (+6,2%)		
Maize (-34,1%)		
Sugar cane (-7,1%)		

R millions (0 – 14 000)

Source: *Trends in the Agricultural Sector, 2004*, Department of Agriculture

Maize prices plunged from more than R1 000 per ton in November 2004 to less than R600 during the first quarter of 2005. The price of maize is expected to remain low. Better-than-expected rains also contributed to the maize price slide.

- Wheat is produced in the Western Cape and the Free State.
- South Africa is the world's 11th-largest producer of sunflower seed.
- South Africa is the world's 12th-largest sugar producer. Some 2,5 mt of sugar is produced per season. About 50% of this sugar is marketed in southern Africa, while the remainder is exported to numerous markets in Africa, the Middle East, North America and Asia.
- South Africa is the leading exporter of protea cut flowers, which account for more than half of proteas sold on the world market.

fact: In 2004, South Africa exported 266,5 million litres of wine worldwide, which is a 12% volume increase from 2003, despite the robust Rand and aggressive competition prompted by a global oversupply. In addition to the United States of America, other high-growth destinations were the Netherlands, which grew by 18%, Germany (34%), Sweden (31%) and Canada (40%).

Agriculture, forestry and land

Total agricultural exports						
	2000	2001	2002	2003	2004	Average: five years
Total South African products R millions	210 022	245 448	314 927	274 640	292 261	267 460
Total agriculture products R millions	15 820	20 075	25 460	23 001	22 187	21 309
Agriculture as % of total exports	7,5	8,2	8,1	8,4	7,6	8,0

Source: Directorate: Agricultural Statistics, Department of Agriculture

Some other crops:

- The Oudtshoorn district in the Western Cape is responsible for about 90% of the lucerne seed produced in South Africa.
- Deciduous fruit exports represent 11% of the country's total earnings from agricultural exports. During 2003, South Africa was the largest exporter in the southern hemisphere of table grapes to Europe and the United Kingdom. Horticulture represents 77% of the total value of agricultural exports, while deciduous fruit make up 60% of horticultural products.
- South Africa is the eighth-largest wine producer in the world. In 2004, the country harvested 312 184 tons of grapes, which resulted in the production of 1,016 billion litres of wine.
- Citrus production is largely limited to the irrigation areas of Limpopo, Mpumalanga, the Eastern and Western Cape, and KwaZulu-Natal. A total of 2 mt of citrus was produced in 2003/04, which was an increase of 4% from 2002/03.

The Department of Agriculture has introduced *sedupe* – sniffer dogs – to detect illegal food items among airport luggage. By April 2005, the dogs had detected 307 illegal smaller consignments in the baggage carousel areas.

Pocket Guide to South Africa 2005/06

Livestock (million)		
		2005
Cattle		13,91
Sheep		25,32
Pigs		1,66
Goats		6,36

Source: Agricultural Statistics, Department of Agriculture

- Pineapples are grown in the Eastern Cape and northern KwaZulu-Natal. Other subtropical crops such as avocados, mangoes, bananas, litchis, guavas, papaya, granadillas, and macadamia and pecan nuts are produced mainly in Mpumalanga and Limpopo and subtropical coastal areas. In 2003/04, South Africa produced 595 000 tons of subtropical fruit.

Livestock

By May 2005, there were an estimated 13,91 million cattle, 25,32 million sheep, 1,66 million pigs and 6,36 million goats in South Africa.

Cattle ranches are found mainly in the Eastern Cape, parts of the Free State and KwaZulu-Natal, Limpopo and the Northern Cape.

Sheep farming is concentrated in the Eastern Cape (30%) Northern Cape (26%), the Free State (20%), Western Cape (10%) and Mpumalanga (7%). Most sheep (18 million) are woolled or dual-purpose sheep.

Strategic Plan for South African Agriculture

This plan recognises the need to improve commercial production, profitability and global competitiveness, while

> **fact**
> On 1 September 2004, government and its partners launched a joint initiative in e-commerce named *Wine Online*, with about 98% of exporters applying online for export certificates and other required certification documents.

Agriculture, forestry and land

Composition of total horticultural gross value during 2004/05

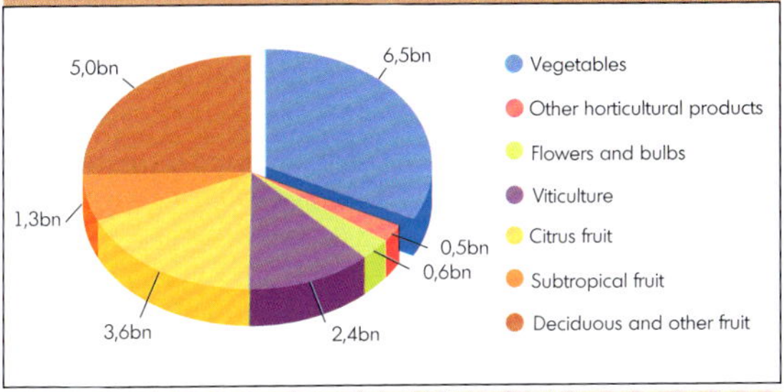

- Vegetables: 6,5bn
- Other horticultural products: 0,5bn
- Flowers and bulbs: 0,6bn
- Viticulture: 2,4bn
- Citrus fruit: 3,6bn
- Subtropical fruit: 1,3bn
- Deciduous and other fruit: 5,0bn

Source: Agricultural Statistics, Department of Agriculture

ensuring equitable access to the sector, deracialising land and enterprise ownership, and ensuring sustainable resource management.

The national Department of Agriculture, the National African Farmers' Union and Agri SA have established an institutional framework for implementing the plan.

Food security

The Integrated Food Security and Nutrition Programme, adopted in July 2002, aims to eradicate hunger, malnutrition and food insecurity by 2015.

By June 2004, the department, working with the provincial departments of agriculture, had distributed production support packages to 37 000 of its target of 50 000 households.

Land and Agricultural Development Bank of South Africa (Land Bank)

The bank provides a comprehensive range of retail and wholesale financial products and services designed to meet the needs of commercial and developing farmers and agriculture-related businesses.

Micro-finance is available to clients with no security who may borrow amounts from R250 to R18 000.

Instalment Sale Finance is a type of medium-term loan where the goods that one buys act as the main security for the loan: the goods belong to the bank until the loan is paid in full. It enables all farmers, especially those with limited assets, to grow their businesses.

This finance package is available for periods between three and 10 years, depending on the expected length of the assets' life.

Forestry

South Africa has developed one of the largest planted forests in the world. Production from these plantations amounted to more than 19,2 million m^3, valued at almost R4,1 billion, in 2003. Together with the processed products, total turnover for the industry was about R14,6 billion in 2003, including R8,4 billion worth of wood-pulp.

The industry was a net exporter to the value of over R3,9 billion in 2004, more than 98% of which was in the form of converted value-added products. Had it not been for this trade surplus in forest products, the country's trade deficit in 2004 of R13 billion would have been 30% higher.

The forest-products industry ranks among the top exporting industries in the country, having contributed 3,09% to total exports and 1,68% to total imports in 2004.

Capital investment in the industry amounted to some R24 billion in 2004. Investment totalled R16,3 billion in 2001 and R9,7 billion in 1999.

The forestry sector employs about 151 000 people. With a claimed multiplier effect of four to one, some 600 000 people owe their employment to forestry.

> **fact**
> South Africa's national tree, the yellowwood tree (*Podacarpus*) can grow to a height of more than 40 m with a girth of 8 m, and can live for up to 800 years.

Agriculture, forestry and land

Plantation yields, 2003

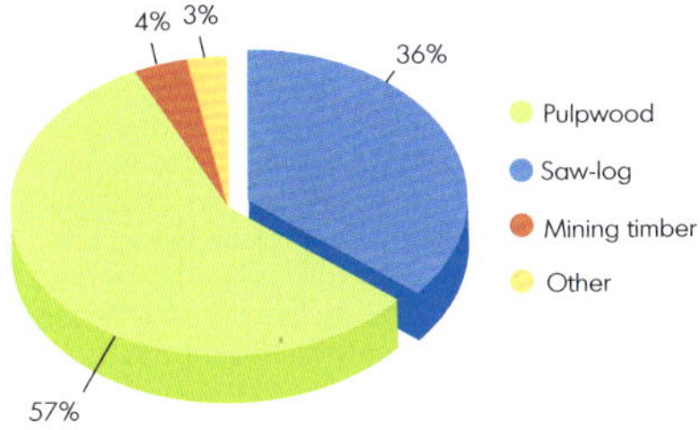

- Pulpwood: 57%
- Saw-log: 36%
- Mining timber: 4%
- Other: 3%

Source: Forestry South Africa

Indigenous forests

There are about 530 000 ha of indigenous or natural forests in the country, which occur mainly along the southern and eastern escarpment, the coastal belt and in sheltered kloofs or ravines.

There has been an increase in the use of natural forests as sources of medicine, building material, fuel wood and food. It is estimated that around 80% of South Africa's population still uses medicinal plants, most of which are sourced from natural forests.

For the first time, South Africa has a detailed inventory of all its natural forests, which will be used to accurately monitor changes in forest areas. The Department of Water Affairs and Forestry also completed a classification of natural forests, represented by 24 broad forest types. The Natural Forests Protected Areas System was also completed for all forests in 2004, and will guide the setting aside and redemarcation of natural forests into protected areas.

> **fact**
> In June 2005, South Africa's reigning world champion shearer Elliot Ntsombo retained his World Blade Shearing title at the World Sheep Shearing and Woolhandling Championship held in Toowoomba, Australia.

> The commercial forestry industry in South Africa is committed to practising Sustainable Forestry Management and is a world leader in forest certification. This is demonstrated by the fact that over a million hectares (ha), or over 80% of the entire planted area of commercial forestry plantations in South Africa, are certified by the Forest Stewardship Council (FSC) and the ISO 14001 certification schemes as being sustainably managed. By March 2005, nearly 1,7 million ha of forestry land in South Africa was certified by the FSC, the second-largest area in the southern hemisphere after Brazil.

Reforming forests

The Department of Water Affairs and Forestry is pursuing a reform programme in the forestry sector, which will eventually see the Government leasing all state-owned forest land to the private sector.

Land affairs

The Department of Land Affairs' responsibilities include deeds registration, surveys and mapping, cadastral surveys, spatial planning and land reform.

A project to upgrade townships surveyed under the apartheid Government has made it possible for thousands of people to register properties as freehold where previously they held lesser rights.

The Chief Directorate: Surveys and Mapping will establish real-time base stations in support of the surveys for the Communal Land Rights Act, 2004 to enable communities previously excluded from the benefits of landownership to hold formal title to their land.

Maps of aerial photography coverage in the rural areas, particularly within the Integrated Sustainable Rural Development Programme nodes, will be updated.

The 1:50 000 topographical map series is the largest scale map series, providing full coverage of South Africa.

The popular large-scale 1:10 000 orthophoto map series provides coverage of predominantly built-up areas, areas of

Agriculture, forestry and land

economic importance and areas experiencing rapid development.

The Chief Directorate: Deeds Registration aims to maintain a public register of land, as well as an efficient system of registration aimed at affording security of title to land and rights to land.

Land reform

The Land Reform for Agricultural Development (LRAD) Programme aims to give previously disadvantaged people access to land, especially agricultural land. Its objective is to redistribute 30% of agricultural land to historically disadvantaged farmers by 2014.

By February 2005, of the 23 520 beneficiaries of the LRAD, 19% were youth and 34,7% women.

By April 2005, the department's 209 000 ha of agricultural land had been transferred to emergent farmers and communities. In her budget vote in April 2005, the Minister of Agriculture and Land Affairs, Ms Thoko Didiza, announced that some 30 400 ha of land was leased with an option to purchase.

Cumulative statistics on settled restitution claims 1995 – 31 March 2004

	Land restoration	Financial compensation	Alternative remedy	Total no of claims settled	Beneficiaries involved
Urban claims settled	14 758	25 477	2 477	42 712	264 480
Rural claims settled	2 873	3 234	6	6 113	397 827
Total	17 631	28 711	2 483	48 825	662 307

1. The above statistics are based on the information reflected in the Database of Settled Restitution Claims.
2. To improve the accuracy of the statistics, the Database of Settled Restitution Claims is subject to an ongoing process of internal auditing.
3. Project Basisa is currently being used to clean/update the Landbase System, as a further mechanism to address any inconsistencies in the statistics.

Source: Department of Land Affairs

Land restitution

The return of land or provision of compensation to those who were dispossessed or forcibly removed through the now defunct Group Areas Act, 1950 is expected to be completed over the next three years.

By February 2005, a total of 57 908 claims had been settled, benefiting 863 138 beneficiaries who had obtained 854 444 ha of land.

In addition to restoring land rights to the rightful owners, these restitution settlements are set to bring money and infrastructure into rural villages. Linked to the restitution programme, government provides agricultural support to emerging farmers and contributes to improved land use and productivity.

An additional R6,5 billion was made available in 2005/06 for land restitution, bringing the total spent since 1994 to R14 billion. The original budget allocated to the Commission on the Restitution of Land Rights for 2004/05 was R933 million, but this was increased to R1,13 billion in line with the increased number of claims settled.

About 80% of the total number of claims lodged were urban, while 20% were rural.

Minerals and mining

South Africa's mineral wealth is staggering. Some of the country's most important minerals are:
- gold – the unique Witwatersrand Basin yields some 96% of South Africa's gold output
- diamonds – the country is among the world's top producers
- titanium – heavy mineral-sand occurrences containing titanium minerals are found along the coasts
- manganese – enormous reserves of manganese are found in the sedimentary rocks of the Transvaal Supergroup
- platinum-group metals (PGMs) and chrome – more than half of the world's reserves occur in the Bushveld Complex in Mpumalanga, Limpopo and North West
- vast coal and anthracite beds occur in the Karoo Basin in Mpumalanga, KwaZulu-Natal and Limpopo
- copper phosphate, titanium, iron, vermiculite and zirconium are found in the Phalaborwa Igneous Complex in Limpopo.

Reserves

South Africa's reserves of the following seven commodities are the biggest in the world:
- manganese
- chromium
- PGMs
- gold
- vanadium
- alumino-silicates
- vermiculite.

South Africa's mineral production, 2004

Commodity	Unit	Production	%	World rank
Aluminium	kt	866	2,6	10
Alumino-silicates	kt	234,4	54,4	1
Antimony	t	4 967	3,1	3
Chrome ore	Mt	7,4		
Coal	Mt	243	4,7	5
Copper	kt	102,6	0,7	18
Diamonds	k car	14 400	9	4
Ferrochromium	Mt	2,8		
Ferromanganese	kt	907,8		
Ferrosilicon	kt	131 555		
Fluorspar	kt	–	–	–
Gold	t	340,2	13,8	1
Iron ore	Mt			
Lead	kt	37,5	1,2	13
Manganese ore	kt	4 206,7		
Nickel	kt	40		
Phosphate rock	kt	–	–	–
Platinum-group metals	kg	286 733	57,8	1
Silicon metal	kt	50 470		
Silver	t	72		
Titanium minerals	kt	–	–	–
Uranium	t	887	2	4
Vanadium	kt	27	41	1
Vermiculite	kt	194,5	52,6	1
Zinc metal	kt	105	1,2	22
Zirconium minerals	kt	–	–	–

Mt=megaton, kt=kiloton, t=ton, kg=kilogram, k car=kilocarats

Source: Minerals Bureau

Gold

World demand for gold decreased by 7,2% to 3 851 tons (t) in 2004. The average gold price traded at a 15-year high of $409/oz.

World mine supply decreased by 128 t to 2 462 t, but South African gold production fell by 8,7% to 340,2 t in

2004. Provisional data for 2004 indicates that total gold sales increased by 4,1% to US$4,55 billion.

Coal
South Africa has around 28,6 billion t of recoverable coal reserves, making it the seventh-largest holder of coal reserves in the world.

Platinum-group metals
South African PGM production increased by 7,7% to 286,7 t in 2004, while PGM revenue increased by 35,7% to $5,17 billion. The average platinum price for 2004 was 22,2% higher at US$846/oz, while the average palladium price was 14,7% higher at US$230/oz.

Base minerals
Refined copper, nickel, cobalt, titanium and zirconium concentrates dominate this sector, with support from zinc, lead and arsenic concentrates. The sector contributes some 12% and 4% respectively to total primary local sales and total primary export sales.

About 44% of total revenue is made up of local sales for further added-value operations.

Ferrous minerals
This sector consists of the ores of iron, manganese and chrome, and is dominated by iron ore. It has been a leading performer in the primary minerals industry in recent years, with revenue in dollar terms growing at about 10,3% annually. Demand depends on the fortune of the world's steel and stainless steel industries.

Gold mining, with 45,7% of the mining industry's labour force, was the largest employer in 2003, followed by platinum-group metals mining with 28,8%. The coal industry employed 11% of the labour force in 2003.

Pocket Guide to South Africa 2005/06

South Africa's share of world mineral exports

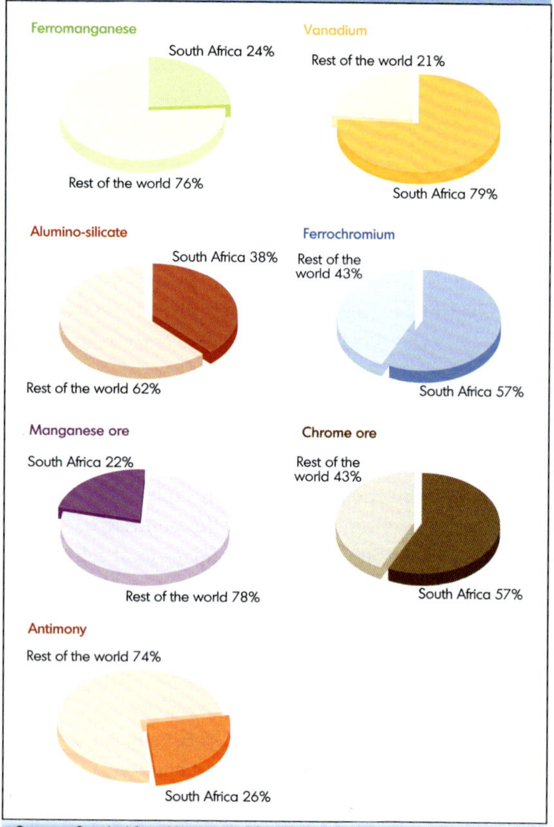

Ferromanganese
- South Africa 24%
- Rest of the world 76%

Vanadium
- Rest of the world 21%
- South Africa 79%

Alumino-silicate
- South Africa 38%
- Rest of the world 62%

Ferrochromium
- Rest of the world 43%
- South Africa 57%

Manganese ore
- South Africa 22%
- Rest of the world 78%

Chrome ore
- Rest of the world 43%
- South Africa 57%

Antimony
- Rest of the world 74%
- South Africa 26%

Source: *South Africa Yearbook 2004/05*

Export earnings from ferrous minerals went up a considerable 16,3% from R4,16 billion in 2003, to R4,84 billion in 2004, despite the fact that higher dollar earnings were severely discounted by a much higher average rand-dollar exchange rate ratio for 2004. Higher prices also affected total ferrous sales, which rose by 18,9% to R6,81 billion.

Minerals and mining

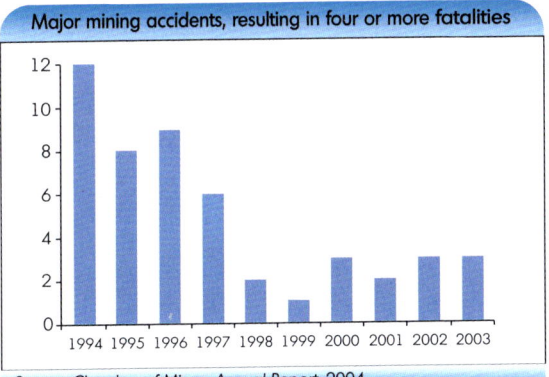

Major mining accidents, resulting in four or more fatalities

Year	Accidents
1994	12
1995	8
1996	9
1997	6
1998	2
1999	1
2000	3
2001	2
2002	3
2003	3

Source: Chamber of Mines, *Annual Report*, 2004

Industrial minerals

This sector comprises a wide variety of mineral products, from which over 80% of revenue is local sales. In dollar terms, domestic total sales increased by 25% in 2004 to US$942 million. In rand terms, local sales increased by 15% to the value of R5,0 billion, while export sales decreased by 21% to R1,0 billion.

During 2004, 83% of local sales comprised aggregate and sand (38%), limestone and lime (24%), phosphate rock concentrate (data withheld) and sulphur (4%).

Exports were dominated by dimension stone (33%), vermiculite (14%), andalusite (20%), fluorspar (17%), and phosphate rock concentrate (data withheld).

---

fact

The mining industry's safety performance improved in 2004. A fatality rate of 0,56 deaths per 1 000 employees was recorded compared with a fatality rate of 0,65 deaths per 1 000 employees in 2003. The reportable injury rates also improved from 10,32 per 1 000 employees in 2003 to 9,63 per 1 000 in 2004. These rates corresponded to 4 254 injuries in 2004 and 4 301 injuries in 2003.

Pocket Guide to South Africa 2005/06

Global supply of platinum

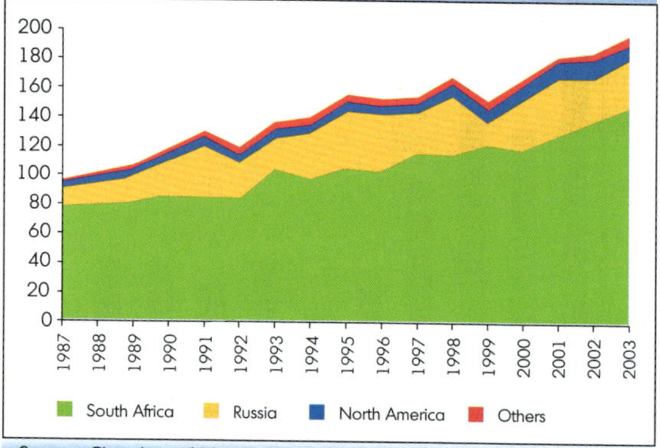

Legend: South Africa, Russia, North America, Others

Source: Chamber of Mines, Annual Report, 2004

Processed minerals

Ferro-alloys and aluminium dominate this sector, with solid support from titanium slag, phosphoric acid, vanadium, zinc metal and low-manganese pig-iron.

International prices of processed minerals surged strongly during 2004 on the back of vigorous growth in demand in China and the East, and as a result, export sales earnings were at an all-time high of US$4,096 billion in 2004, up 42% from US$2,889 billion in 2003.

Other minerals

This sector is dominated by diamonds, with support from hydrocarbon fuel, uranium oxide and silver.

Due to the strong Rand, revenue from these minerals slumped by 12,6% to R117,8 million in 2003.

New investment potential remains strong in this sector, which has recovered enormously through new investments

> **fact:** The biggest diamond ever found, the Cullinan diamond, was found in South Africa. Its largest fragments today adorn Britain's crown jewels.

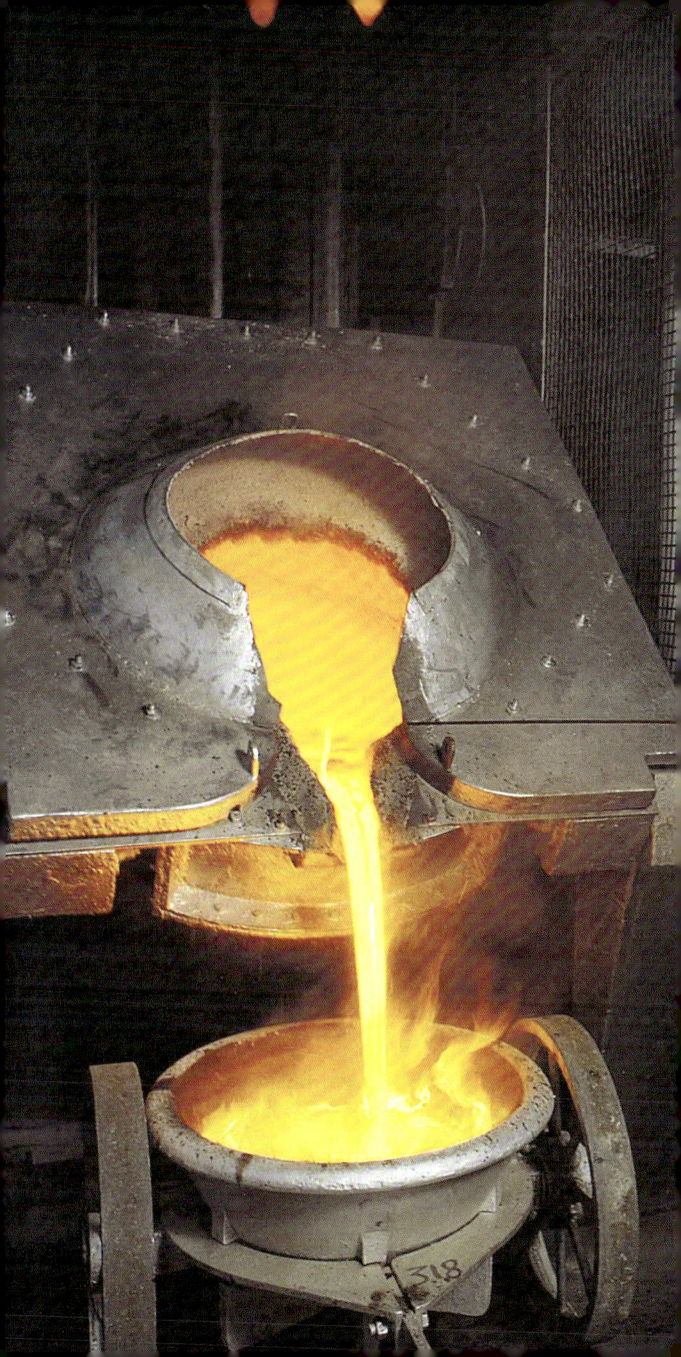
318

Gold price in US dollar and rand terms

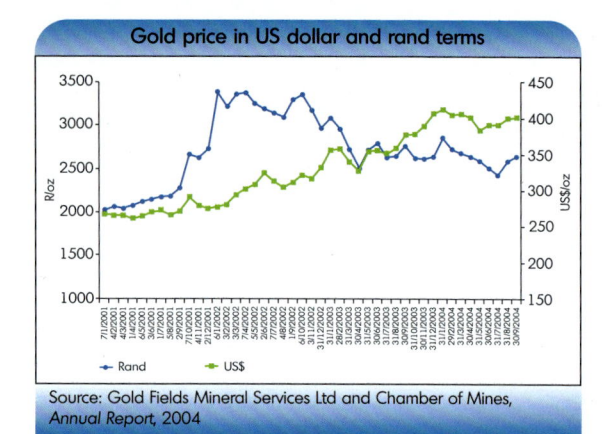

Source: Gold Fields Mineral Services Ltd and Chamber of Mines, Annual Report, 2004

in operations since 1994, compensating for the rapid demise in the demand for uranium oxide in nuclear applications since the late 1980s.

The industry

Mining continues to play an important role in the national economy. Preliminary figures for 2004 indicate that South Africa's mining contributed R87,1 billion or 7,1% gross value added, an increase of R8,6 billion from the previous year. The trend where foreign revenue earnings are dominated by PGMs at US$4,6 billion, followed by gold at US$4,5 billion, also continued in 2004.

Over the last few years, South African mining houses have transformed into large, focused mining companies that include Anglo Platinum, AngloGold, De Beers, Implats and Iscor. The Chamber of Mines represents 85% of mining production.

Including suppliers and considering the multiplier effect, many millions rely on the industry for their livelihood.

Minerals and mining

South Africa's mineral reserves, 2004

Commodity	Unit	Reserves	%	World ranking
Alumino-silicates	kt	50	37	1
Antimony	t	250	6,4	3
Chrome ore	Mt	5 500	72,4	1
Coal	Mt	33,8	3,6	7
Copper	kt	13	1,4	14
Fluorspar	Mt	80	17	2
Gold	t	36 000	40,7	1
Iron ore	Mt	1 500	0,9	9
Lead	Mt	3	2,1	7
Manganese ore	kt	4 000	80,0	1
Phosphate rock	kt	2 500	5	n/a
Platinum-group metals	kg	70 000	87,7	1
Silver	t	10	1,8	9
Titanium minerals	kt	244	29	2
Uranium	t	298	1,0	4
Vanadium	kt	12 000	44,4	1
Vermiculite	kt	14	40	1
Zinc metal	kt	15	3,3	6
Zirconium minerals	kt	14	19,4	2

Mt=megaton, kt=kiloton, t=ton, n/a=not available, kg=kilogram

Source: Minerals Bureau

Policy

The Minerals and Petroleum Resources Development Act, 2002 aims to:
- recognise that mineral resources are the common heritage of all South Africans
- promote the beneficiation of minerals
- guarantee security of tenure for existing prospecting and mining operations
- ensure that historically disadvantaged people (HDP) participate more meaningfully
- promote junior and small-scale mining.

In terms of the Act, new order rights may be registered, transferred and traded, while existing operators are guaranteed security of tenure. Mining rights are valid for a maximum of 30 years, renewable for another 30 years, while prospecting rights are valid for up to five years, renewable for another three.

An empowerment charter for the industry, which is supported by mining houses and labour, targets:
- 15% ownership of mines by HDP within five years
- 40% of junior and senior management positions to be held by HDP within five years
- 26% ownership within 10 years
- 10% participation by women within five years.

Government is committed to helping junior and small-scale miners upgrade their operations into economically viable units. The first step is to legalise these mines.

The South African Small-Scale Mining Chamber was launched in July 2005 in Kimberley in the Northern Cape.

Energy and water

Bringing clean and affordable water and energy within everyone's reach is a key national goal. At the same time, planning ensures that these key drivers of economic growth are delivered reliably and cost-effectively to industry, commerce and agriculture.

The Department of Minerals and Energy's Energy Policy is based on the following key objectives:
- attaining universal access to energy by 2014
- accessible, affordable and reliable energy, especially for the poor
- diversifying primary energy sources and reducing dependency on coal
- good governance, which must also facilitate and encourage private-sector investments in the energy sector
- environmentally responsible energy provision.

Current estimates suggest that R107 billion will be needed between 2005 and 2009 to meet the country's growing energy needs. Eskom will invest R84 billion over the next five years. The balance of R23 billion is reserved for independent power-producer entrants.

Energy in South Africa

- Electricity prices in South Africa are among the lowest in the world.
- The production and distribution of energy contributes 15% of gross domestic product (GDP), creating about 250 000 jobs.

South Africa has the world's 11th-highest commercial primary energy intensity, with large-scale, energy-intensive primary mineral beneficiation industries and mining industries being vast consumers of power.

Power sources

Coal

In 2004, South African mines produced 242,82 megatons (Mt) of coal, making it the fifth-largest coal-producing country in the world. Of this figure, 178,37 Mt was used locally, at a value of R13,6 billion, with export sales totalling 67,94 Mt, at a value of R14,47 billion.

South Africa has around 28,6 billion t of recoverable coal reserves, making it the seventh-largest holder of coal reserves in the world.

With South Africa's present production rate there should be more than 50 years of coal supply left.

As a result of new entrants to the industry, operating collieries were increased to 64 during 2004.

Nuclear

Eskom Koeberg Nuclear Power Station's two reactors outside Cape Town supply 1 800 megawatts to the national grid when both are operating at full power, contributing about 6% of South Africa's electricity.

The National Nuclear Regulator is the prime safety regulator and is responsible for the protection of persons, property and the environment against nuclear damage through the establishment of safety standards and regulatory

fact: The refurbishment of three mothballed power stations – Camden in Ermelo (1 600 megawatts [mw]), Grootvlei in Balfour (1 200 mw) and Komati in Middleburg (1 000 mw) – will result in an additional 3 800 mw to the system. Eskom will spend about R12 billion (nominal rand) on the recommissioning of these three stations.

Implementation of the Kyoto Protocol came into effect on 16 February 2005. Government established a designated national authority (DNA) office in the Department of Minerals and Energy to handle clean development mechanism transactions. It opened its doors for business on 1 December 2004. The DNA office is receiving a number of project proposals for review from the private sector. These projects, when implemented, will reduce South Africa's carbon dioxide emissions and generate revenue of R618 million by the year 2012 from sales of certified emission reductions.

practices. It exercises regulatory control related to safety over the siting, design, construction and operation of nuclear installations and other actions.

The Nuclear Energy Corporation of South Africa (Necsa) undertakes and promotes research and development in the field of nuclear energy, radiation sciences and technology, medical isotope manufacturing, nuclear liabilities management, waste management and decommissioning. It is a public entity reporting to the Minister of Minerals and Energy.

Necsa's reactor-produced radioisotopes are exported to more than 50 countries.

The research reactor at Pelindaba, SAFARI-1, is the most commercialised such reactor in the world with ISO 9001 accreditation. It is earning South Africa millions of rands worth of foreign revenue.

Liquid fuels

South Africa consumed 21 267 million litres (ML) of liquid-fuel products in 2002 and 25 338 ML in 2003. Thirty-six percent of the demand is met by synthetic fuels (synfuels) produced locally, largely from coal and a small amount from natural gas. The rest is met by products refined locally from imported crude oil. The petrol price in South Africa is linked to the petrol price in United States (US) dollars in certain international petrol markets. This means that the domestic price is influenced by supply and

Pocket Guide to South Africa 2005/06

Brent crude oil prices

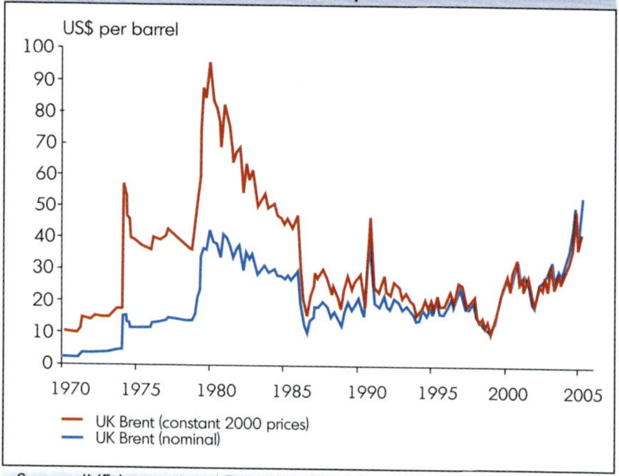

Source: IMF, International Financial Statistics

demand for petroleum products in the international markets, combined with the Rand/Dollar exchange rate.

PetroSA is responsible for the exploration and exploitation of oil and natural gas, as well as producing and marketing synthetic fuels produced from offshore gas at the world's largest commercial gas-to-liquids plant in Mossel Bay.

Sasol

The Sasol group of companies comprises diversified fuel, chemical and related manufacturing and marketing operations, complemented by interests in technology development, oil and gas exploration, and production.

> On 3 March 2005, Cabinet approved cleaner fuels for South Africa with effect from January 2006. This will see an end to lead being added to petrol and lower sulphur standards for diesel. This forms part of a process that will see newly formulated fuels being introduced, which will contribute to the improvement of urban air quality.

Energy and water

The Department of Minerals and Energy continues to support Black Economic Empowerment (BEE) suppliers in pursuance of the Liquid and Petroleum Charter. On 30 November 2004, the department and individual members of the South African Petroleum Industry Association signed a memorandum of understanding aimed at creating a supplier development agency. The agency opened its doors for trading on 1 April 2005.

The primary objectives of the agency are to source potential BEE suppliers to the industry, accredit the suppliers to combat fronting, develop suppliers to meet the performance levels of the industry and source opportunities for BEE suppliers from industry.

Its principal feedstocks are obtained from coal, which the company converts into value-added hydrocarbons through Fischer-Tropsch process technologies.

Indigenous oil, gas resources and production

The EM gasfield complex off Mossel Bay started production in the third quarter of 2000, and will ensure sufficient feedstock to PetroSA to maintain current liquid-fuel production levels at 36 000 barrels (bbls) of petroleum products a day until 2009.

PetroSA's gas-to-liquid plant supplies about 7% of South Africa's liquid-fuel needs.

PetroSA's new oilfield, Sable, situated about 150 km south off the coast of Mossel Bay, is expected to produce 17% of South Africa's oil needs.

The field, which came into operation in August 2003, was initially projected to produce 30 000 to 40 000 bbls of crude oil a day and 20 million to 25 million bbls in the next three years.

Eskom

Eskom generates about 95% of South Africa's electricity.

The utility is among the top 11 utilities in the world in terms of generation capacity and among the top seven in

> The proposed wind farm in the Darling district of the Western Cape was approved in March 2005. This facility will consist of four Danish-designed wind turbines that will produce 1,3 megawatts (mw) of electricity each, bringing the total output of the wind farm to 5,2 mw.
>
> This is the first renewable energy power-generating facility to be developed by a private company that will feed into the national power network. It will also be the first commercial wind farm in South Africa.
>
> Klipheuwel, funded by Eskom, is the biggest wind farm in sub-Saharan Africa.

terms of sales. Eskom was incorporated as a public company on 1 July 2002.

Eskom does not have exclusive generation rights but does enjoy a practical monopoly on bulk electricity. It also operates the integrated national high-voltage transmission system and supplies electricity directly to large consumers and some residential consumers.

Restructuring of the electricity distribution industry

The Minister of Minerals and Energy, Ms Lindiwe Hendricks, launched South Africa's first regional electricity distributor (RED 1) on 4 July 2005 in Cape Town. RED 1 will pave the way for five other REDs, following the amalgamation of the distribution function of Eskom with that of 187 municipalities already distributing electricity in the country.

REDs will provide competitive electricity tariffs, and offer an efficient and reliable electricity service. These entities will in the long term enable access to electricity for all.

The REDs will consist of Eskom Distribution and the local authorities. They will buy electricity from power generators such as Eskom on wholesale prices determined by the National Energy Regulator.

Integrated National Electrification Programme (INEP)

Significant progress has been made towards universal access to electricity. By May 2005, the INEP had delivered 232 287 household connections at R582 million, 2 233 schools at R100 million and 50 clinics at R118 million. The programme focuses on creating bulk infrastructure, especially in areas where it has become impossible to connect new households to the network without reinforcement.

In April 2004, South Africa celebrated the electrification of 7,5 million households – an achievement of four million new electricity connections since 1994. By May 2005, access to electricity was at 71%.

Government gazetted the national Electricity Basic Services Support Tariff Policy in July 2003. The policy aims to bring relief, through government intervention, to low-income households and to ensure optimal socio-economic benefits from the INEP. Qualifying customers are eligible for 50 kWh of free electricity per month. By July 2005, 64% of South Africa's 284 municipalities were providing free basic electricity to 49% of the population.

Energy and the environment

South Africa's per capita production of greenhouse gases is well above global averages and that of other middle-income developing countries.

The economy is carbon intensive, producing only US$259 per ton of carbon dioxide emitted, as compared with US$1 131 for South Korea, US$484 for Mexico and US$418 for Brazil.

Coal is used by about 950 000 households countrywide, resulting in indoor air-pollution problems.

Fuel wood is the primary energy source of three million rural households. Studies have shown that fuel-wood users are exposed to even higher levels of particulate emissions than coal users.

To address this situation, the Department of Minerals and Energy is investigating improved woodstoves and other alternatives, such as solar cookers and biogas, as well as speeding up electrification.

Eskom is looking at harnessing biomass as a grid supply option, while also planning to pilot a new technology aimed at providing rural power in a remote area in the Eastern Cape. This technology, called a gasifier system, will use waste from a rural sawmill to provide electricity to power the creation of business ventures in the area. The system was expected to be installed in 2005.

Water

South Africa is largely a semi-arid, water-stressed country. The country's average rainfall is about 450 mm per year, well below the world average of about 860 mm per year. To overcome the problem of variable river flows, many large storage dams have been built.

Dams experience high evaporation rates, further reducing available water, as do commercial afforestation and sugar-cane farming.

The total net abstraction of water from surface water resources amounts to about 10 200 million m^3 per year for the whole of South Africa, after allowing for the re-use of return flows. This represents about 20% of the total mean annual run-off of 49 200 million m^3 per year (all standardised to 98% assurance of supply). A further 8% is

---

The Working for Water Programme is a labour-intensive initiative to clear invasive alien plants. It is a mulltidepartmental initiative led by the departments of water affairs and forestry, of environmental affairs and tourism, and of agriculture. It started in 1995 with a budget of R25 million and has grown into one of government's key poverty-relief programmes.

During 2004, R440 million was spent and the programme employed about 32 000 people.

Energy and water

Major dams in South Africa		
Dam	Full supply capacity (10m^3)	River
Gariep	5 341	Orange
Vanderkloof	3 171	Orange
Sterkfontein	2 616	Nuwejaarspruit
Nuwejaarspruit Vaal	2 603	Vaal
Pongolapoort	2 445	Pongola

Source: Department of Water Affairs and Forestry

estimated to be lost through evaporation from storage and conveyance along rivers, and 6% through land-use activities. As a national average, about 66% of the natural river flow (mean annual run-off) therefore still remains in the country's rivers.

Free basic water (FBW)

The focus of the Department of Water Affairs and Forestry broadened in 2001 to include the provision of free basic services to all indigent people in the country. By March 2005, 162 of the 170 water-service authorities were providing FBW. The 2004/05 target that FBW should be accessible to 75% of the population served with water, was achieved. By February 2005, more than 31 million people were receiving FBW.

Water policy

Cabinet approved the first edition of the National Water Resource Strategy (NWRS) in September 2004. The NWRS

By the end of March 2005:
- 44,5 million people had access to an improved water supply
- basic water infrastructure had been supplied to 15 million people, over 10 million of this supplied by the Department of Water Affairs and Forestry.
- 31,9 million people (66,3%) had access to free basic water.

> In response to drought conditions seriously affecting many parts of the country since 2003, the Government allocated additional funds for emergency water supplies. In 2003/04, R295 million was made available through two allocations. About R203 million of this amount went to municipalities for emergency water provision at local authority level, while about R92 million was used by the Department of Water Affairs and Forestry to supplement regional water supplies. During 2004/05, an additional R280 million was allocated to municipalities for emergency water provision, via the Department of Provincial and Local Government, while an additional R50 million was allocated to the Department of Water Affairs and Forestry to strengthen national and regional water supplies.

describes how South Africa's water resources will be protected, used, developed, conserved, managed and controlled in accordance with the requirements of the National Water Policy, 1997 and the National Water Act, 1998, which are founded on government's vision of a transformed South African society in which every person has the opportunity to participate in productive economic activity and lead a dignified and healthy life.

One of the most ambitious binational water projects ever is the Lesotho Highlands Water Project between South Africa and Lesotho.

The first phase, which was completed in 1998, consisted of the construction of three dams, various tunnels and a hydroelectric plant.

Education

The right to education is enshrined in South Africa's Bill of Rights – not only for children but also for adults.

Learners

In 2004, the South African public education system accommodated more than 11,8 million school learners, more than 450 000 university students, more than 200 000 university of technology students, and over 460 000 Further Education and Training (FET) college students. There were almost 26 000 primary, secondary, combined and intermediate schools, with 350 000 educators.

The national matriculation pass rate declined from 73,3% in 2003 to 70,7% in 2004; 18,2% of matriculation candidates passed with university endorsement in 2004, compared with 18,6% in 2003. However, the actual number of learners who passed with endorsements increased from

---

In 2005/06, R6,9 billion was allocated to the Department of Education to contribute to improving salaries for educators. Some R4,2 billion of the R6,9 billion would be used for expanding pay progression for performance rewards and targeted incentives.

The Masifunde Sonke Library Project was initiated by the Ministry of Education and civil society to address the challenges of illiteracy, and to promote a love of reading. The project is tasked to profile reading and to encourage stakeholders to promote reading.

Pocket Guide to South Africa 2005/06

Number of schools for learners with disabilities and special needs	
Eastern Cape	43
Free State	21
Gauteng	100
KwaZulu-Natal	62
Limpopo	23
Mpumalanga	18
North West	40
Northern Cape	9
Western Cape	68
National	384

Source: Department of Education

School enrolments		
Education	Period	Enrolment
Enrolment (Early Childhood Development)	1999 – 2002	150 000 – 280 000
Primary school enrolment	1995 – 2001	95,5%
Secondary school enrolment	1992 – 2001	85% (+15%)

Source: Towards a Ten Year Review

82 000 to 85 117. This was possibly due to an increase of 5,9% in the number of candidates who wrote the exam.

Some 537 schools obtained a 100% pass rate. Some 13 480 girl learners passed Mathematics at Higher Grade (HG) and 17 566 passed Physical Science at HG. A total of 40 098 learners passed with merit and 9 213 passed with distinction.

Over the past 10 years, the National Student Financial Aid Scheme (NSFAS) assisted more than 400 000 students with awards amounting to over R5 billion. A student may receive between R2 000 and R30 000, depending on need that is determined through a national means test.
In 2004/05, over R200 million was paid back by past students and made available to future students.
In 2005/06, the NSFAS was allocated a budget of R776 million.

Education

Matric pass rates

Year	Percentage
1999	48,9%
2002	68,9%
2003	73,3%
2004	70,7%
2005	68,3%

Source: Department of Education

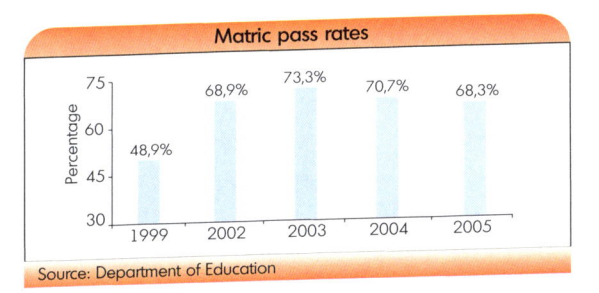

Girl learners' performance in matric Mathematics HG improved, with 74,4% passing the exam in 2004, compared with 50,9% in 1999. The national matric pass rate in 2005 was 68,3%.

By mid-2005, South Africa had more than 11 373 libraries, of which 9 416 were school libraries.

The new institutional landscape for Higher Education (HE) consists of eight separate and incorporated universities, three merged universities, five universities of technology and six comprehensive universities.

Structures

South Africa has a single national education system, which is organised and managed by the national Department of Education and the nine provincial departments.

Policy

Schooling is compulsory between the ages of seven and 15. All learners are guaranteed access to quality learning. There

---

fact

By September 2005, more than 22 000 people had been recruited nationwide to prepare and serve school meals, enabling them to gain income through stipends. Meals are served at about 15 000 schools to more than five million learners.

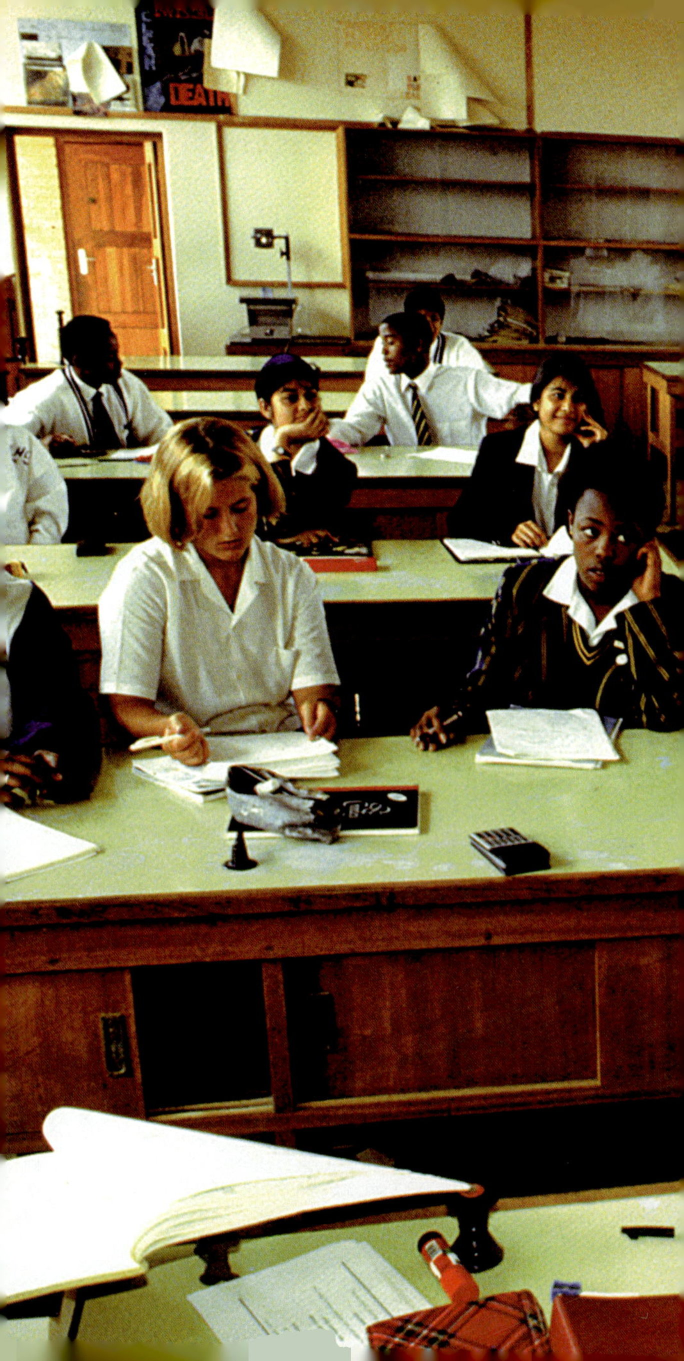
DEATH

Education

Number of farm school learners by province, 1996 and 2000

	1996	2000	% decrease 1996-2000
Eastern Cape	50 307	18 333	-64
Free State	104 268	56 618	-46
Gauteng	25 297	12 576	-50
KwaZulu-Natal	192 615	55 304	-71
Limpopo	48 294	24 877	-48
Mpumalanga	93 352	32 847	-65
Northern Cape	16 528	8 321	-50
North West	61 107	35 503	-42
Western Cape	47 264	11 769	-75
Total	639 032	256 148	-60

Source: Department of Education

are two types of schools: independent (private) and public.

At public schools, parents vote on the level of school fees. Poor parents are given exemption or reductions.

According to a plan of action to improve access to free, quality education, released in June 2003, compulsory school fees were abolished for 40% of learners in the poorest schools.

The Department of Education has developed proposals for improving the targeting of funding for schools and the regulations governing school fee exemption.

Curriculum 2005

Curriculum 2005 is based on the concept of outcomes-based education, which regards learning as an interactive process between educators and learners. The focus is on what learners should know and be able to do (knowledge, skills, attitudes and values). The goal is to produce active and lifelong learners with a thirst for knowledge and a love of learning.

Further Education and Training

FET provides learning and training from National Qualifications Framework (NQF) levels 2 to 4, or the equivalent of grades 10 to 12 in the school system, and Further Education and Training Certificate (FETC) General Vocational and FETC Trade Occupational, on NQF levels 2 to 4 in FET colleges. The FETC will replace the current Senior Certificate in 2008.

The FET curriculum is shifting towards a balanced learning experience that provides flexible access to lifelong learning, HE and training, and productive employment.

The implementation of the FET curriculum in 2006 is expected to complete the circle of transformation of the schools' curriculum. The FET curriculum provides for a fundamental component comprising four compulsory subjects: two official languages, Mathematical Literacy or Mathematics, and Life Orientation, as well as three approved subjects.

In addition to the 21 approved subjects, 13 non-official languages have been added to the curriculum.

In 2002, the 152 technical colleges were merged to form 50 multicampus FET colleges.

In 2005/06, government invested R1 billion over the next three years for improved facilities, equipment and support for FET colleges in the country.

Higher Education transformation

According to a strategic plan for HE, enrolment at these institutions will rise from 15% to 20% of school leavers within 15 years. Within five years, enrolments in the humanities will decline, while those in Business and Commerce, and Science, Engineering and Technology will rise.

The 2001 National Plan for HE also envisaged:
- research being funded through a separate formula based on research output

> By May 2005, the South African Council for Educators had registered about 490 000 educators, of which 18 000 were provisionally registered.

- targets being set to increase the numbers of black and female students and academic staff.

The total cost for the restructuring of the HE system is estimated at R1,9 billion for the period 2001/02 to 2006/07.

Institutional restructuring

The new HE landscape consists of the following institutions:
- University of the Witwatersrand
- University of Cape Town
- University of Stellenbosch
- Rhodes University
- University of the Western Cape (which incorporated the Dental Faculty of Stellenbosch University)
- University of Zululand
- University of Venda
- University of the Free State (which incorporated the QwaQwa Campus of the University of the North and the Bloemfontein Campus of Vista)
- North West University (which incorporated the University of Potchefstroom and Vista Sebokeng Campus
- University of Pretoria (retained its name after incorporating the Mamelodi Campus of Vista University)
- UNISA (retained its name after merging with the Vista University Distance Education Campus and Technikon SA)

Since the launch of the National Strategy for Mathematics, Science and Technology Education, the number of African learners performing better has increased almost two-fold nationally. About 11% of these learners are from 102 dedicated schools. In these schools, performance tripled, especially at higher-grade level. There has also been an improvement in participation by female learners, especially in the dedicated schools, where there are currently more female than male learners taking Mathematics and Science.

- Tshwane University of Technology (from the merger of technikons Pretoria, North West and Northern Gauteng)
- Durban Institute of Technology (from the merger of Natal Technikon and Technikon M.L. Sultan)
- Central University of Technology (formerly Technikon Free State)
- Mangosuthu Technikon
- University of Johannesburg (from the merger of the Rand Afrikaans University with Technikon Witwatersrand, which incorporated the Soweto and East Rand campuses of Vista University)
- University of Limpopo (from the merger of the Medical University of South Africa [Medunsa] and the University of the North)
- Nelson Mandela Metropolitan University (from the merger of the University of Port Elizabeth, Port Elizabeth Technikon and Port Elizabeth Campus of Vista)
- Eastern Cape University of Technology (from the merger of the University of Transkei, Border Technikon and the Eastern Cape Technikon)
- University of Fort Hare (which incorporated the East London Campus of Rhodes University)
- Cape Peninsula University of Technology (from the merger of the Cape Technikon and Peninsula Technikon)
- Walter Sisulu University for Technology and Science (from the merger of the University of Transkei, Border Technikon and Eastern Cape Technikon)
- Northern Cape Institute of Learning
- Mpumalanga Institute of Learning.

Science and technology

South Africa's science and research are world class. The Department of Science and Technology seeks to realise the full potential of science and technology (S&T) in social and economic development, through the development of human resources, research and innovation.

Strategies

The department's Research and Development (R&D) Strategy, which was launched in 2002, enhances the National System of Innovation through which a multitude of role-players collaborate to pursue the goals of economic development and progress.

Government has recommitted itself to the R&D Strategy of 1% of gross domestic product to be invested by both public and private sectors by 2008. This implies an additional R2 billion investment across both sectors.

The department continues to develop strategies in new areas of knowledge and technology. Strategies for indigenous knowledge, nanotechnology, astronomy and intellectual property derived from publicly funded research, have been developed.

The Southern African Large Telescope at Sutherland in the Northern Cape, is one of South Africa's flagship scientific projects. It is the largest single optical telescope in the southern hemisphere.

> South Africa is bidding to host the ambitious Square Kilometre Array (SKA) radio telescope, a telescope that will have multiple receiving surfaces and will provide radio astronomers with one million m^2 of collecting area. The Northern Cape is an ideal location for the SKA's core array.

Innovation centres

The Department of Science and Technology has created trusts as agencies for driving the development of the biotechnology sector in South Africa. These are the biotechnology regional innovation centres, the PlantBio Innovation Centre and the National Bioinformatics Network. These institutions – individually, collectively, and in partnership with the incubators, industry, and with the broader biotech role-players – must develop their leadership role to grow the South African biotechnology sector.

Backed by the European Union, the Godisa National Incubation Programme was launched in 2001. The programme aims to encourage technology transfer and to help small businesses compete in the global economy. By 2005, Godisa had supported 1 280 small, medium and micro enterprises (SMMEs).

Supporting innovators

Technology for Human Resources for Industry Programme (THRIP)

The programme aims to increase participation by SMMEs, Black Economic Empowerment entities, black and women

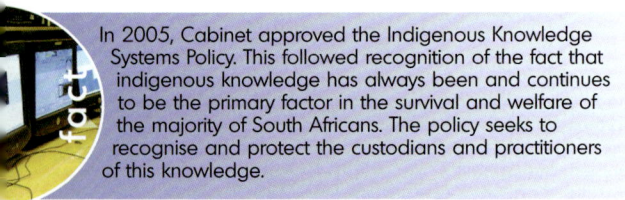

> In 2005, Cabinet approved the Indigenous Knowledge Systems Policy. This followed recognition of the fact that indigenous knowledge has always been and continues to be the primary factor in the survival and welfare of the majority of South Africans. The policy seeks to recognise and protect the custodians and practitioners of this knowledge.

Science and technology

International alliances being forged with the European Union, within the New Partnership for Africa's Development structure and the India-Brazil-South Africa partnership are gaining momentum. Prior to 1994, foreign funding of South African research and development (R&D) was almost zero. By 2005, it had grown to at least 6% of total expenditure.

The Department of Science and Technology manages 36 signed international bilateral agreements, which have resulted in over 300 R&D projects.

researchers and students; as well as to increase the share of the THRIP budget allocation to historically disadvantaged individuals and universities of technology.

The Medium Term Expenditure Framework budget allocation for THRIP was R143 million in 2005/06.

Innovation Fund

The Innovation Fund was created to promote technological innovation, increase networking and cross-sectoral collaboration, increase competitiveness, improve quality of life, ensure environmental sustainability and harness Information Technology. The Innovation Fund's budget increased to R171 million in 2004/05.

Research capacity-development programmes

These seek to boost historically black universities by supporting individual researchers and encouraging a postdoctoral research culture.

National research facilities

South Africa's national research facilities are managed by the National Research Foundation (NRF). The NRF is responsible for promoting and supporting basic and applied research.

The following national research facilities are managed under the mandate of the NRF:
- South African Astronomical Observatory
- Hartebeesthoek Radio Astronomy Observatory

- Hermanus Magnetic Observatory
- South African Institute for Aquatic Biodiversity
- South African Environmental Observation Network, an emerging national research facility
- National Zoological Gardens
- iThemba Laboratory for Accelerator-Based Sciences (iThemba LABS).

Science councils

Council for Scientific and Industrial Research (CSIR)

The CSIR is one of the largest scientific and technology research, development and implementation organisations in Africa. The organisation undertakes and applies directed research and innovation in S&T to improve the quality of life of South Africans.

The organisation's staff complement is in the order of 2 500 with a core of technical and scientific specialists.

The CSIR's portfolio includes:
- research, development and implementation
- technology transfer and assessment
- scientific and technical education and training
- policy and strategic decision support
- global S&T links as well as perspectives
- specialised technical and information consulting
- prototyping and pilot-scale manufacturing
- commercialisation of intellectual property, including venture establishment.

Mintek

Mintek, South Africa's national mineral research organisation, is one of the world's leading technology organisations specialising in mineral processing, extractive metallurgy and related areas. Working closely with industry and other R&D institutions, Mintek provides service testwork, process development, consulting and innovative products to clients worldwide.

Science and technology

Mintek is an autonomous statutory organisation and reports to the Minister of Minerals and Energy. About 35% of the annual budget of R278 million is funded by the State science vote, with the balance provided by contract R&D, sales of services and products, technology licensing agreements, and joint-venture operating companies. Mintek has some 480 permanent staff members, over half of whom are scientists, engineers and other technical R&D personnel.

Human Sciences Research Council (HSRC)

The HSRC is South Africa's statutory research agency dedicated to the applied social sciences. It has about 130 researchers, mainly specialists, 30 interns and 110 support staff. Its revenue is derived roughly equally from its parliamentary grant and from earnings through tenders, commissions, and local and international foundation grants.

According to a survey by the Centre for Science, Technology and Innovation Indicators, South Africa spent R10,1 billion or 0,81% of gross domestic product on research and development (R&D) in 2003/04.

This was an increase from R7,5 billion in 2001/02.

While South Africa's R&D expenditure is fairly high compared with that of other developing countries, the total number of researchers is low at 2,2 researchers per 1 000 employees.

Women researchers make up 38% of the total researchers, compared with 11,2% in Japan and 28,4% in Norway. In developing countries, Argentina leads the way with 50,5% women researchers.

The largest amount, 28%, of R&D is performed in the field of engineering sciences. This is followed at 21,9% in natural sciences and 13,5% in the medical and health sciences.

The major performer and financier of R&D is the business sector, which performs 55,5% of all R&D undertaken and finances 52% of the total spent in this field.

Government financed 28%, while 10% of R&D is financed from abroad.

Higher Education performs 20,5% of national R&D, and government 21,9%.

The HSRC conducts social-science research concerned with all aspects of development and poverty alleviation in South Africa, the region and in Africa.

Medical Research Council (MRC)

Established in 1969, the MRC conducts research through six national programmes, and collaborates with most of the world's top health-research agencies to improve the nation's health status and quality of life.

The MRC disseminates research information through the National Health Knowledge Network. The council recently established the African Biotechnology Information Centre in co-operation with various universities.

The MRC National HIV/AIDS Lead Programme co-ordinates the South African AIDS Vaccine Initiative (SAAVI).

This initiative has grown from a small core group of researchers into a large biotechnology consortium which works on various aspects of developing and testing novel HIV vaccines.

By 2005, SAAVI had developed three candidate vaccines that had entered the regulatory process in preparation for trials. Human clinical trials with the DNA vaccine began in 2004. The development team completed the pre-investigational new drug application with the United States Food and Drug Administration (FDA) in 2003, which was the first-ever from a developing country to be lodged with the FDA.

Agricultural Research Council (ARC)

The ARC is committed to the promotion of agriculture and

> In 2004, South Africa was represented at the International Workshop on the Changing Role of Science Centres in Vietnam. The Vietnam Agreement resolved to strengthen the science centre network in developing countries. Nearly 600 000 people visit science centres in South Africa every year; about two thirds of whom are learners.

Science and technology

> In June 2005, the South African Biodiversity Information Facility (SABIF) and its portal were launched at the Innovation Hub in Pretoria.
>
> SABIF aims to contribute to South Africa's sustainable development by facilitating access to biodiversity and related information on the Internet. The SABIF Portal will serve as South Africa's national gateway to open and free scientific biodiversity information. In doing this, SABIF will contribute towards a co-ordinated international scientific effort to enable users throughout the world to discover and put to use vast quantities of biodiversity data.

related sectors through research and technology development and transfer.

Council of Geoscience (CGS)
The CGS supplies the country with geoscience data to establish a safe cost-effective physical infrastructure.

South African Bureau of Standards (SABS)
The SABS produces, maintains and disseminates standards. It promotes standardisation in business and government, and administers compulsory standards on behalf of the State. It also certifies international quality standards such as ISO 9000 and ISO 14001.

Other important research bodies
The National Institute for Tropical Diseases in Tzaneen, Limpopo, does ongoing assessment of various malaria-control programmes.

The South African National Antarctic Programme manages three bases, one at Vesleskarvet in Dronning Maud Land, Antarctica; a second on Marion Island in the south Indian Ocean; and a third on Gough Island, a British territory in the South Atlantic Ocean.

South Africa is the only African country with a presence in Antarctica, and which is also conducting research there in physics, engineering, Earth sciences, biological and oceanographic sciences.

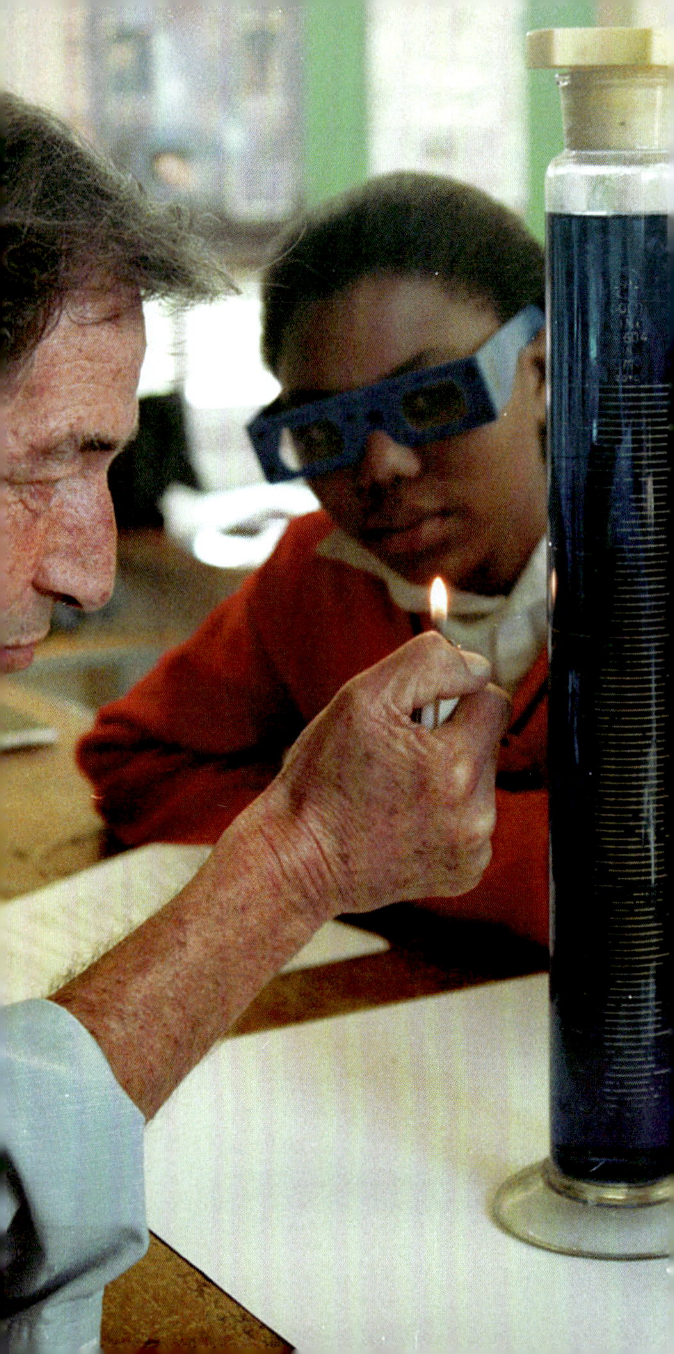

Science and technology

The South African base, SANAE IV, is one of few country bases built on hard rock as opposed to the ice shelf, and is regarded as one of the more modern bases on Antarctica. The Department of Science and Technology has finalised the Antarctic Research Strategy for South Africa.

Mine-safety research
The Safety in Mines Research Advisory Committee aims to advance mineworkers' safety. It has a permanent research management office overseeing research in rock engineering, engineering and occupational health.

Energy research
The Chief Directorate: Energy of the Department of Minerals and Energy manages a policy-directed research programme. This includes transport energy, renewable energy and energy for developing areas, coal, electricity, energy efficiency, energy economy and integrated energy-policy formulation.

Agricultural research
Agricultural research is conducted by the ARC, several universities and the private sector.

Water research
Water research in South Africa is co-ordinated and funded by the Water Research Commission in Pretoria.

In 2004/05, government allocated funds to the Pebble Bed Modular Reactor (PBMR) project. The funding enables the PBMR to secure strategic contracts for the development of key components such as the turbine machinery being developed by Mitsubishi Heavy Industries from Japan and a helium test facility at Pelindaba. Government wants to produce between 4 000 and 5 000 megawatt (mw) of power from pebble bed reactors in South Africa. This equates to between 20 and 30 PBMR reactors of 165 mw each. The project is factored into the country's future energy planning from about 2010 onwards. The PBMR will place the country at the forefront of energy technology.

The organisations most active in water research are:
- universities and universities of technology (56,25% of the total number of contracts)
- professional consultants (16,6%)
- science councils (22,9%)
- water/waste utilities (2%)
- non-governmental organisations (2%).

Coastal and marine research

The Chief Directorate: Marine and Coastal Management advises on the use of marine living resources and the conservation of marine ecosystems, by conducting and supporting relevant multidisciplinary scientific research and monitoring the marine environment. Sustainable use and the need to preserve future options in the use of marine ecosystems and their resources are guiding objectives in the research and advice provided by the chief directorate.

Environmental research

The Chief Directorate: Environmental Management of the Department of Environmental Affairs and Tourism annually finances several research and monitoring programmes.

The programmes comprise subjects such as waste management and pollution, nature conservation, river management, the coastline and marine environment, and the atmosphere.

Housing

Access to housing and secure accommodation is an integral part of government's commitment to reduce poverty and improve the quality of people's lives.

Achievements

Between 1994 and June 2005, a total of 2,4 million housing subsidies were approved. During this period, 1,7 million housing units were provided to more than seven million people.

In 2004/05, some 178 612 housing units were completed.

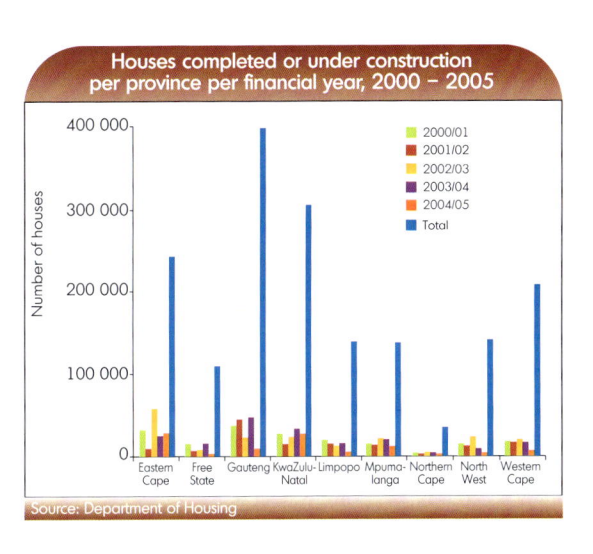

Houses completed or under construction per province per financial year, 2000 – 2005

Source: Department of Housing

Pocket Guide to South Africa 2005/06

Number of houses completed or under construction, September 2005

- 13 042
- 6 511
- 25 321
- 21 287
- 6 666
- 19 884
- 11 108
- 17 553
- 56 239

- Eastern Cape
- Free State
- Gauteng
- KwaZulu-Natal
- Limpopo
- Mpumalanga
- Northern Cape
- North West
- Western Cape

Source: Department of Housing

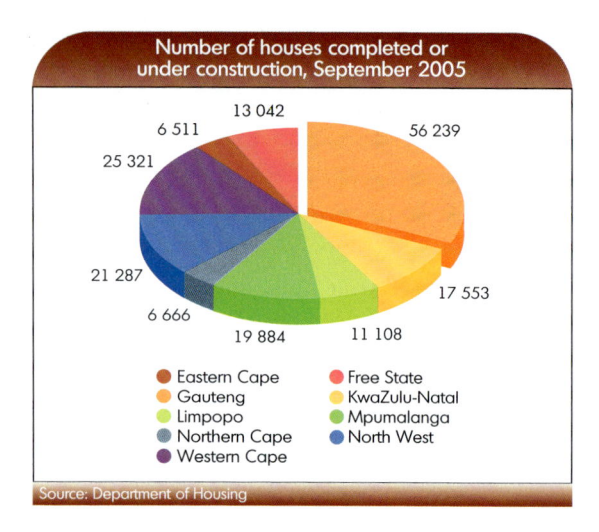

Comprehensive Housing Plan

In September 2004, government unveiled the Comprehensive Housing Plan for the Development of Integrated Sustainable Human Settlements.

Cabinet approved the plan as a framework for housing programmes in the next five years. It provides for comprehensive oversight by government in promoting the residential property market. This includes the development of low-cost housing, medium-density accommodation and rental housing; stronger partnerships with the private sector; social infrastructure; and amenities.

The plan also aims to change spatial settlement patterns, informed by the need to build multicultural communities in a non-racial society.

Human Settlement Redevelopment Programme

This programme aims to improve the quality of the urban environment and addresses the legacy of dysfunctional urban structures, frameworks and imbalances through multiyear housing development plans.

Housing

Total number of approved housing projects, September 2005

- Eastern Cape: 1 096
- Free State: 559
- Gauteng: 513
- KwaZulu-Natal: 360
- Limpopo: 256
- Mpumalanga: 233
- Northern Cape: 568
- North West: 594
- Western Cape: 613

Source: Department of Housing

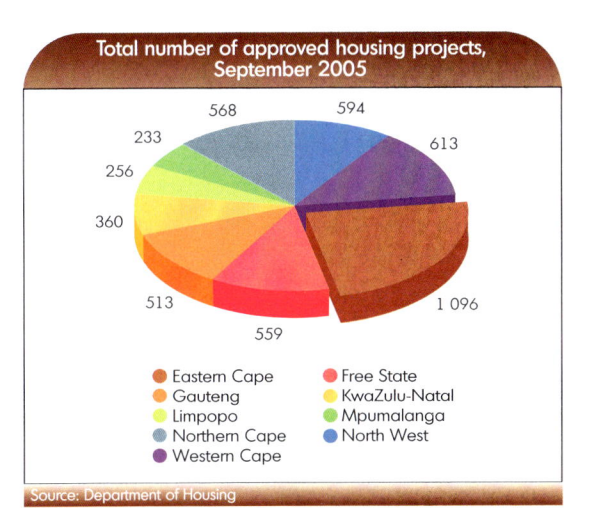

A multipronged approach, this programme aims to redevelop depressed areas, counter spatial distortion, provide essential community facilities and re-plan existing settle-ments. This could entail slum clearance and resettlement.

By February 2005, more than 180 projects to improve dysfunctional human settlements had been approved and were funded through the Human Settlement Redevelopment Programme.

The Human Settlement Redevelopment Grant and the Housing Subsidy Grant have been consolidated into a single integrated housing and human settlement grant to accommodate this responsive, area-based approach to housing delivery.

In the 2005 Budget, an additional allocation was made of R50 million for 2005/06 to step up the housing programme so that all informal settlements can be upgraded by 2014.

Additional funding amounting to R500 million in 2006/07 and R1,5 billion in 2007/08 has been allocated.

In January 2005, South Africa hosted the African Ministerial Conference on Housing and Urban Development (AMCHUD) at the International Convention Centre in Durban.

At the event, South Africa was elected chair and Kenya a rapporteur until 2007. Other members of the Bureau of AMCHUD are Senegal, Algeria and Chad. In various follow-up fora, South Africa presented the common African position on the eradication of slums relating to the inadequacy of the presently agreed upon slum target that is contained in the millennium development goals, the need for the international community to meet their commitments in respect of finance, as well as debt relief and cancellation.

In March 2005, the Minister of Housing, Dr Lindiwe Sisulu, signed a memorandum of understanding (MoU) with the Banking Association of South Africa in Pretoria.

The MoU is in line with the commitment of the Financial Services Charter and the Comprehensive Plan on Sustainable Human Settlements to extend housing finance on a sustainable basis to low-income borrowers.

The banking sector has pledged R42 billion to be released into the affordable housing market by 2008.

Housing projects today aim to encourage previously marginalised communities and particularly women contractors.

Legislation

Recent housing legislation has been aimed, among other things, at:

- The construction of more rental housing. (Special tribunals have been set up in three provinces to mediate disputes between landlords and tenants.)
- Requiring lending institutions to disclose mortgage information to prevent discriminatory lending.
- Requiring all home-builders to register new houses with the official Defect Warranty Scheme managed by the National Home-Builders Registration Council (NHBRC). The NHBRC registered 3 739 home-builders (an increase of 23,7% from 2003) and enrolled 48 305 housing units by March 2004 (an 11,5% increase from 2003).

Housing

Delivery partners

The Department of Housing collaborates with various organisations towards breaking new ground in housing delivery.

- The National Housing Finance Corporation (NHFC) has made significant strides towards making affordable housing finance accessible to the low- and moderate-income communities. The NHFC had disbursed more than R1,7 billion by mid-2005.

  Through its funding, the lives of almost two million people were improved. The NHFC is the implementing agent for the first rental housing projects initiated through the Presidential Job Summit pilot project on rental housing.

- By March 2005, the National Urban Reconstruction and Housing Agency – a partnership between the Government and the Open Society Institute of New York – had financially supported the building of 146 984 houses.

- As a joint venture between the Department of Housing and the Council of South African Banks, Servcon Housing Solutions manages non-performing loans (NPLs) and properties in possession (PIPs) in areas where normal legal processes have broken down. Servcon inherited 33 306 properties with a value of R1,277 billion. By 31 March 2005, Servcon had normalised 21 953 properties and anticipated achieving the full target of 33 306 by 31 March 2006.

- Thubelisha Homes, a not-for-profit company, helps the owners of PIPs or NPLs to relocate to more affordable homes. By May 2005, Thubelisha had serviced 3 000 stands and built 3 674 houses, using skills such as project and construction management and subsidy administration.

- Another not-for-profit company, the Social Housing Foundation (SHF), aims to build capacity for social housing institutions. The SHF and the social housing sector have shown significant growth. By March 2004, there were 83 social housing institutions in South Africa.

In 2005/06, government awarded the SHF a grant of R18 million.
- The Rural Housing Loan Fund's (RHLF) main purpose, as a wholesale lending institution, is to enable retail institutions to provide loans to low-income earners to finance housing in rural areas.

By March 2004, the RHLF-funded intermediaries had made available more than 53 209 loans to rural borrowers for incremental housing and home improvement, totalling R250 million.

Safety, security and defence

The Department of Safety and Security's strategic plan for 2004 to 2007 lays down four key strategic priorities for the medium term:
- combat organised crime, focusing on drug and firearm trafficking, vehicle theft and hijacking, commercial crime and corruption among public officials
- combat serious and violent crimes through strategies to, among other things, counter the proliferation of firearms, improve safety and security in high-crime areas, combat crimes such as taxi and gang violence and faction fighting, and maintain security at major public events
- reduce the incidence of crimes against women and children, and improve the investigation and prosecution of these crimes

In September 2005, the South African Police Service released the following crime statistics for 2004/05:
- attempted murder decreased by 18,8%
- assault decreased by 4,5%
- common assault decreased by 5,1%
- robbery with aggravating circumstances decreased by 5,5%
- common robbery decreased by 5,3%
- burglary at residential premises decreased by 8,1%
- theft of motor vehicles and motorcycles decreased by 5,3%
- theft from motor vehicles decreased by 14%
- stock-theft decreased by 21,2%
- illegal possession of firearms and ammunition decreased by 8,3%
- drug-related crimes increased by 33,5%
- car hijackings decreased by 9,9%
- shoplifting decreased by 7,9%
- commercial crime decreased by 3,8%
- murder decreased by 5,6%
- rape increased by 4%.

- improve the services provided by the South African Police Service (SAPS) in general.

Reducing crime

The total staff establishment of the SAPS on 15 August 2005 was 148 113 members. Some 11 000 trainees were allocated for the 2005/06 financial year, while 4 410 recruits reported for basic training in July 2005. The remaining recruits were expected to commence basic training in January 2006.

Government has expanded the number of police areas for focused multidisciplinary interventions from 63 to 69.

By May 2005, all of the top 200 criminals identified earlier by the SAPS had been arrested.

In reducing crime levels by between 7% and 10% per year, the socio-demographic profiling for 148 priority police-station areas had been completed by June 2005. Action plans aimed at addressing the social causes of crime were developed for 116 priority police stations responsible for combating 50% of all contact crime in South Africa.

Firearms control

The Firearms Control Act, 2000 and the Firearms Control Amendment Act, 2003 intend to help the SAPS prevent the

Number of guns recovered: January – June 2005	
Province	Quantity
Gauteng	32 014
Western Cape	18 021
KwaZulu-Natal	14 532
Free State	9 092
Eastern Cape	9 057
North West	4 354
Northern Cape	2 675
Limpopo	2 747
Mpumalanga	2 139
Source: South African Police Service	

proliferation of illegal firearms and remove them from society, as well as to control legally owned firearms.

The Firearms Control Act, 2000 came into effect on 1 July 2004. People seeking firearm licences are compelled to undergo a competency test before being granted a licence.

In November 2004, the Minister of Safety and Security, Mr Charles Nqakula, declared a firearm amnesty for people in possession of illegal firearms and ammunition. In terms of the amnesty, as defined in Section 138 of the Firearms Control Act, 2000, illegal firearms and ammunition had to be surrendered at police stations nationwide from 1 January to 31 March 2005.

By 31 March 2005, some 46 190 firearms had been recovered, of which 14 987 illegal and 22 520 legally licensed firearms were voluntarily handed over, and 8 683 confiscated by the SAPS.

The minister extended the amnesty period to 30 June 2005.

By 30 June 2005, 94 631 guns and 1 764 246 rounds of ammunition had been surrendered to the police.

Crime intelligence

Between 21 May 2004 and the end of January 2005, the police arrested the following number of suspects in the 63 priority areas:
- murder: 2 317
- rape: 3 942
- robbery: 4 687.

Further, 278 organised crime leaders and 896 runners were arrested on charges relating to organised crime. Following the arrest of those criminals, more information came to light implicating accomplices. Consequently, the police netted a total of 3 810 suspects in connection with organised crime.

Community involvement

Crime prevention in South Africa is based on the principles of community policing, that is, partnerships between the

> The South African Police Service has made significant strides to address the matter of gender balance in the service. By mid-2005, the contingent of female members stood at 28,6%. This is the highest representation of females in any police service in the world. Additionally, 17% of the Senior Management Service is female.

community and the SAPS. Partnerships between police officers (who are appointed as sector managers) and communities strengthen existing community police fora.

Sector policing was introduced in 2002/03 to increase the visibility and accessibility of police officers, particularly in areas that have limited infrastructure and high levels of crime. By mid-2005, 81 sectors had been established and were operationalised at 30 police stations.

Building for security

- Community safety centres (CSCs) bring all relevant departments under one roof, including the SAPS and the departments of justice, correctional services, health and social development. The focus is on deep rural and informal settlements. The first CSC was opened at Tembalethu near George in the Western Cape in 2000. In 2004/05, two more CSCs were completed – at Tshidilamolomo in North West at a cost of R8,5 million and at Galeshewe in the Northern Cape at a cost of R35 million.
- In 2002/03, a three-year plan was developed to provide victim-friendly facilities for handling violent crimes such as rape and domestic abuse. By mid-2005, 227 such

> In terms of the firearms control legislation, 510 non-official firearm institutions, 144 shooting ranges and 158 training-providers had been accredited by the South African Police Service by June 2005. A total of 3 788 applications for the renewal of firearm licences, permits and authorisations were received.

facilities had been established at police stations. An additional 150 such facilities were expected to be established in 2005/06. The SAPS Victim Support Programme has been reviewed to ensure that SAPS training and guidelines support the Service Charter for Victims of Crime in South Africa.

Defence

The mission of the Department of Defence is to defend and protect South Africa, its territorial integrity and its people.

The department, under the auspices of the New Partnership for Africa's Development, participates in various initiatives to secure peace and stability on the continent.

The South African National Defence Force (SANDF) is an all-volunteer force consisting of a regular force core and a reserve force.

In addition to military matters, the Department of Defence is involved in search-and-rescue operations, hydrography and securing national key points.

Uniformed members of the SANDF have the right to join trade unions. They may not, however, go on strike or picket.

Border control and security

In keeping with the Department of Defence's strategy for a phased withdrawal from internal security to external peace-support operations and the rejuvenation of the SANDF, the process to transfer functions and personnel from the

---

Government has started establishing and maintaining centres for homeless children in big cities throughout the country. Three such centres have been launched in Gauteng and the Western Cape.

These centres provide homeless children with shelter, food and various social service programmes, including sports activities, education and arts programmes.

Pocket Guide to South Africa 2005/06

SANDF to the SAPS's Protection and Security Division was underway by mid-2005.

This forms part of the phasing out of the commando system by closing down 183 commando units by 2009. At least 17 units had been closed down by the end of March 2005 and 55 units are expected to be closed down by 2006.

This process is intended to release SANDF forces to pursue government's regional and continental obligations to peace support, conflict resolution and post-conflict reconstruction.

Peace support

Members of the SANDF have been deployed in Africa to contribute to peacekeeping, democracy and capacity-building efforts.

The biggest deployment of SANDF personnel has been to the Democratic Republic of Congo, where by mid-2005 1 347 personnel were stationed. They perform duties ranging from emergency work and integration and training to infantry battalion duties.

The next biggest deployment is in Burundi where SANDF personnel have been active since August 2004. The majority of the personnel formed part of the United Nations contingent. The remainder of the SANDF group performs VIP-protection duties as part of an African Union mission.

In 2005, some 277 SANDF personnel were deployed to Sudan, partly as military observers and partly as an infantry protector company.

The Department of Defence's Youth Foundation Training Programme is a critical vehicle to ensure continuous supply of competent specialists such as engineers, pilots, doctors and navy combat officers, among others. During 2005/06, the Department of Defence spent R11 million on 225 learners registered with the programme.

By September 2005, some 883 members had completed the programme since 2001. A total of 715 new members were appointed in the Department of Defence.

Safety, security and defence

Requirement of main equipment

The SANDF's core capabilities will be maintained to allow it to execute its mandate and play a meaningful role in peace missions. The procurement of corvettes, submarines, helicopters and fighter and trainer aircraft will go a long way in ensuring credible defence capabilities.

South Africa is on track in building and re-equipping the SANDF for both its primary and secondary roles. Over the last five years, the SANDF has been building and equipping the SA Air Force and the SA Navy. The focus is now on the modernisation of armaments and equipment for landward defence.

The development of the Rooivalk combat helicopter progressed well and it was envisaged that the first helicopters would be deployed in peace missions during the second half of 2005.

Armaments Corporation of South Africa (Armscor)

Armscor's primary function is to acquire defence products and services for the SANDF, and to co-manage, with the Department of Defence, the development of technologies for future weapon systems and products. It also manages the disposal of excess, forfeited, redundant or surplus defence material for the SANDF and subsidiary companies, which directly support defence technology and acquisition strategies.

Armscor provides the department with tender-board functions, project security and arms-control compliance assurance.

Denel Group of South Africa

Denel is a profit-driven company wholly owned by the State. Fifty-one percent of its airmotive division, however, is owned by France's Turbomeca. It is recognised as a world leader in artillery systems.

> On 15 December 2004, government signed a declaration of intent with Airbus Military, the European consortium for the development of the A400M multirole military transport craft.
> The A400M programme is aimed at boosting the revitalisation of the South African aerospace sector, which possesses knowledge, experience and capability in aircraft design, manufacturing, support and maintenance.
> South Africa is expected to deliver between eight and 14 aircraft on completion as the programme matures between 2010 and 2014.

Through offset deals, Denel supplies aerostructures for Gripen and Hawk aircraft to BAE Systems and Saab. It has started licensed manufacturing of the Agusta A119 Koala helicopters for AgustaWestland and provides parts to the Boeing Company.

Intelligence services

South Africa has two civilian intelligence structures: the National Intelligence Agency (NIA) and the South African Secret Service (SASS).

The NIA's mission is to provide government with domestic intelligence and counter-intelligence. The NIA's mandate has been divided into seven areas of interest: counter-intelligence, political intelligence, economic intelligence, border intelligence, terrorism, organised crime and corruption.

The SASS is South Africa's foreign-intelligence capacity. Executive control is exercised by a civilian ministry and a Cabinet committee.

The objective of the SASS is to forewarn, inform and advise government on real and potential threats to South Africa's security, and on socio-economic opportunities for the country.

Justice and correctional services

Judicial authority is vested in the courts, which are independent and subject only to the Constitution and the law. No person or organ of state may interfere with the functioning of the courts.

Over the next five years, the Department of Justice and Constitutional Development will focus on the following three key strategic result areas: ensuring access to justice for all, modernising justice services, and transforming the justice system.

The courts

Constitutional Court
This is the highest court in all constitutional matters and deals only with constitutional issues. The court's work includes deciding whether Acts of Parliament and the conduct of the President and executive are consistent with the Constitution, including the Bill of Rights.

The court's decisions are binding on all persons including organs of state, and on all other courts. It consists of the Chief Justice of South Africa, the Deputy Chief Justice and nine Constitutional Court judges.

In June 2005, Justice Pius Langa replaced Justice Arthur Chaskalson as the new Chief Justice following Justice Chaskalson's retirement. The deputy is Justice Dikgang Moseneke.

Supreme Court of Appeal
The Supreme Court of Appeal is the highest court in respect

of all other matters. The court has jurisdiction to hear and determine an appeal against any decision of a high court. Decisions of the Supreme Court of Appeal are binding on all courts of a lower order.

It is composed of the President and Deputy President of the Supreme Court of Appeal and a number of judges of appeal determined by an Act of Parliament.

High courts

There are 10 court divisions and three local divisions which are presided over by judges of the provincial courts concerned.

A provincial or local division has jurisdiction in its own area over all persons in that area. These divisions hear matters that are of such a serious nature that the lower courts would not be competent to make an appropriate judgment or impose a penalty. Except where minimum or maximum sentences are prescribed by law, their penal jurisdiction is unlimited and includes life imprisonment.

In 2004/05, high courts attained their conviction rate target of 85% for the first time.

The Land Claims Court and the Labour Court have the same status as the High Court. In the case of labour disputes, appeals are made to the Labour Appeal Court.

Regional courts

Regional courts established in each regional division have jurisdiction over all offences, except treason. Unlike the High Court, the penal jurisdiction of the regional courts is limited.

Regional courts can impose a sentence of not more than 15 years' imprisonment or a fine not exceeding R300 000. Regional courts attained their conviction rate of 70% in 2004/05 for the first time since 2000.

Magistrate's courts

Magisterial districts are grouped into 13 clusters. By March 2005, there were 366 magistrate's offices, 50 detached

Justice and correctional services

offices, 103 branch courts and 227 periodical courts in South Africa, with 11 767 magistrates.

A magistrate's court has jurisdiction over all offences except treason, murder and rape.

Small claims courts

Cases involving civil claims not exceeding R7 000 are heard by a commissioner in the Small Claims Court. Thirteen new small claims courts, seven of which are in rural areas and townships, were opened in 2004.

By June 2004, there were 152 such courts throughout the country. The commissioner is usually a practising advocate or attorney, a legal academic or other competent person who offers his or her services free of charge.

Neither the plaintiff nor the defendant may be represented or assisted by counsel at the hearing. There is no appeal to a higher court.

Equality courts

These courts enforce legislation which outlaws unfair discrimination and upholds equality.

By May 2005, 220 equality courts were in operation. By mid-2004, 75 cases had been heard, including 31 complaints of racial discrimination; 23 of hate speech; 17 of sexual harassment; and four of discrimination against people with HIV and AIDS.

Community courts

Modelled on the Hatfield Community Court in Pretoria, community courts focus on the appropriate handling of

---

A comprehensive human resource development strategy to widen the pool of women and black legal practitioners is expected to be finalised during 2006/07.

Of the 204 judges by February 2005, 76 were black and 23 were women, while of a total of 1 662 magistrates, 794 were black and 428 were women.

> The Thuthuzela care centres are 24-hour, one-stop service centres where victims have access to all services including police, counselling, doctors, court preparation and prosecutors. The main objectives of these centres are to eliminate secondary victimisation, reduce case cycle time, and increase convictions.

lower-court cases from the area, specifically offences such as handbag and cellphone theft, offences relating to drug and alcohol abuse, municipal by-law offences and petty offences.

By September 2005, there were 13 community courts, of which four were operational. The total number of cases finalised was 9 685, with a 96% conviction rate.

Specialised commercial crimes courts
These courts deal with commercial crimes such as fraud, corruption and the violation of 52 statutes.

Court for income tax offenders
In October 1999, the South African Revenue Service (SARS) opened a criminal courtroom at the Johannesburg Magistrate's Office dedicated to the prosecution of tax offenders. The court deals only with cases concerning failure to submit tax returns or failure to provide information requested by SARS officials. It does not deal with bigger cases such as tax fraud.

Municipal courts
Municipal courts are being set up in the larger centres of South Africa in conjunction with municipalities. They deal only with traffic offences and contraventions of municipal by-laws.

Chief's courts
An authorised African headman or his deputy may hear and determine civil claims arising from indigenous law and

custom, brought before him by an African against another African within his area of jurisdiction.

Litigants have the right to choose whether to institute an action in a chief's court or in a magistrate's court. Proceedings in a chief's court are informal. An appeal against a judgment of a chief's court is heard in a magistrate's court.

National Prosecuting Authority (NPA)

The NPA structure includes the National Prosecuting Services, the Directorate: Special Operations (DSO), the Witness-Protection Programme, the Asset Forfeiture Unit (AFU) and units such as the Sexual Offences and Community Affairs Unit and the Specialised Commercial Crime Unit.

A priority crimes litigation unit was set up in the Office of the National Director of Public Prosecutions in 2003/04. Its mandate is to focus on serious national and international crimes, including treason, sedition, terrorism, sabotage, and foreign military crimes committed by mercenaries.

Asset Forfeiture Unit

The AFU made 212 seizures in 2003/04, well above the target of 150. In 2003/04, 124 forfeitures were completed, resulting in the recovery of R54 million, of which R39 million was deposited in the Criminal Assets Recovery Account.

During the first eight months of 2004/05, 111 new seizures were made to the value of R164 million, 98 forfeitures were completed to the value of R137 million, and about R20 million was deposited into the Criminal Asset Recovery Account.

The Legal Aid Board has a national network of 58 justice centres, 13 high-court units and 27 satellite centres countrywide. It provides publicly funded legal advice and representation in criminal and civil matters to people in need.

Assets valued at nearly R700 million were placed under restraint over the past five years.

Directorate: Special Operations

The DSO is committed to the investigation of matters that are national in scope, and concentrates on those crimes that threaten national security and economic stability. The more complex and protracted the investigations and higher up the criminal target, the more appropriate the matter would be for DSO selection. In many instances, these high-impact investigations fall outside the scope and capacity of the South African Police Service.

The DSO achieved a conviction rate of 94% in the 203 prosecutions finalised by the end of 2004. From April to December 2004, personnel successfully completed 203 prosecutions, 292 investigations and 127 high-impact cases. In the process, there were 1 117 arrests, searches, seizures and traps, with operational support providing 432 ancillary support activities. Through interdiction, R2,5 billion worth of contraband was seized.

During 2005, President Thabo Mbeki appointed a judicial commission to investigate the location of the DSO in government.

Sexual Offences and Community Affairs Unit

Various concrete steps have been taken to give effect to the national crackdown on sexual offences:

- Multidisciplinary rape-care centres, known as the Thuthuzela care centres, have been established. Here rape investigations are speeded up and 'humanised'. A play, *Speak Out*, designed to encourage children to report sexual offences committed in the home, has been commissioned and piloted in 51 schools in KwaZulu-Natal. It was subsequently rolled out in Mpumalanga and the Free State. Some 120 359 learners saw the play.
- New child-witness rooms have one-way glass partitions enabling child witnesses to testify in a friendly and secure

Justice and correctional services

environment without the risk of being intimidated.
- Some 54 sexual offences courts, with a conviction rate of 62%, have been established. A further 20 such courts were planned for 2005/06.

Integrated justice system

This system aims to use technology to improve the co-ordination of the activities of departments in government's Justice, Crime Prevention and Security Cluster.

The system will entail, among other things:
- a virtual private network
- an automated fingerprint identification system and DNA database
- an integrated case-flow management system, including case, person (offender, victim and witness) and exhibits
- better tracking of people, including inmates.

Improving court productivity

Court performance continues to improve. Statistics indicate that court productivity has increased, that the number of cases finalised has increased, that courts on average sit longer hours, and that conviction rates are higher, especially in the specialised courts.

Court productivity in the lower courts has shown a slight improvement.

According to the *Estimates of National Expenditure*, between July and September 2004 the integrated case-flow management centres (previously known as integrated justice court centres) yielded the following key results:

The Department of Correctional Services is expected to spend about R80 million on the installation of advanced technological equipment at 65 correctional centres. Equipment to be installed includes items such as closed-circuit television cameras, biometric readers and scanning devices.

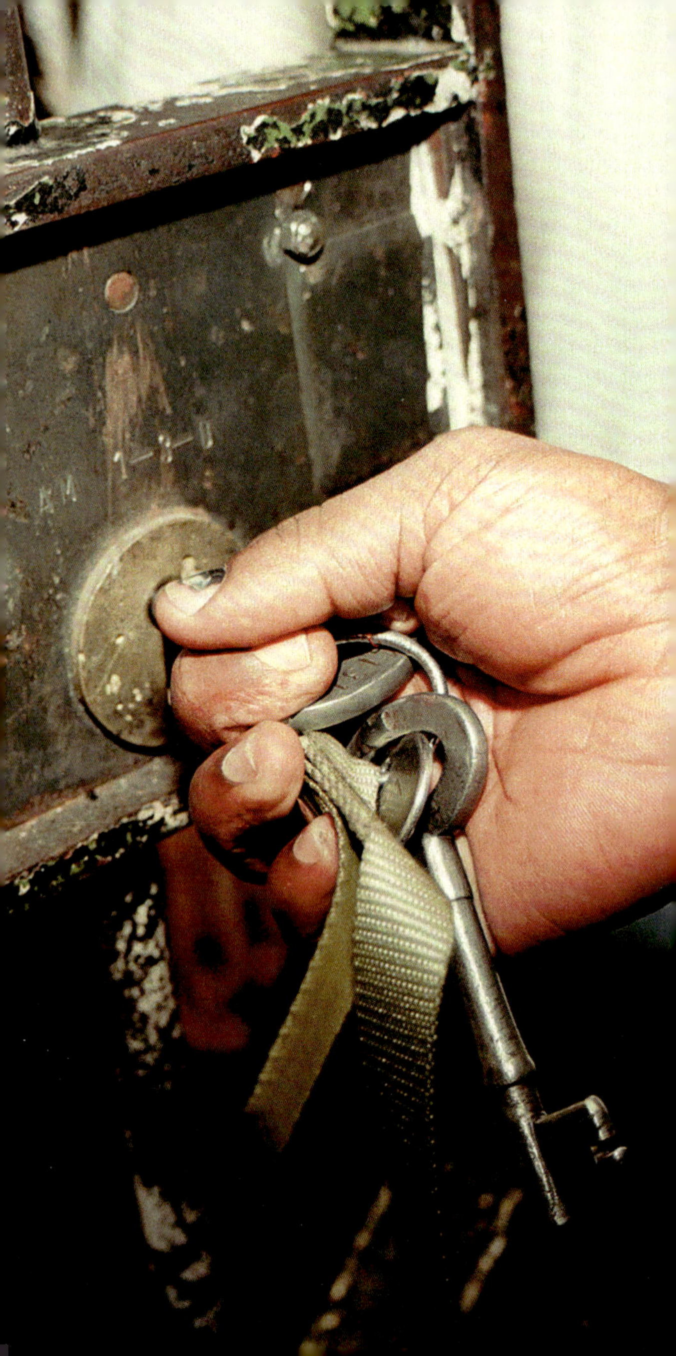

Justice and correctional services

- Court hours on average improved by 21 minutes, from four hours and two minutes to four hours and 23 minutes. The national average court hours for district courts are four hours and 14 minutes.
- Case preparation cycle time was reduced on average by 27 days, from 105 days to 78 days.
- The percentage of cases on the court rolls for fewer than 60 days increased from 54,8% to 56,5%.
- The management of trial-ready cases improved by 3% (measured against the percentage of outstanding cases on the court roll waiting to be tried), decreasing from 39,7% to 36,6%. The ideal is that between 25% and 33% of outstanding cases on the court roll should be trial-ready.

Improving the justice system

- According to the *Estimates of National Expenditure*, some 82 maintenance investigators and 100 clerks for maintenance and domestic violence courts have led to improvements in the maintenance system.
- A short messaging service was introduced for individuals to notify the court if maintenance is not paid.
- Twenty-six additional family advocates were appointed in previously disadvantaged and rural areas.
- Some 35 673 pieces of high-court documentation (including divorce papers and settlement agreements) were scrutinised and 5 286 enquiries finalised.
- The Chief Family Advocate has been designated as the central authority in international child abduction matters in terms of The Hague Convention on the Civil Aspects of International Child Abduction. Thirty-two such applications were processed in 2003/04.
- By 2005, the department had raised the number of female officials to 7 372 compared with 4 000 in 1995. At least 33 female correctional officials were at senior management level.

Public Protector

The Public Protector is independent of government and is responsible for investigating any improper conduct in state or public affairs.

In 2003/04, the Public Protector received 17 295 new cases, 1 627 more than in 2002/03, and 15 946 cases were finalised. Some 8 869 cases were carried forward from 2002/03 to April 2004.

Victims' charter

The Service Charter for Victims of Crime in South Africa and minimum standards for services for victims of crime, introduced in December 2004, are important instruments elaborating and consolidating rights and obligations relating to services applicable to victims and survivors of crime in the country.

The charter identifies the following seven rights of crime victims:
- to be treated with fairness, respect, dignity and privacy
- to offer information
- to receive information
- protection
- assistance
- compensation
- restitution.

Correctional services

The total inmate population at 28 February 2005 was 187 000, while prison capacity was 113 825. Those awaiting

> The Department of Correctional Services' budget for 2005/06 amounted to R9,234 billion. It provided for the establishment of 36 000 personnel and operational costs for a daily average offender population of 192 000 incarcerated persons, as well as 76 000 community correctional supervision cases and parolees.

Justice and correctional services

> The Department of Correctional Services estimated that it would receive revenue of about R89,7 million during 2005/06, mostly generated through the sale of products from correctional-centre workshops, hiring out of offenders' labour and letting official personnel accommodation. Part of the income generated by offenders' labour is paid to them as a gratuity.

trial accounted for 52 000, with 135 000 sentenced offenders.

To alleviate overcrowding, unsentenced juveniles have been transferred to places of secure care, some sentences have been converted to correctional supervision, and facilities have been renovated or upgraded.

National and provincial action plans to fast-track all children awaiting trial from prisons and police cells, since October 2004, have led to a reduction in children awaiting trial, from 2 200 monthly, to 1 500 monthly.

On 21 January 2005, some 1 389 children under 18 years awaiting trial were in correctional centres nationally. This figure was reduced to 885 children by 21 June 2005.

No prisoners may be released before they have served at least half their sentence. The Criminal Law Amendment Act, 1997 provides for much harsher sentences for serious crimes. These changes are expected to place an even greater burden on prisons.

> In June, 2005, government granted a maxium of six and 14 months special remission of sentence to 18 171 sentenced offenders, probationers, parolees and day parolees, irrespective of the crime category.
> However, prisoners convicted of aggressive crimes – especially firearm-related, sexual and drug-related crimes – did not qualify.
> This was in line with the Department of Correctional Services' newly adopted policy of correcting behaviour and development as opposed to punitive measures.

An independent judicial inspectorate regularly visits all prisons to report on conditions and prisoners' treatment.

South Africa's inmate tracking system, launched as a pilot project at the Durban Westville Correctional Centre, has been extended to the Johannesburg Medium A Correctional Centre. The main functions of this project are to accurately identify awaiting trial detainees (ATDs), to decrease the time spent in processing ATDs for court appearances and visits, and to monitor the movements of ATDs through a personal tracking device.

The building of four new-generation prisons in Kimberley, Klerksdorp, Leeuwkop and Nigel is expected to be completed by April 2007. Similar facilities are expected to be erected in East London, Allandale, KwaZulu-Natal and Limpopo. All eight prisons will have 3 000 beds each. Over the next three years, accommodation capacity in correctional services will be increased by 12 000 beds.

Social development

The Department of Social Development works with religious groups, non-governmental organisations, business, labour and communities to uplift society and eradicate poverty.

Legislation

By February 2005, three sets of legislation to strengthen the framework for the protection and support of children, people with disabilities, older persons and women were before Parliament.

The Children's Bill and the Older Persons' Bill provide for programmes and services that give effect to the rights of children and older persons respectively, while the Child Justice Bill addresses the protection of children who are in conflict with the law.

The Policy Framework and Strategic Plan for the Prevention and Management of Child Abuse will ensure the swift implementation of the Child Protection Register, which will link provincial and national databases of children under 18 years who have allegedly been abused.

Payment of social grants

Beneficiaries of social grants increased from 3,8 million people in April 2001 to more than 10 million in September 2005.

By September 2005, 6,2 million people were receiving the Child Support Grant (CSG), 286 131 the Foster Care Grant, and 87 093 the Care Dependency Grant.

By September 2005, there were about 1,3 million

Pocket Guide to South Africa 2005/06

Uptake of child support grants		
	1998	2005
Number of children	58 000	6,2 million

beneficiaries of the Disability Grant while 2,1 million people were receiving the Old-Age Grant.

Social assistance grant transfers increased from around 2% of gross domestic product (GDP) in 2000/01 to more than 3% of GDP in 2004/05. They were expected to reach 3,4% of GDP in 2005/06.

Food security

The department's National Food Emergency Scheme, introduced by Cabinet in 2002, is aimed at distributing food parcels to the most vulnerable sections of the population.

These include children and child-headed households, people with disabilities, female-headed households with insufficient or no income, and households affected by HIV, AIDS and tuberculosis.

In 2005/06, the department set aside R388 million to ensure improved access to food in vulnerable and impoverished families. The scheme distributed over 490 000 food parcels for each of the three months of distribution in 2004/05.

Over 400 000 food hampers that will benefit over two million of the poorest people, especially vulnerable children, including child-headed households, were expected to be distributed in 2005.

In 2005, social-security programmes accounted for 14% of consolidated non-interest expenditure, up from 9,5% in 2000.

> In March 2005, the Department of Social Development and the Umsobomvu Youth Fund signed a partnership agreement. The department has established a youth development directorate to develop policies and programmes to help young people become self-reliant. About R15 million will be invested in about 940 unemployed youth over the next three years, starting in June 2005.

Social development

HIV and AIDS

In 2005/06, the department was allocated R74 million for its HIV and AIDS Programme. In 2004/05, the programme reached 109 267 families with 73 048 food parcels, distributed 1 005 school uniforms, and provided material support (clothing, blankets, food supplements, bereavement support and burial assistance) to 4 615 families.

About 570 caregivers were trained in HIV counselling, lay counselling, project management and in-service training. The special-allocations increase from R70,2 million in 2003/04 to R142,8 million in 2007/08 will enable the department to expand the Home- and Community-Based Care Programme in the provinces, mostly through non-profit organisations and community organisations.

By February 2005, some 117 000 orphans and about 5 000 children of child-headed households had been identified and were receiving care and support.

National councils

The department strives to strengthen the capacity of civil society to actively engage in social and economic development, by supporting the following national councils:
- National Council for Persons with Physical Disabilities
- Deaf Federation of South Africa
- South African National Epilepsy League
- South African Federation for Mental Health
- Cancer Association of South Africa.

Statutory bodies include the National Development Agency (NDA), relief boards and the Central Drug Authority.

National Development Agency

The NDA is a statutory funding agency that aims to contribute to the alleviation of poverty, address its causes, and strengthen the capacity of civil-society organisations to combat poverty.

The key strategic objectives of the NDA are to, among other things, grant funds to civil-society organisations to

Pocket Guide to South Africa 2005/06

meet the development needs of poor communities; proactively strengthen organisations' institutional capacity for long-term sustainability; source funds for the NDA; and promote consultation, dialogue and the sharing of development experiences.

Anti-fraud campaign

On 12 December 2004, the Department of Social Development launched a nationwide anti-fraud and anti-corruption campaign.

It granted indemnity to all people illegally accessing social grants and requested them to come forward before 31 March 2005.

Over 30 000 people responded and their fraudulent payments were stopped, translating into an estimated saving of R12 million per month or R446 million between 2005/06 and 2007/08.

These savings are expected to result in an additional 66 000 children receiving the CSG.

To root out fraud and corruption, the department has set aside R57,9 million and entered into a co-operation agreement with the Special Investigating Unit (SIU).

Some 200 staff were trained and utilised in the fight against fraud and corruption. They probed the details of all beneficiaries of social grants.

The department, in collaboration with all national and provincial law-enforcement agencies, including the South African Police Service and the SIU, was expected to establish the Inspectorate for Social Security by March 2006.

> **fact**
> The South African Social Security Agency (SASSA) is expected to be fully functional by April 2006. The SASSA is tasked with the management, administration and payment of social grants.

Environment

The overarching vision of the Department of Environmental Affairs and Tourism is a prosperous and equitable society living in harmony with its natural resources. The department manages the development and implementation of policies governing three interrelated components of South Africa's socio-economic development: tourism, the fishing industry and environmental management.

Government leads protection of the environment by example. National and provincial departments must compile environmental implementation and management plans.

South Africa has taken several concrete steps to implement the United Nations' (UN) Agenda 21 on sustainable development. These include reforming environmental policies, ratifying international agreements, and participating in many global and regional sustainable-development initiatives.

Environmental heritage

South Africa enjoys the third-highest level of biodiversity in the world.

> **fact**
> South Africa won a gold medal at the 2005 Chelsea Flower Show – the 27th gold that the team from Kirstenbosch has won in 30 years of competing at the prestigious show.
> The show – an annual event since 1826 – ran from 24 to 28 May at the Royal Hospital in Chelsea, London.

Some remarkable aspects of the abundance of life in this country include:
- over 3 700 endemic marine species
- some 18 000 vascular plant species, 80% of which occur nowhere else
- there are more plant species in the Cape Peninsula National Park than the whole of the British Isles
- South Africa has 5,8% of the world's mammal species, 8% of bird species and 4,6% of reptile species
- in terms of the mammal, bird, reptile and amphibian species, South Africa is the 24th-richest country in the world and the fifth-richest in Africa
- one third of the world's succulent species are found in South Africa.

South Africa is one of only six countries with an entire plant kingdom within its national confines. South Africa is ranked first in the world for its floral kingdom.

The Cape Floral Kingdom has the highest recorded species diversity for any similar-sized temperate or tropical region in the world. It is a World Heritage Site.

Biomes

There are eight major terrestrial biomes, or habitat types, in South Africa. These biomes can, in turn, be divided into 70 veld types. The biomes are savanna, Nama-Karoo, succulent Karoo, grassland, fynbos, forest, thicket and desert. The fynbos biome is one of only six floral kingdoms worldwide.

---

fact: The National Spatial Biodiversity Assessment was launched in April 2005 – the first-ever comprehensive spatial evaluation of biodiversity throughout the country. It deals with terrestrial, freshwater, estuarine and marine environments. This assessment will inform the National Biodiversity Framework.

Environment

Biodiversity values by province

Province	Plant	Mammal	Bird	Amphibian	Reptile
Eastern Cape	6 383	156	384	51	57
Free State	3 001	93	334	29	47
Gauteng	2 826	125	326	25	53
KwaZulu-Natal	5 515	177	462	68	86
Limpopo	4 239	239	479	44	89
Mpumalanga	4 593	160	464	48	82
Northern Cape	4 916	139	302	29	53
North West	2 483	138	384	27	59
Western Cape	9 489	153	305	39	52

Source: Department of Environmental Affairs and Tourism

Conservation victories
- The population of southern white rhinoceros in South Africa has risen from less than 20 in 1910 to 8 000 today.
- By mid-2002, more than 200 000 seedlings of endangered cycad species had been sold to the public, reducing the threat to wild populations.
- Many cheetah are bred in captivity and relocated to protected areas.

Conservation areas
Some 34% of South Africa's 440 terrestrial ecosystems are threatened. Of these, 5% are critically endangered (mostly

---

In April 2005, the United Nations (UN) Environment Programme recognised President Thabo Mbeki and the people of South Africa for outstanding achievements in the field of the environment.

The Champion of the Earth Award was presented during the meeting of the UN Commission on Sustainable Development held in New York in the United States of America.

South Africa was recognised for its commitment to cultural and environmental diversity, as well as its strong leadership role in Africa through the environmental component of the New Partnership for Africa's Development.

in the fynbos and forest biomes), 13% are endangered (mostly in the grassland and savanna biomes), and 16% are vulnerable (mostly in the fynbos and grassland biomes).

The total percentage of the country's land area in protected areas is nearly 6%. However, the percentage of well-protected ecosystems is higher, at 15%. Most of these well-protected ecosystems are in the fynbos mountains and the savanna biome, while the most severely underprotected ecosytems tend to be in the succulent Karoo, the grasslands, and the fynbos lowlands.

The Threatened Species Programme (TSP) aims to facilitate the conservation of South Africa's rare and endangered species. The project currently focuses on plant biodiversity, but will soon address the full spectrum of biodiversity.

By mid-2005, the TSP was in the process of producing an updated and comprehensive national *Red List of South African Plant Species*, which was expected to be available in printed and electronic form by March 2006.

Scientific reserves

These are sensitive, undisturbed areas managed for research, monitoring and the maintenance of genetic sources. Access is limited. Examples are Marion Island and the Prince Edward islands near Antarctica.

Wilderness areas

These areas are extensive in size, uninhabited, under-developed, and access is strictly controlled. Examples are the Cedarberg Wilderness Area and Dassen Island in the Western Cape.

---

fact: In South Africa, there are 180 000 indigenous vascular plant species of which 80% do not occur anywhere else in the world.

Environment

National parks and equivalent reserves

South African National Parks (SANParks) manages a vast system of national parks. Commercial and tourism-conservation development, as well as the involvement of local communities, are performance indicators.

There are currently six transfrontier conservation areas (TFCAs) along borders with neighbouring countries. The proposed 38 600 km^2 Greater Limpopo Transfrontier Park includes South Africa's Kruger National Park and parks in Mozambique and Zimbabwe. It will be bigger than the Yellowstone National Park in the United States of America.

Other TFCAs include the Ais-Ais/Richtersveld, Kgalagadi, Lubombo, Maloti-Drakensberg and Limpopo-Shashe.

South African national parks

Park	Date proclaimed	Size (ha)
Addo Elephant	1931	74 339
Agulhas	1999	5 690
Augrabies Falls	1966	41 676
Bontebok	1931	2 786
Camdeboo	2005	14 500
Golden Gate Highlands	1963	11 633
Kgalagadi	1931	959 103
Karoo	1979	77 094
Knysna National Lakes Area	1985	15 000
Kruger	1926	1 962 362
Marakele	1993	50 726
Mapungubwe	1989	5 356
Mountain Zebra	1937	24 663
Namaqua	2001	60 000
Richtersveld	1991	162 445
Table Mountain	1998	24 310
Tankwa-Karoo	1986	43 899
Tsitsikamma	1964	63 942
Vaalbos	1986	22 697
West Coast	1985	36 273
Wilderness	1985	10 600

Source: SANParks

Pocket Guide to South Africa 2005/06

South Africa's national parks

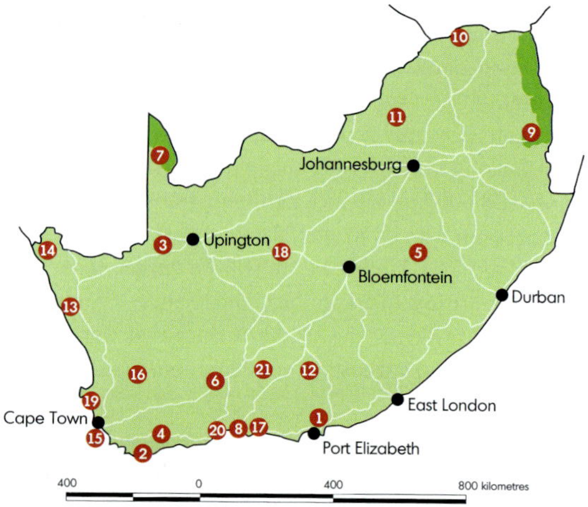

1. Addo Elephant National Park
2. Agulhas National Park
3. Augrabies Falls National Park
4. Bontebok National Park
5. Golden Gate Highlands National Park
6. Karoo National Park
7. Kgalagadi Transfrontier Park
8. Knysna National Park
9. Kruger National Park
10. Mapungubwe National Park
11. Marakele National Park
12. Mountain Zebra National Park
13. Namaqua National Park
14. Richtersveld National Park
15. Table Mountain National Park
16. Tankwa Karoo National Park
17. Tsitsikamma National Park
18. Vaalbos National Park
19. West Coast National Park
20. Wilderness National Park
21. Camdeboo National Park

The transfrontier conservation initiative originated in Africa, and by mid-2005 there were 169 such areas involving 113 countries and 667 protected areas.

TFCAs offer southern Africa important vehicles to ensure that South Africa's hosting of the 2010 Soccer World Cup brings real benefits to neighbouring states as well.

In addition to the R159 million invested in TFCA projects during 2004/05, a further R193 million is expected to be invested in new projects, including more than R25 million in Limpopo/Shashe, more than R50 million in

Environment

Climate of provincial capitals

Province	Capital	Average temperature (°C)	
		January	July
Eastern Cape	Bisho	22,1	13,8
Free State	Bloemfontein	23,0	7,7
Gauteng	Johannesburg	20,1	10,4
KwaZulu-Natal	Pietermaritzburg	22,9	12,9
Mpumalanga	Nelspruit	24,0	14,8
Northern Cape	Kimberley	25,3	10,8
Limpopo	Polokwane	22,6	12,2
North West	Mafikeng	24,1	12,0
Western Cape	Cape Town	20,9	12,2

Source: Department of Environmental Affairs and Tourism, South African Weather Service

Greater Limpopo, and more than R60 million in Maloti-Drakensberg.

The Giriyondo Border Post between the Kruger National Park and the Limpopo National Park in Mozambique was officially opened in December 2005.

National and cultural monuments

These are natural or cultural features, or both, and may include botanical gardens, zoological gardens, natural heritage sites and sites of conservation significance.

In December 1999, Robben Island, the Greater St Lucia Wetlands Park and the Cradle of Humankind were proclaimed World Heritage Sites by the United Nations Educational, Science and Cultural Organisation (UNESCO).

The Ukhahlamba-Drakensberg Park was nominated as a mixed site. In July 2003, the site of the Mapungubwe civilisation became the fifth heritage site. The Cape Floral Region also became a World Heritage Site at the end of June 2004.

The Vredefort Dome in the Free State was declared as South Africa's seventh World Heritage Site at the 29th session of the UNESCO World Heritage Conference held in

> **The Kruger National Park**
> More than a million people visit Kruger National Park every year. Comprising almost two million hectares, the park has over 500 bird, 336 tree and 147 mammal species. It also has 49 species of fish.

Durban in July 2005. It was the first time the body met in sub-Saharan Africa.

Makapans Valley in Limpopo and the Taung Cave in North West were declared extensions of the Cradle of Humankind.

Habitat and wildlife management areas

These areas include conservancies; provincial, regional or private reserves created for the conservation of species, habitats or biotic communities; marshes; lakes; and nesting and feeding areas.

Sustainable-use areas

These areas emphasise the utilisation of products on a sustainable basis in protected areas such as the Kosi Bay Lake system in KwaZulu-Natal.

Wetlands

Wetlands include a wide range of inland and coastal habitats – from mountain bogs and fens and midland marshes to swamp forests and estuaries, linked by green corridors of streambank wetlands.

Botanical gardens

There are eight botanical gardens in five provinces. The

> **fact**
> The top 50 air-polluting industries in South Africa will be targeted in a bid to improve South Africa's air quality. The Department of Environmental Affairs and Tourism will train and employ at least 30 air-quality licensing officers in each of the nine provinces.

Environment

largest is Kirstenbosch in Cape Town. It houses 5 300 indigenous plant species, and was voted one of the top seven botanical gardens in the world in 2000.

The Pretoria National Botanical Garden houses the National Herbarium of South Africa, the largest in the southern hemisphere.

The botanical gardens collectively attract over a million visitors per year. All the gardens are signatories to the International Agenda for Botanic Gardens in Conservation and are founding members of the African Botanic Gardens Network.

Zoos

The 80-ha National Zoological Gardens (NZG) of South Africa in Pretoria is one of the world's 10 best. It attracted more than 550 000 visitors in 2004. The national zoo is responsible for two breeding centres in Lichtenburg and Mokopane and the satellite zoo and animal park at the Emerald Animal World complex in Vanderbijlpark.

The NZG was declared a national research facility, subject to the provisions of the National Research Foundation, in March 2004. The declaration of the zoo as a national research facility presents a remarkable opportunity for the zoo to reposition itself as one of the world leaders in breeding and researching endangered species.

The zoo houses more than 10 000 animals.

There are a number of zoological gardens in South Africa

Marine protected areas (MPAs)

The Minister of Environmental Affairs and Tourism, Mr Marthinus van Schalkwyk, officially announced four new MPAs in June 2004.

The MPAs are modelled on the success of the Greater St Lucia Wetlands Park – with strict zoning of both marine and coastal protected areas. The four MPAs are Aliwal Shoal on the south coast of KwaZulu-Natal, the coastal and marine environment next to Pondoland in the Eastern

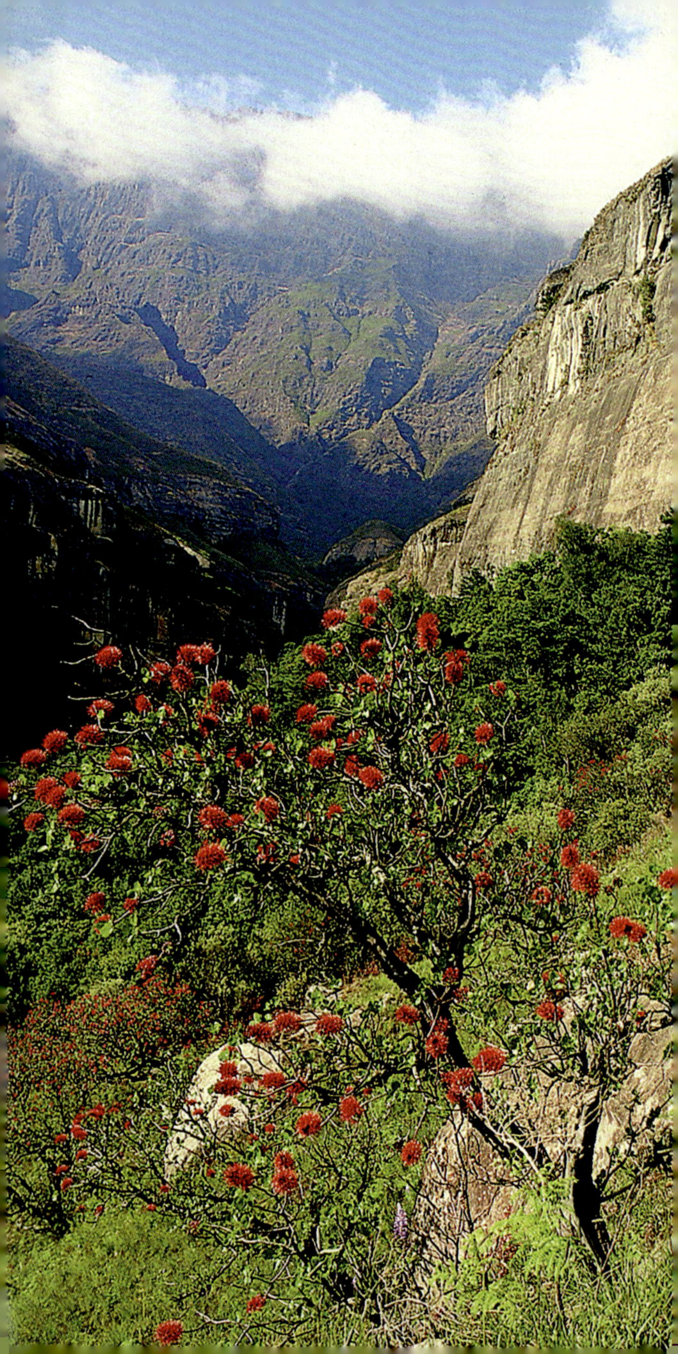

Environment

Cape, Bird Island at Algoa Bay, and the Cape Peninsula in the Western Cape. Negotiations are underway for the creation of an MPA off Namaqualand.

Some of the protection measures to be implemented in the MPAs are restrictions for people who want to fish, as well as restrictions for stowing fishing gear when fishing from a vessel.

Spear fishers will not be allowed entry to these areas and scuba divers will be required to obtain permits.

Marine resources

The sustainable exploitation of marine resources on the one hand and the demand for fish products from local and foreign consumers on the other, pose a growing challenge globally, and South Africa is no exception. South Africa's coastline covers some 3 000 km.

The Marine Living Resources Act, 1998 sets out the broad objectives of fishery management and access rights. It also sets empowerment and broad transformation objectives for the fishing industry.

South Africa's fisheries are among the best-managed in the world.

In February 2003, the first Environmental Court in South Africa was opened in the southern coastal town of Hermanus, in the Western Cape. It had an immediate impact on poaching.

The second Environmental Court was launched in Port Elizabeth in February 2004.

The department's precautionary policy on managing the country's marine resources has resulted in pilchard and anchovy populations reaching record highs.

On 30 May 2005, South Africa launched the final set of 19 fishery-specific policies and one general policy that will guide the allocation of long-term commercial fishing rights for periods between eight and 15 years. This industry is estimated to be worth about R70 billion.

Pocket Guide to South Africa 2005/06

In September 2005, South Africa took delivery of the last of four environmental protection vessels, the *Victoria Mxenge*.

The other three vessels, *Lilian Ngoyi*, *Sarah Baartman* and *Ruth First*, were received in September 2004, January 2005 and May 2005, respectively.

The patrol vessels – all named after women who showed courage, dedication and commitment to the struggle for freedom – are used in assisting with high-speed disaster relief, search and rescue, evacuations, fire-fighting, pollution control, towing and other emergency operations.

In 2005/06, South Africa had 34 beaches participating in the *Blue Flag* Campaign.

South Africa's coastal management policy is one of the best in the world, with the country being the first outside Europe to gain Blue Flag status for coastal management.

Some of the most popular beaches in South Africa are:
- Camps Bay, Western Cape
- Clifton, Western Cape
- Llandudno, Western Cape
- Muizenburg, Western Cape
- Hobie Beach, Eastern Cape
- Humewood Beach, Eastern Cape
- Margate, KwaZulu-Natal
- Umhlanga Rocks, KwaZulu-Natal
- Grotto Beach, Western Cape
- Marina South Coast, KwaZulu-Natal.

The Working for the Coast Programme was launched in October 2000. It has succeeded in upgrading the environment and improving the lives of many people living along the coast.

More than 55 teams of workers have been formed along South Africa's coast to upgrade the environment, with many of them having started their own small businesses.

Arts and culture

The Department of Arts and Culture is the custodian of South Africa's diverse cultural, artistic and linguistic heritage. It is directly responsible for several public entities including museums, art galleries, the National Archives and six playhouses.

A large proportion of the department's budget is dedicated to supporting and developing institutional infrastructure to showcase, restore and preserve South Africa's heritage for future generations.

The department funds six playhouses. In 2004/05, it contributed R89,140 million towards the running of these institutions.

National coat of arms

South Africa's coat of arms was adopted in 2000.

Symbolism
Rising sun: a life-giving force
Protea: beauty and the flowering of the nation
Ears of wheat: fertility of the land
Elephant tusks: wisdom, steadfastness and strength
Knobkierie and spear: defence of peace
Drum: love of culture.

The motto, !Ke e:/xarra//ke, written in the Khoisan language of the !Xam people, means 'diverse people unite'.

National anthem

The national anthem is a combined version of *Nkosi Sikelel' iAfrika* (God bless Africa) and *The Call of South Africa* (*Die Stem*).

Pocket Guide to South Africa 2005/06

National flag

The national flag of the Republic of South Africa was brought into use on Freedom Day, 27 April 1994. The design and colours are a synopsis of the principal elements of the country's flag history.

National symbols

South Africa's national symbols are:

National animal: springbok

National bird: blue crane

National fish: galjoen

National flower: king protea

National tree: real yellowwood

National orders

South Africa's national orders are:

The Order of the Baobab

The Order of Mapungubwe

The Order of the Companions of O.R. Tambo

The Order of Luthuli

The Mendi Decoration for Bravery

The Order of Ikhamanga

Arts and culture

In 2005/06, the performing arts institutions received a budget of just over R97,685 million. The combined budget for the declared cultural institutions was over R237 million.

The National Arts Council's budget increased to R47,9 million in 2005/06. The Pan South African Language Board received R26,2 million while the National Film and Video Foundation (NFVF) received R24,609 million. The National Heritage Council received R1,4 million and the South African Heritage Resources Agency R24,298 million.

Cultural tourism

Cultural festivals, African-cuisine projects, cultural villages, heritage routes and story-telling are areas that can benefit from South Africa's booming tourist industry.

The department works with various players to extend the Cultural Industries Growth Strategy, which aims to enhance the potential of cultural industries.

2005 South African Music Awards winners

Best African Gospel Album - Deborah for *Ngixolele*
Best Contemporary Gospel Album - Joyous Celebration for *Joyous Celebration 8*
Best South African Traditional Jazz - McCoy Mrubata for *Livumile Icamagu*
Best Contemporary Jazz Album - Tlala Makhene
Best Adult Contemporary Album - Thandiswa Mazwai for *Zabalaza*
Best Adult Contemporary Album Afrikaans - Coenie de Villiers
Best Adult Contemporary Album English - Nianell
Best Music Video - Supervillain for *Indoda* by Mandoza
Best Pop Album - Mandoza and Danny K for *Same Difference*
Best Rock Album - Sugardrive
Best Dance Album - Lebo Mathosa for *Drama Queen*
Best Rap Album - Mr Selwyn
Best Afro Pop - Mafikizolo
Best Newcomer - Simphiwe Dana
Best Duo or Group - Revolution
Best Kwaito Album - Brown Dash
Best Female Artist - Thandiswa Mazwai
Best Male Artist - Themba Mkhize
Song of the Year - Brown Dash for *Phansi Komthunzi Welanga*

Domestic music sales (R millions)

	Local	International	Total
2001	R157	R453	R610
2002	R192	R512	R704
2003	R225	R479	R705

Source: Recording Industry of South Africa

Arts festivals

The National Arts Festival, held annually in July in Grahamstown, Eastern Cape, is one of the largest and most diverse arts gatherings in Africa. Other major festivals are held in Oudtshoorn, Johannesburg, Durban, Cape Town, Potchefstroom and Bloemfontein.

Theatre

South African theatre is internationally acclaimed as being unique and of top quality.

Johannesburg's celebrated Market Theatre has built its reputation on local content productions. There is a growing trend towards the establishment of smaller theatres.

Music

While local music styles such as South African jazz have influenced African and world music for decades, today gospel and kwaito are the most popular and most recorded styles. Kwaito combines elements of rap, reggae, hip-hop and other styles into a distinctly South African sound.

Orchestras

In 2004/05, the department funded the establishment of two large instrumental ensembles – one in Cape Town and

---

fact

South Africa is the 25th-largest market for recorded music, with the industry employing more than 20 000 people. Local music accounts for a third of all the music bought by South Africans.

Arts and culture

the other in Johannesburg. A music training programme directed at township youth in Gauteng also received a grant towards its work.

Dance

Contemporary work ranges from normal preconceptions of movement and performance art or performance theatre, to the completely unconventional. Added to this is the African experience, which includes traditional dance inspired by wedding ceremonies, battles, rituals and everyday life.

The Dance Factory in Johannesburg provides a permanent platform for all kinds of dance and movement groups, while the Wits (University) Theatre is home to the annual Dance Umbrella, a showcase for new work.

The Cape Town City Ballet is the oldest ballet company in the country.

Visual arts

South Africa has a range of art galleries that showcase collections of indigenous, historical and contemporary works.

Crafts

The crafts industry employs more than 1,2 million people, with products being widely exported. The department co-ordinates initiatives to finance, market and develop the sector. Training is a particular focus.

Film

The film and video sector generates around R518 million a year. Film production is being actively supported by govern-

---

The 10-year celebrations of democracy in 2004 created opportunities for individual exposure, the branding of South African music and practitioners, and short-term employment for 597 arts and culture practitioners through their participation in activities in over 30 countries.

> **fact**
> In February 2005, Ladysmith Black Mambazo won the award for Traditional World Music Album at the 47th annual Grammy Awards in Los Angeles. The group has sold over six million albums, making it the number one record seller in Africa.
> In a career spanning 30 years, the group has been nominated for nine Grammys. Its previous Grammy win came in 1987 for the album *Shaka Zulu*.

ment; just one initiative is the Film and Television Production Rebate introduced by the Department of Trade and Industry.

South Africa offers foreign producers world-class film facilitation, logistics, facilities, talent and administration-management services.

Television production accounts for more than a third of total film/television revenue, with local-content quotas increasing the demand for programming.

The NFVF develops and promotes the film and video industry in South Africa. During 2004, the NFVF made grants of R36,9 million available for the production of films and for the development of the film industry. It was also involved in the development of projects that appeal to targeted audiences and have greater commercial returns. It ensured a South African presence at major international film markets, festivals, trade fairs and exhibitions.

Legacy projects

Cabinet approved these projects as a mechanism to establish commemorative structures to celebrate South Africa's past.

Some of the initiatives include:
- the Women's Monument

> **fact**
> The crafts industry generates an income of R3,5 billion a year and employs over 1,2 million people. The music industry generates R900 million a year and employs over 12 000 people. The film and video industry generates R518 million a year, and printing and publishing R2 billion a year.

Arts and culture

In February 2005, *U-Carmen eKhayelitsha*, the acclaimed version of Bizet's opera *Carmen* set in the context of Cape Town's Khayelitsha township, won the prestigious Golden Bear Award at the 55th Berlin Film Festival.

The South African film *Yesterday* was nominated for an Academy Award in the category Best Foreign Film in 2005. *Yesterday* was funded by various South African bodies, including the National Film and Video Foundation.

Hotel Rwanda, a co-production partnership involving South Africa, Italy and the United Kingdom, was also nominated for an Oscar.

Yesterday opened at the Cannes Film Festival in 2004. It won the Human Rights Award at the Venice Film Festival and the Best Film Award at the Puna Film Festival in India. *The Zulu Love Letter* won the Silver Award at the Carthage Film Festival in Tunisia; *Hotel Rwanda* won the Audience Award for Best Film at the Toronto Film Festival; and *Forgiveness* won the Best African Film Award at the Sithengi Film Festival. South Africa is the only African country that regularly participates in these prestigious international festivals.

- the Chief Albert Luthuli Legacy Project
- the Nelson Mandela Museum
- Constitution Hill
- Freedom Park.

The construction of the first phase of Freedom Park was completed in March 2004, namely the garden of remembrance, access routes and parking, water and sanitation, and power and telecommunications. The second phase will include the building of a museum and intrepretation centre.

The Albert Luthuli Inaugural Commemorative Lecture took place on 21 July 2004 at the University of KwaZulu-Natal. It was followed by the opening of the Luthuli Museum in August 2004. President Thabo Mbeki gave the

During 2003/04, the Film and Publication Board classified 3 424 films and interactive computer games. As part of its efforts to protect children from being used in pornography, the board has established a hotline for members of the public to report child pornography. The number is 0800 148 148.

Pocket Guide to South Africa 2005/06

By early 2005, there were 39 international agreements for the joint development of arts and culture projects in place, valued at R94,5 million. The two biggest are the joint Swedish/South Africa Institutional Development Fund (R57 million over three years) and the Flanders/South Africa agreement (R25 million). The Department of Arts and Culture received a grant in aid of R2,5 million from Japan on behalf of the State Theatre. Two co-production treaties with France and Germany and a programme of co-operation with Mexico and Tunisia were signed.

inaugural lecture at the ceremony, and a doctorate was conferred on Chief Albert Luthuli posthumously.

Museums

More than 300 of the approximately 1 000 museums in Africa are in South Africa. Most museums are subsidised by the Department of Arts and Culture, but are otherwise autonomous.

The department pays an annual subsidy to 13 national museums, thereby ensuring the preservation of artefacts and collections that are important to all South Africans.

National Library of South Africa

The construction of the new building in Pretoria that will house the National Library of South Africa, started in January 2005. The project is planned for completion in November 2007. The facility is intended to improve access through its design and available space to support a culture of reading.

In September 2005, *Tsotsi* won the People's Choice Award at the Toronto International Film Festival. It is South Africa's official entry for the 2006 Academy Award for Best Foreign Film.
In 2006, it was also nominated for a Golden Globe Award and two British Academy Film Awards

Tourism

Often described as 'a world in one country', South Africa offers the visitor a breathtaking variety of scenery, from desert and lush forest, to soaring mountains and vast empty plains. Culturally as diverse as the landscape, many visitors are drawn to experience for themselves the miracle of the peaceful overthrow of apartheid. Others are attracted by the endless golden beaches, big game, diving or snorkelling, or bird watching. Whatever their reasons, visitors will find South Africa positively inviting, with world-class infrastructure, transport and accommodation.

Since 1994, tourism in South Africa has emerged as a leading economic growth sector. It is now one of the largest contributors to gross domestic product (GDP), and offers significant employment and enterprise-development

---

The School for Tourism and Hospitality in Johannesburg, the first combined hospitality and tourism training school in the country, was officially opened by Deputy President Phumzile Mlambo-Ngcuka in August 2005.

The school is situated on the Auckland Park Campus of the University of Johannesburg. Some 750 students enrolled, but the intake was expected to increase to 1 000 a year.

The school has various modern facilities, including two restaurants catering for fine dining, à la carte, buffet and fast food; a bar; a wine cellar; six en-suite bedrooms; computer rooms; and museums featuring the hotel school and the history of catering and cuisine in South Africa.

Students can obtain national diplomas or master's degrees in Technology (MTech) in Hospitality Management, Tourism, and Food and Beverage Management, preparing them for employment in all sectors of the tourism and hospitality industry.

Top 10 tourist attractions

1. Kruger National Park
2. Table Mountain
3. Garden Route
4. Cape Town's Victoria & Alfred Waterfront
5. Robben Island
6. Beaches
7. Sun City
8. Cultural villages
9. Soweto
10. The Cradle of Humankind

Source: SA Venues

opportunities. Tourism is the fastest-growing economic sector in South Africa, contributing close to 7,1% of GDP. It is a labour-intensive industry that attracts foreign revenue and stimulates a broad range of other industries.

The global travel industry showed real signs of recovery in 2004. Total foreign arrivals to South Africa increased by almost 1% during the first nine months of the year – to more than 4,77 million compared with 4,72 million in 2003. Some 27 000 new direct tourism jobs were created in 2004. In the first quarter of 2005, there were 1,7 million foreign tourist arrivals – the highest in South Africa's history. At the same time, foreign tourism spending increased by more than 25% to R12,9 billion.

> **fact**
> According to Statistics South Africa, the country offers an average of 1,6 million room-nights a month and registers an average occupancy of 54,2%. The average monthly revenue for accommodation in the country amounts to almost R593 million.

> **fact**
> The Tourism Black Economic Empowerment Charter was officially launched at the Annual Tourism Indaba in Durban, in May 2005.
> The charter is a ground-breaking commitment by industry to greater access for all communities to the benefits of tourism.

Tourism

Arrivals and departures of foreign travellers, 1999-2004

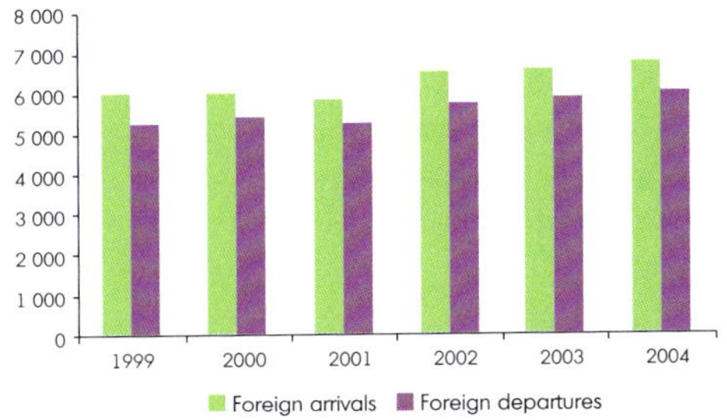

Foreign arrivals ■ Foreign departures

Source: Statistics South Africa

Travel formalities

- Foreign visitors should check before arriving whether a visa is required. Visas are issued free of charge.
- Visitors must have at least one blank page in their passports.
- Tourists must have return or onward tickets.
- Visitors from yellow-fever areas must have proof of inoculation.
- Foreign tourists may have their value-added tax refunded upon departure.
- For safety, emergency and other information, phone 083 123 2345 (24 hours a day) when in South Africa.

In June 2005, the first of four new hiking trails in the Table Mountain National Park (TMNP) was launched. The new trail forms part of the long-term plan to upgrade and reinvigorate 350 km of trails within the TMNP to help cater for the 4,5 million annual visitors. Lasting two days and one night, the People's Trail begins at Constantia Nek and winds along Disa Gorge to the Woodhead Dam where hikers overnight. The next morning the group descends either via Platteklip Gorge or Kasteel's Poort.

Tourism in the provinces

Western Cape

The Western Cape continues to be one of the most favoured destinations for foreigners. Everyone wants to see Cape Town, one of the world's most beautiful cities.

Some attractions in Cape Town are:
- the Victoria & Alfred Waterfront
- the Company's Garden
- the District Six Museum
- the houses of Parliament and the South African National Gallery
- a boat trip to Robben Island, the place where former President Nelson Mandela spent most of his 27 years in jail.

Table Mountain is a popular site for visitors and provides a majestic backdrop to the vibrant and friendly 'Mother City'. The top of the mountain can be reached by an ultra-modern cableway.

Newlands is home to the world-renowned Kirstenbosch National Botanical Garden, and the famous rugby stadium.

Cape Point, part of the Table Mountain National Park, offers many drives, walks, picnic spots and a licensed restaurant. This is the point where the Atlantic and Indian oceans meet. The park has a marine protected area encompassing almost 1 000 km^2.

Hout Bay is well-known for its colourful working harbour. Seafood outlets, round-the-bay trips to the nearby seal island, and a harbour-front emporium attract many visitors.

The Wine Route outside Cape Town offers the chance to taste first-class wines in arguably the most beautiful winelands in the world. Superb accommodation is available in historic

> **fact**: South Africa is ranked among the top 30 global convention countries in the world, with business tourism generating about R20 billion a year in revenue. Business tourism is estimated to sustain almost 260 000 jobs.

towns such as Paarl, Stellenbosch and Franschhoek, as well as on many estates and farms.

The Garden Route

The Garden Route has a well-developed tourist infrastructure, spectacular scenery and a temperate climate, making the region popular all year round.

Not to be missed
- The city of George is at the heart of the Garden Route and is the mecca of golf in the southern Cape. It is home to the renowned Fancourt Country Club and Golf Estate.
- Knysna, nestling on an estuary, is one of South Africa's favourite destinations, famous for its indigenous forests, lakes and beaches.
- Just 26 km from Oudtshoorn, the ostrich-feather capital of the world, are the remarkable Cango caves, a series of 30 spectacular subterranean limestone caverns. The cave system is 5,3 km long.

Central Karoo

The Central Karoo forms part of one of the world's most interesting and unique arid zones. This ancient, fossil-rich land, with the richest desert flora in the world, also has the largest variety of succulents found anywhere on Earth.

Key attractions
- Matjiesfontein, a tiny railway village in the middle of nowhere, offers tourists a peek into the splendour of colonial Victorian England.
- Prince Albert is a well-preserved town which nestles at the foot of the Swartberg mountains. The Fransie Pienaar Museum offers interesting cultural history displays, a fossil room and an exhibit of gold-mining activities in the 19th century.
- The museum in Beaufort West, birthplace of famous heart surgeon Prof Chris Barnard, depicts the story of the

world's first heart transplant. The Karoo National Park on the outskirts of the town is also worth a visit.

Northern Cape

The Augrabies Falls National Park, with its magnificent falls pressing through a narrow rock ravine, remains the main attraction of the Northern Cape. Game drives reveal a variety of bird life and animals such as klipspringer, steenbok, wild cats and otters.

Key attractions

- The Big Hole in Kimberley is the largest man-made excavation in the world. The Kimberley Mine Museum is South Africa's largest full-scale open-air museum. Underground mine tours are a big attraction. The Freddy Tate Golf Museum at the Kimberley Golf Club was the first golfing museum in Africa. The Kimberley Ghost Trail has become a popular tourist attraction.
- The Robert Sobukwe House in Galeshewe was once the residence of Robert Sobukwe, an important figure in South African history and a major role-player in the rise of African political consciousness.
- The Orange River Wine Cellars Co-op in Upington offers wine-tasting and cellar tours. The South African Dried Fruit Co-operative is the second-largest in the world.
- Moffat's Mission in Kuruman is a tranquil place, featuring the house of missionary Robert Moffat, who was also the father-in-law of explorer David Livingstone.
- Namaqualand, the land of the Nama and San people, puts on a spectacular show in spring when its floral splendour covers vast tracts of desert in a kaleidoscope of colour.
- A cultural centre at Wildebeestkuil outside Kimberley features !Xun and Khwe artwork for sale and a tour of rock engravings by these indigenous people.
- The 100-m high, 9-km long, 2-km wide white sand dune at the Witsand Nature Reserve near Postmasburg.

Tourism

Free State

In the capital, Bloemfontein, the *Eerste Raadsaal* (First Parliament Building) was built in 1849 as a school and is the city's oldest surviving building still in its original condition. It is still in use as the seat of the Provincial Legislature.

The National Women's Memorial is a sandstone obelisk, 36,5 m high, which commemorates the women and children who died in concentration camps during the Anglo-Boer/South African War.

Not to be missed
- Clarens, the jewel of the Free State, is surrounded by spectacular scenery.
- The Golden Gate Highlands National Park outside Clarens has beautiful sandstone rock formations.
- The King's Park Rose Garden in Bloemfontein boasts more than 4 000 rose bushes.
- The Vredefort Dome, recently declared a World Heritage Site, is the oldest and largest meteorite impact site in the world. It was formed an estimated two billion years ago when a giant meteorite hit the earth.

Eastern Cape

The Eastern Cape is the only province in South Africa, and one of the few places on Earth, where all seven biomes (major vegetation types) converge.

What to see and do
- the rugged beauty of the Wild Coast, including Hole in the Wall

---

fact

South Africa has seven World Heritage Sites, namely: Robben Island, the Greater St Lucia Wetland Park, uKhahlamba-Drakensberg Park, Mapungubwe, Sterkfontein Cradle of Humankind, the Cape Floral Kingdom and the Vredefort Dome.

Pocket Guide to South Africa 2005/06

- Port Elizabeth, sunshine capital of the Eastern Cape, with its friendly people and excellent beaches
- the Tsitsikamma National Park, forests and rivers
- East London, South Africa's only river port, originally established as a supply port to serve the military headquarters at King William's Town
- the village of Qunu, former President Mandela's childhood home
- the world's highest bunjee jump (180 m) at the Bloukrans Bridge on the Storms River
- outstanding, and varied game reserves, including the Addo Elephant, Mountain Zebra and Mkambati parks.

Limpopo

Limpopo is well endowed with cultural diversity, historical sites and tourist attractions. This is an excellent destination for a get-away-from-it-all holiday in the bush – with first-class accommodation and service.

Not to be missed

- The Mokopane vicinity has several nature reserves. The Arend Dieperink Museum offers a fine cultural-historical collection, and the Makapan caves are famous for their fossils. The Makapan Valley is the only cultural heritage site of its kind. It reflects the history of the Ndebele people and resistance wars dating back 151 years. South Africa's application for the extension of the fossil

---

fact

South Africa stood out as one of the hottest destinations in the 2004 World's Best Awards survey by international travel magazine *Travel & Leisure*, sweeping the World's Best Hotels category with five of the 10 highest-rated properties in the world.

Other hotels in the country ranked at numbers 13, 46, 49, 50, 61 and 74, giving South Africa more top 100 hotels than any country except the United States of America.

hominid sites of Sterkfontein to include Makapan Valley was approved in July 2005.
- The Thabazimbi district is one of the fastest-growing ecotourism areas in South Africa, thanks to its outstanding game reserves.
- Bela-Bela is well-known among South Africans, and increasingly foreigners, for its hot springs, fun water slides and scenery.
- The Waterberg mountain range is rich in indigenous trees, streams, springs, wetlands, bird life and dramatic vistas.
- The Modjadji Nature Reserve, north of Tzaneen, is named after the legendary Rain Queen, Modjadji, the inspiration for Rider Haggard's *She*.
- Phalaborwa has one of the country's top-rated golf courses – just watch out for animals on the fairways!
- The Schoemansdal Voortrekker Town and Museum, west of Mokhado, is built on the site of an original Voortrekker village and depicts their lifestyle in the mid-18th century.

North West

The province abounds with attractions, including wild animals and fun nights at the famous Sun City and Lost City resorts.

Key attractions
- The Historic Route of Mafikeng includes the town which was besieged during the Anglo-Boer/South African War.
- The Groot Marico region, mampoer (moonshine) country, is famous among South Africans for storytelling.
- The Hartbeespoort Dam is a popular spot for weekend outings, breakfast runs and yachting.
- The Pilanesberg National Park supports over 7 000 head of game, including the Big Five and 350 bird species.
- Sun City and the Palace of the Lost City are hugely popular tourist attractions offering gambling, golf,

extravaganza shows, water sport and an artificial sea.
- South Africa's application for the extension of the fossil hominid sites of Sterkfontein to include the Taung Skull fossil site was approved in July 2005. The site marks the place where in 1924 the celebrated Taung Skull – a specimen of the species *Australopithecus africanus* – was found.
- Madikwe Game Reserve is home to 66 large mammal species including the Big Five, and about 300 resident and migrant bird species. It is one of South Africa's largest game reserves.

Mpumalanga

Mpumalanga – the place where the sun rises – is situated in the north-eastern part of South Africa, bordered by Mozambique to the east and the Kingdom of Swaziland to the south-east.

Scenic beauty and wildlife are found in abundance.

Tourist attractions
- Historical sites and villages, old wagon routes and monuments mark the lives of the characters who came to Mpumalanga seeking their fortune. The town of Pilgrim's Rest is a living monument reflecting the region's gold fever period.
- The Blyde River Canyon Nature Reserve near Graskop has striking rock formations and a rich diversity of plants.
- Within the Blyde River Canyon Nature Reserve, the Bourke's Luck potholes were formed by river erosion and the action of flood water. The spectacular Blyde River Canyon is a 26-km long gorge carved out of the face of the escarpment, the only green canyon in the world.
- The southern section of the Kruger National Park falls in this region. The park draws a million visitors a year.
- An annual frog-watching festival is held at Chrissiesmeer, South Africa's largest freshwater lake.

Tourism

- Dullstroom has become a popular destination for trout- and fly-fishing enthusiasts.

Gauteng

Gauteng, the economic heart of southern Africa, offers a vibrant business environment and many tourist attractions, including a rainbow of ecological and cultural diversity.

Key attractions

- The Vaal Dam covers some 300 km^2 and is a popular venue for water sport. Numerous resorts line the shore. The dam is also popular with birders and anglers.
- The Sterkfontein caves near Krugersdorp are the site of the discovery of the skull of the famous Mrs Ples (now believed to be Mr Ples), an estimated 2,5 million-year-old hominid fossil; and Little Foot, an almost complete hominid skeleton more than 3,3 million years old.
- The Walter Sisulu National Botanical Garden boasts a 70-m high waterfall and stunning displays of indigenous plants.
- Forty kilometres north of Pretoria lies a ring of hills a kilometre in diameter and 100 m high. These hills are the walls of an impact crater, the Tswaing Meteorite Crater, left by an asteroid 200 000 years ago.
- The National Zoological Gardens in Pretoria is considered to be one of the 10 best in the world.
- Constitution Hill Precinct is set to become one of South Africa's most popular landmarks.
- The old mining town of Cullinan is the place where the world's biggest diamond, the 3 106-carat Cullinan diamond, was found.
- A guided tour of Soweto makes a lasting impression of this vast community's life and struggle against apartheid.
- The Apartheid Museum in Johannesburg tells the story of the legacy of apartheid through photographs, film and artefacts.

- The Union Buildings in Pretoria, venue for the inauguration of presidents Nelson Mandela and Thabo Mbeki.

KwaZulu-Natal

Also known as the Zulu Kingdom, KwaZulu-Natal is a combination of natural wonders, fascinating culture and ultra-modern facilities.

Durban's Golden Mile skirts the main beaches of the Indian Ocean. Drawcards include an amusement centre, paddling pools, paved walkways and fountains.

Enticing attractions

- The uShaka Marine World theme park, oceanarium, dolphinarium and oceanographic research institute on Durban's Point.
- Dolphin spotting or lazing the days away on the coastline between the Umdloti and Tugela rivers – the Dolphin Coast.
- The Hluhluwe-Umfolozi Park, one of the largest game parks in South Africa and home to the Big Five, as well as cheetah and wild dogs.
- The eMakhosini Valley, birthplace of King Shaka. The Valley of Zulu Kings gives visitors insight into the history and culture of the Zulu nation.
- The Greater St Lucia Wetland Park, with some of the highest forested dunes in the world, and an abundance of fish and birds.
- Travelling the Hibiscus Coast between Umkomaas and the Wild Coast on the Banana Express.
- The Royal Natal National Park offers many scenic highlights, including the Amphitheatre, Mont-aux-Sources and the Tugela falls.
- The Battlefields Route in northern KwaZulu-Natal has the highest concentration of battlefields and related military sites in South Africa.
- Every year around June/July, millions of sardines leave their home on the Aghulas banks and move up to the

coast of Mozambique. Thousands of dolphins, Cape gannets, sharks and game fish follow the 'Sardine Run' northwards.

Things to see and do in South Africa

Just a few of the attractions that make South Africa an exceptional destination:

- breathtaking Cape Town nestling at the foot of Table Mountain
- Cape Point, where two oceans meet
- Cape Town's laid-back, welcoming attitude and fabulous nightlife
- Robben Island in Cape Town's Table Bay where former President Mandela was incarcerated
- the delights of Sun City and the Lost City, and many other first-rate casino resorts
- walking in the spectacular Drakensberg mountains
- the chance to learn how to say 'hello' in 11 official languages
- the country's Blue Flag beaches
- the variety of national parks and transfrontier conservation areas
- seven World Heritage Sites
- the lilac-breasted roller, the blue crane and the other 900 bird species to be spotted in southern Africa
- the Big Five and other wild animals that abound in the many parks and game reserves

---

The Minister of Environmental Affairs and Tourism, Mr Marthinus van Schalkwyk, announced in April 2005 that the South African Government would, over the next three years, invest another R193 million in transfrontier conservation areas, creating visitor centres, upgrading access routes, building rest camps and improving tourism infrastructure.

Originating in Africa, the transfrontier conservation initiative has been spearheaded by the Southern African Development Community region. By April 2005, there were 169 such areas globally, involving 113 countries and 667 protected areas.

- the strange *halfmens* (half-human) and the exotic baobab, just some of South Africa's many amazing trees and plants
- evocative battlefields on which imperial Britain fought Zulus, Xhosas and Boers
- the dazzling floral displays which carpet Namaqualand once a year
- the mountains, forests and beaches of the Garden Route
- the silence and solitude of the Karoo's wide-open spaces
- country hospitality (and home cooking) in hundreds of picturesque towns and villages across South Africa
- the endless golden beaches of the Eastern Cape
- fly fishing in stunning scenery with first-class accommodation
- fabulous golf courses that produced the likes of Gary Player, Ernie Els and Retief Goosen
- an array of cultural villages, arts festivals, rock paintings and museums
- the adrenaline rush of the many adventure tourism opportunities available in the country.

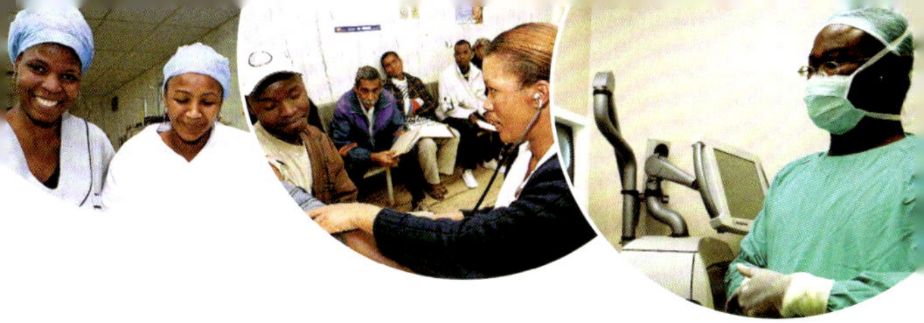

Health

One of the challenges that has confronted government since the advent of democracy was the process of reforming the health system. This included the creation of a single, unified national health system and strengthening institutional capacity at national, provincial and district levels.

In 1994, government started to provide free public primary healthcare (PHC) services for children under six years, and pregnant and lactating women. During the same period, government initiated a clinic-building and upgrading programme, which resulted in the building and upgrading of more than 1 300 clinics between 1994 and February 2005.

PHC services include immunisation, communicable and endemic disease prevention, maternity care, screening of children, integrated management of childhood illnesses and child healthcare, health promotion, counselling, management of chronic diseases, and diseases of older persons, rehabilitation, accident and emergency services, family planning, and oral health.

Where necessary, patients with complications are referred to higher levels of care, such as hospitals.

Health budget

The total health budget for 2005/06 was R9,825 billion. This was an increase of 11,4% compared with the previous financial year. This allocation is projected to rise to R10,658 billion in 2006/07 and to R11,184 billion in 2007/08.

Source: Estimates of National Expenditure, 2004

Health-delivery system

The major emphasis in the development of health services at provincial level has been the shift from curative hospital-based healthcare to that provided in an integrated community-based manner.

Provincial-hospital patients pay for examinations and treatment in accordance with their income and number of dependants. A provincial government may partly or entirely finance patients' treatment.

Clinics
A network of mobile clinics run by government forms the backbone of primary and preventive healthcare.

Hospitals
According to the Health Systems Trust (HST), there were 382 provincial public hospitals in 2004.

The Hospital Revitalisation Grant increased by 12,7% from R911 million in 2004/05 to R1,027 billion in 2005/06. Government completed the revitalisation of four hospitals in 2004, with another 37 nearing completion.

There were 357 private hospitals in 2004 according to the HST. Private hospital fees are generally higher than those of provincial hospitals.

South Africa has 18 state mental-health institutions with 10 000 beds.

Emergency medical services
Emergency medical services, including ambulance services, are run by the provinces, but training is nationally standardised.

> **fact:** During 2005, 287 dental practitioners registered for continuing professional development. A total of 488 pharmacists commenced community service in 2005, compared with 49 in 2000.

Annual malaria cases and deaths, 1999 – July 2005

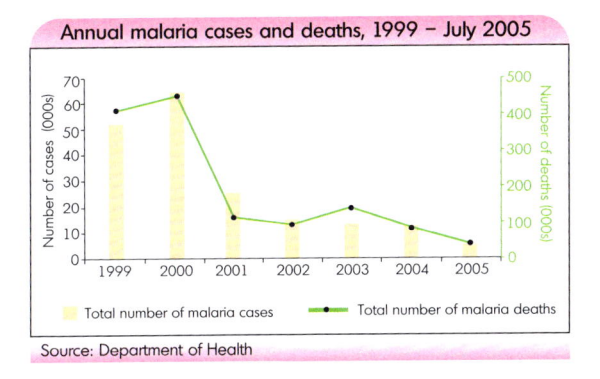

Source: Department of Health

Private ambulance services also provide services to the community. Some of these also render aeromedical services.

Legislation

The National Health Act, 2003 is critical legislation that provides a framework for a single health system for South Africa. It highlights the rights and responsibilities of health-providers and users, and ensures broader community participation in healthcare delivery from a health facility up to national level.

Among other things, the National Health Act, 2003 will enable government to establish the Office of Standard Compliance.

President Thabo Mbeki promulgated the Traditional Health Practitioners Act, 2004 early in 2005. It provides, among other things, for the establishment of a council for traditional health practitioners.

The Nursing Bill addresses developments in nursing education and classification of nurses into different categories. This Bill will also assist in introducing the nursing profession into the community-service programme, which already covers all other categories of health professionals.

The Mental Healthcare Act, 2002, enforces the culture of human rights within the mental-health services and ensures that mental-health patients are treated with respect and dignity.

National School Health Policy

A policy and set of guidelines, launched in July 2003, aim to ensure that all children have equal access to school-health services. A comprehensive programme to train nurses is being rolled out. The training programme is expected to be implemented across the country by 2007.

Health team

The core team consists of:
- 32 368 registered doctors (May 2005)
- 4 500 dentists (end of 2001)

Allied health professionals:

In May 2005, the following practitioners were registered:
- Ayurveda — 122
- Chinese medicine and acupuncture — 656
- chiropractors — 506
- homoeopaths — 726
- naturopaths — 158
- osteopaths — 62
- phytotherapists — 28
- therapeutic aromatherapists — 1 123
- therapeutic massage therapists — 346
- therapeutic reflexologists — 1 935

Supplementary health professionals include the following*:

Basic ambulance assistants	24 784
Psychologists	5 875
Radiographers	5 196
Medical technologists	4 833
Ambulance emergency assistants	4 857
Occupational therapists	2 759
Environmental health officers	2 662
Optometrists	2 458
Physiotherapists	4 739

* May 2005

Health

	Registered nurses	Enrolled nurses	Nursing auxiliaries	Students in training
Eastern Cape	12 025	3 073	5 155	2 908
Free State	7 199	1 302	3 070	966
Gauteng	26 864	8 391	14 749	9 045
KwaZulu-Natal	18 995	10 929	9 039	8 524
Limpopo	7 284	2 913	4 170	1 947
Mpumalanga	4 674	1 768	1 803	568
North West	6 382	2 097	3 884	1 189
Northern Cape	1 919	531	928	210
Western Cape	13 148	4 262	7 905	1 800
Total	98 490	35 266	50 703	27 157

Source: South African Nursing Council

- 11 145 pharmacists (May 2005)
- 184 459 nurses and nursing auxiliaries (end of 2004).

South Africa has a severe shortage of health professionals such as physiotherapists, dietitians and radiographers.

National Health Laboratory Service (NHLS)

The NHLS consists of 234 laboratories. It provides cost-effective and efficient laboratory services to all public and private healthcare providers.

Medical schemes

The Council of Medical Schemes regulates the more than 170 registered private medical schemes.

In South Africa, about 25 000 people die from smoking diseases every year.

However, government's policies are beginning to have an impact on reducing the levels of smoking in the country. Research indicates that smoking prevalence among the adult population decreased from 36% in 1996 to 22% in 2003. Among the youth, smoking decreased from 23% in 1999 to 18,5% in 2002.

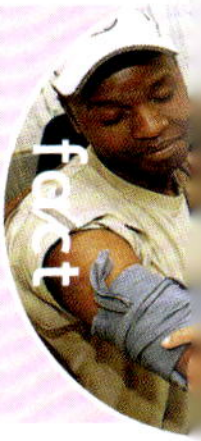

Community health

The most common communicable diseases in South Africa are tuberculosis (TB), malaria, measles and sexually transmitted infections.

In South Africa, it is recommended that children under the age of five be immunised against the most common childhood diseases. Immunisation should be administered at birth, six weeks, 10 weeks, 14 weeks, nine months, 18 months and five years of age. Childhood immunisations are given to prevent polio, TB, diphtheria, pertussis, tetanus, haemophilus influenzae type B, hepatitis B and measles.

The set routine immunisation coverage target for fully immunised children under one year is 90%. In 2005, the overall routine immunisation coverage for South Africa stood at 82%, but some districts were still lagging behind with less than 60% immunisation coverage.

The last confirmed case of polio was reported in 1989.

Malaria is endemic in the low-altitude areas of Limpopo, Mpumalanga and north-eastern KwaZulu-Natal. The highest-risk area is a strip of about 100 km along the Zimbabwe, Mozambique and Swaziland borders.

The success of the country's malaria-control programme has not been limited to the affected areas in South Africa but extended to other countries in the Southern African Development Community region where South Africa initiated joint efforts in malaria control with its neighbours. Between July/August 2004 and July/August 2005, there was a 72% reduction in malaria cases and a 50% reduction in malaria-related deaths in South Africa.

Immunisation coverage	
1998	63%
2005	82%

Source: *South Africa Yearbook 2005/06*

Health

Malaria risk areas

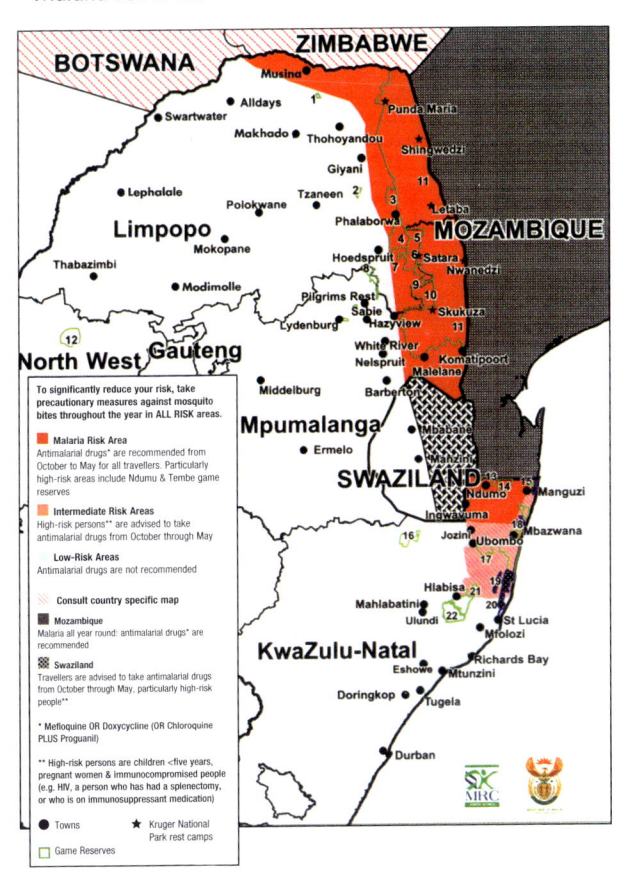

Child and maternal health

In 1998, the infant mortality rate was measured to be 45,4 per 1 000 live births. This decreased in 2003 to 42,5 per 1 000 live births.

The proportion of births attended to by either a nurse or doctor increased from 84% in 1998 to 92% in 2003. This

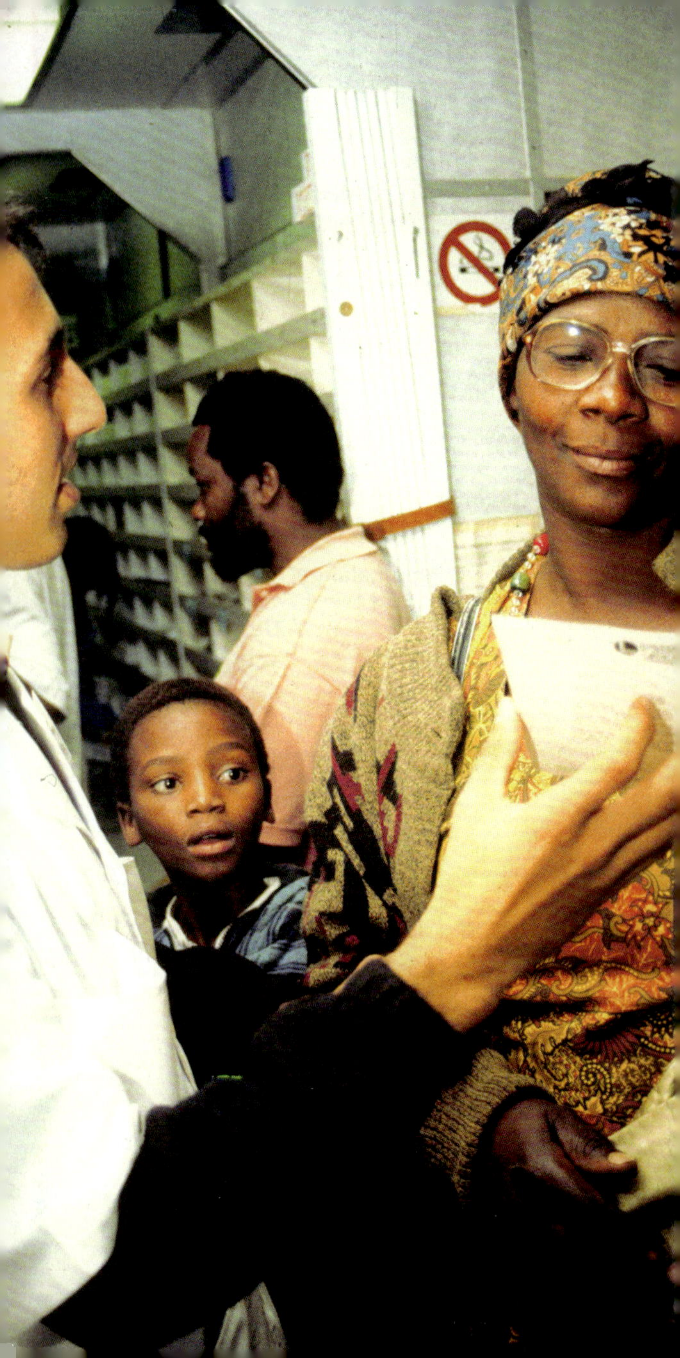

could be attributed to the increased access to health services both in terms of availability of health facilities in various communities and free health services for pregnant and lactating women, as well as for children under the age of six years.

Tuberculosis

South Africa has 188 000 new TB cases a year. Free testing is available at public clinics countrywide.

Countrywide efforts have now been brought to bear on this disease. These efforts include:
- implementation of the Directly Observed Treatment Strategy
- the establishment of a national TB team
- a countrywide reporting system.

HIV and AIDS

The Government's Comprehensive Plan for Management, Care and Treatment of HIV and AIDS centres around preventing the spread of HIV-infection and improving the health system to enable it to provide a series of interventions aimed at improving the lives of those infected and affected by HIV and AIDS.

By October 2005, there were 192 sites spread across all the 53 health districts. By the end of August 2005, 78 078 patients were receiving antiretroviral treatment.

Because of its commitment to curb the spread of HIV-infection and reduce the impact of AIDS, government

---

In 2004/05, the Department of Health focused on, among other things, eliminating the backlog in the provision of assistive devices which are critical in enabling people with disabilities to actively participate in everyday life. In that period, the department supplied 10 407 wheelchairs and buggies, 1 131 pressure care cushions and 4 547 hearing aids. These are in addition to the devices procured and distributed by provinces.

Pocket Guide to South Africa 2005/06

increased the conditional grant by 45% from R782 million in 2004/05 to R1,135 billion in 2005/06.

Condoms are available free of charge at all clinics. The distribution of male condoms increased from 302 million in 2003 to 346 million in 2004. A total of 1,2 million female condoms were distributed through 203 sites nationwide in 2004.

The South African AIDS Vaccine Initiative is a public-private partnership funded at a level of about R50 million per year. It is a holistic vaccine-development initiative that has three South African developed products that are going through the regulatory process preceding Phase 1 trials.

Sport and recreation

South Africans have more than made their mark in international sport. The country has successfully hosted major international soccer events, as well as the Rugby, Cricket and Women's Golf World Cups and will be sure to impress when it hosts the *Fédération Internationale de Football Association* Soccer World Cup in 2010.

Taking part

Government aims to encourage all South Africans (particularly the historically disadvantaged) to take part in organised sport for the sake of social integration, health and the sheer enjoyment of it. The mass participation programme was launched in 2004/05 with the opening of 60 hubs aimed at getting the youth involved in mass-based sport activities. A further 36 were envisaged for 2005/06.

Facilities

Since 2001, government has built more than 360 basic, multi-purpose facilities and has established some 360 community sports councils. More than 15 500 temporary jobs were created over a four-year period. The 2004/05 Budget provided for 121 facilities to be built or upgraded.

Between 2001 and 2005, funding for upgrading existing facilities and creating new ones came from the Poverty Relief, Infrastructure Investment and Job Summit funds. The allocation for 2004/05 also allowed Sport and Recreation South Africa (SRSA) to undertake projects in the areas where

Pocket Guide to South Africa 2005/06

the 2010 Soccer World Cup matches are planned, to benefit the poor in those urban areas. The projects are, however, not restricted to soccer or to these areas alone.

International achievements in 2005

- In January 2005, world indoor 800-m champion, Mbulaeni Mulaudzi, won the International Association of Athletics Federation's Permit Flanders Indoor race in Ghent, Belgium, in 1:48,05 seconds.
- In January 2005, Oscar Pistorius, the 18-year-old 200-m Paralympic champion and world record holder for double leg amputees, continued his astonishing career at a Gauteng North open athletics meeting at Pilditch Stadium in Pretoria. He set a new global 400-m record in the same category with a time of 47,43 seconds.
- In February 2005, Fancourt Golf Estate near George hosted the Women's World Cup of Golf. The event was won by Japan. The event was won by Sweden in 2006.
- In February 2005, South African cyclist Ryan Cox won the Tour de Langkawi in Malaysia.
- In February 2005, South Africa beat England 4-1 in a seven-match one-day international cricket series.
- In February 2005, Ryk Neethling followed his opening day world record with two more golds at the FINA World Cup short-course swimming competition in New York. He notched a world record in the men's 100-m individual medley and a United States (US) Open record in the 200-m freestyle, finishing in 1:43,12 seconds.
- In April 2005, Makhaya Ntini claimed the best match bowling figures in South African cricket test history to help his team dismiss the West Indies on the final day of the second test at Queen's Park Oval. South Africa won the test series 2-0.

Fast bowler Ntini took seven wickets for 37 as the home team slumped from 170 for five at the start of the day to 194 all out.

Sport and recreation

In May 2005, *Golf Digest USA* ranked the top 100 golf courses outside the United States of America. South Africa achieved five listings, with Leopard Creek Golf Estate and Country Club coming in at number 25.

The survey covered 1 005 courses worldwide, and was overseen by a panel of over 800 course-rating specialists, 22 editors of *Golf Digest* and its affiliates, and an undisclosed number of other expert panelists.

The five listed South African courses are all regular stops on the Sunshine Tour annual calendar.

Leopard Creek ranked 25th, followed by the Gary Player Country Club, home to the multimillion-dollar Nedbank Golf Challenge and the Dimension Data Pro-Am, at 29th.

The Links at Fancourt, venue of the 2003 President's Cup, was placed at number 59, followed at number 62 by the Durban Country Club. Arabella Estate and Country Club, which plays host to the annual Nelson Mandela Invitational, completed the list at number 100.

- In April 2005, the South African Baby Boks won the 2005 International Rugby Board Under-19 Rugby World Championship title when they defeated New Zealand 20-15 at the Absa Stadium in Durban.
- In April 2005, South African wheelchair athlete Ernst van Dyk won the Boston Marathon for a record fifth consecutive time, coming home almost six minutes clear of his nearest challenger.

  Van Dyk's winning time of 1:24:11 was some way off the world record 1:18:27 he posted in 2004.

  A week prior to the Boston Marathon, Van Dyk won the Paris Marathon.
- At the beginning of May 2005, Ernie Els recorded his third win of the season in record-breaking style at the Tomson Shanghai Pudong Golf Club in Shanghai. He carded a tournament-best 26-under par 262 to win by 13 shots.
- In May 2005, Natalie du Toit broke four world records in the pool at the Visa Paralympic World Cup in Manchester. Ernst van Dyk won the men's wheelchair pursuit with a time of 4:20:80. He also won gold in the 1 500 m with a time of 3:21:85. Oscar Pistorius followed with gold in the

100 m in a time of 11,23 seconds and gold in the 200 m with a time of 22,01 seconds.
- In May 2005, South African ski paddler Oscar Chalupsky won a record 11th Molokai Challenge, widely regarded as the unofficial world surf ski championship.
- In June 2005, South African game ranger Sibusiso Vilane summited Mount Everest. Vilane, who was the first black African to reach the top of Everest in May 2003, summited with fellow mountaineer Alex Harris.
- On 16 June 2005, Sipho Ngomane won South Africa's annual premier athletic event, the Comrades Marathon.
- In June 2005, South Africa defeated Australia 24-20 to win the Under-21 Rugby World Championship.
- Also in June 2005, South Africa defeated the French 27-13 in Port Elizabeth to clinch the rugby test series. The first test was drawn 40 all.
- In July 2005, second seeds Cara Black of Zimbabwe and Liezel Huber of South Africa won the Wimbledon women's doubles title by defeating Amelie Mauresmo of France and Svetlana Kuznetsova of Russia 6-2, 6-1 in the final.

Sports of most interest to adult South Africans, June 2004

Sport	June 2004	Feb 2003	June 2000	May 1999
	%	%	%	%
	Multi-mention	One only	One only	One only
Soccer	78	45	49	47
Rugby	47	10	14	12
Cricket	39	16	14	16
Wrestling	25			
Athletics	22	4	1	3
Tennis	22	2	2	3
Boxing	18	2	1	4
Motorsport	12			
Golf	12			
Netball	11	4	3	3

Source: SABC Markinor

Sport and recreation

South Africa's Wesley Moodie teamed up with Australia's Stephen Huss to beat Bob and Mike Bryan, the American second seeds, 7-6 (7/4), 6-3, 6-7 (2/7), 6-3, to become the first qualifiers to clinch the title.

- In July 2005, South African golfer Tim Clark holed a 20-foot birdie putt at the last to shoot a four-under 67 and clinch his third European Tour title by two shots at the Scottish Open in Loch Lomond.
- In July 2005, Roland Schoeman set a world record in the semi-finals of the men's 50-m butterfly at the World Championships in Montreal. He went on to win South Africa's first world swimming title by setting another new world record in the final of the men's 50-m butterfly. He also won the men's 50-m freestyle final in 21,69 seconds, the second-fastest time in history and only 0,05 outside Russian Alexander Popov's world record of 21,64. South Africa returned home with five medals in total.
- In July 2005, the Springbok rugby team ensured that the Nelson Mandela Challenge Plate stayed in South Africa by beating Australia 33-20 at Ellis Park stadium in Johannesburg. Two weeks earlier they went down 12-30.
- At the end of July 2005, South Africa beat Australia 22-16 in the first match of the Tri-Nations rugby tournament. A week later they also beat the All Blacks 22-16 at Newlands in Cape Town.
- In August 2005, Retief Goosen overcame the American Brandt Jobe to win the Golf International at Castle Rock, Colorado.
- In October/November 2005, South Africa won the one-day international cricket series against New-Zealand.
- In November 2005, Ernst van Dyk won the New York Marathon.
- In November 2005, Ryk Neethling won six gold medals at the FINA World Cup Series in Durban.

South African sports awards

At the South African Sports Awards 2005 function held on 24 November 2005, rugby player Bryan Habana and cricketer Jacques Kallis were named as the joint winners of the SA Sportsman of the Year award. Natalie du Toit scooped the SA Sportswoman of the Year title. Lucas Radebe was named Sports Personality of the Year and Makhaya Ntini the Bonitas Sports Star of the Year. Team Shosholoza (sailing) clinched the Sports Team of the Year title.

The President honours exceptional achievement in sport and recreation through the national orders. President Thabo Mbeki bestowed the Order of Ikhamanga (silver class) to Fanie Lombaard (Paralympic gold medallist) and Lucas Radebe (soccer) in September 2005.

Sports tourism project

South Africa's hosting of the 2003 Cricket World Cup attracted 20 000 foreign fans over 44 days. They spent some R1,1 billion and generated 3 500 jobs during the hugely successful event.

South Africa will host the 2010 Soccer World Cup, which is expected to attract some 400 000 visitors. It is the first Soccer World Cup to be held in Africa. An economic-impact study predicts that 2,72 million tickets will be sold, generating revenue to the tune of R4,6 billion.

South Africa has hosted a number of international sporting events since 1994:
- Rugby World Cup 1995
- African Cup of Nations 1996
- IAAF World Cup in Athletics 1998
- All Africa Games 1999
- Cricket World Cup 2003
- President's Cup 2003
- Women's World Cup of Golf 2005 and 2006
- Women's World Cup of Cricket 2005

It is estimated that capital expenditure to upgrade stadiums and other infrastructure will amount to R2,3 billion and the event will lead to direct expenditure of R12,7 billion, while contributing R21,3 billion to the country's gross domestic product. Some 160 000 new employment opportunities will be created and some R7,2 billion will be paid to government in taxes.

Television coverage of the Soccer World Cup will bring South Africa into the homes of new tourism markets such as Brazil, Argentina, eastern Europe, Russia, Japan and South Korea.

Sports administration

The South African Sports Commission (SASC) Act, 1998 provided for a commission to administer sport and recreation under the guidance of the Minister of Sport and Recreation. By May 2005, a Repeal Act was before Parliament to de-establish the SASC. The functions of the SASC are now shared between SRSA and the newly established South African Sports Confederation and Olympic Committee that will take responsibility for high-performance sport in South Africa.

Disability Sport South Africa (DISSA)

DISSA aims to promote, manage, administer and co-ordinate the competitive and recreational participation in sports activities by disabled South Africans.

It is responsible for the selection and funding of South African national teams attending the Paralympic Games or any world championships recognised by the International Paralympic Committee (IPC). It is the South African member of the IPC.

Pocket Guide to South Africa 2005/06

IMPORTANT TELEPHONE NUMBERS/NOTES